LEFT-WING DEMOCRACY IN THE ENGLISH CIVIL WAR

LEFT–WING DEMOCRACY IN THE ENGLISH CIVIL WAR

GERRARD WINSTANLEY AND THE DIGGER MOVEMENT

DAVID W. PETEGORSKY

FOREWORD BY **CHRISTOPHER HILL**
with a new introduction by **Ivan Roots**

sandpiper books

A Sutton Publishing Book

This edition published in 1999 by Sandpiper, an imprint of
Sandpiper Books Ltd, London

First published in 1940 as *Left-Wing Democracy in the English Civil War: A
Study of the Social Philosophy of Gerrard Winstanley*
by Victor Gollancz Ltd, London
First published in this editon in 1995 by Sutton Publishing Limited

Copyright, text © David W. Petegorsky, 1940
Copyright, foreword © Christopher Hill, 1995
Copyright, introduction © Ivan Roots, 1995

A catalogue record for this book is available from the British Library

ISBN 1 8400 4004 1

Printed in Great Britain by
Redwood Books Limited,
Trowbridge, Wiltshire.

CONTENTS

DAVID W. PETEGORSKY

David W. Petegorsky, a young Canadian scholar, pursued a doctoral degree course at the London School of Economics in the late thirties under the supervision of Harold Laski. The result of his research, *Left-Wing Democracy in the English Civil War*, was published by Victor Gollancz in 1940 in the Left Book Club series. It was his only book. He died in 1959.

FOREWORD

Petegorsky's book was a shining light in the dark days of 1940. It is now perceived primarily as a pioneering study of Gerrard Winstanley, and it still offers the best analysis of his ideas, establishing him as a serious and highly significant figure in the history of political thought. But Winstanley is only half of Petegorsky's book. The first two chapters add up to an analysis of the English Revolution, and of the political ideas to which it gave rise, which was remarkably innovative in 1940. Petegorsky places Winstanley firmly against a background of "religious" and political thought, emphasizing that Winstanley's social ideas represented a logical development of his theological concepts.

"More than any of his contemporaries", Petegorsky wrote, Winstanley "was able to . . . perceive, with remarkable clarity, that the Civil War had been above all else a struggle for economic and political supremacy between the monarchy and the rising gentry whose development the monarchy had retarded" (p. 195). With massive quotations from contemporary sources Petegorsky shows that there was a continuous demand for "common property" among the religious radicals, though only Winstanley worked out a "comprehensive social philosophy" and "political programme" to achieve this result (pp. 149–51). Petegorsky's introductory chapters make it clear that seventeenth-century "Puritanism" was something very different from nineteenth-century nonconformity. It all depends on what you mean by religion.

Petegorsky's book did not attract the attention it deserved. Publication by the Left Book Club ensured a wide circulation, but was hardly calculated to win "scholarly" readers. Petegorsky, alas, did not live to publish the major works which would have transformed our understanding of the English Revolution.

Christopher Hill, FBA, D.Litt.
Formerly Master of Balliol College, Oxford

INTRODUCTION TO
THE SECOND EDITION

In 1649, on April 1 (an appropriate day, some might say), a
small group of landless labourers, led by one Gerrard
Winstanley, a failed cloth-merchant, and (briefly) a visionary
ex-soldier, William Everard, came on to the common at St.
George's Hill, near Cobham, Surrey, and proceeded to "dig
and plant" together as a first step towards making the earth
"a common treasury". This seemingly futile gesture was, in
fact, a practical expression of a radical theological and
philosophical process, set off in Winstanley during a trance
and continued in a series of pamphlets, initially obscurely
mystical, but which would go on to ravel up together spiritual,
economic, political and social aspects of the human
condition. In them Winstanley concluded that nothing would
be well until, working with Reason – or the Creator – men
devised a more equal society, without private property,
buying and selling, and the exploitation of one man's labour
by another. Though sporadically and ephemerally copied
elsewhere "Digging" at Cobham was a failure, not least
because of harassment by alarmed local landlords, among
them Parson Platt, "a tithing priest" of the sort condemned
by Winstanley. A nine-days wonder, digging soon went, in
Thomas Carlyle's phrase, historically "submarine". It would
be rediscovered, largely because of a burgeoning modern
interest in the radicalisms – there were many varieties – of the
1640s and 1650s, increasingly seen as expressing with
remarkable vigour and adventurousness ideas some of which
at least seemed to chime with the reforming spirit of the late
nineteenth and the twentieth centuries. What clinched
concern for Winstanley himself was the canon of his
published writings from the slight *The Mysterie of God
Concerning the whole Creation* (1648) to the substantial *The
Law of Freedom in a Platform* (1652), which detailed the

conduct of a society on its way to becoming a common treasury. Writing in a maturing style, which (it is generally agreed) makes him a master of seventeenth-century prose, and presenting a body of thought and feeling capable of sustaining a plethora of interpretations, the works of Gerrard Winstanley have set in motion a historiography of industrial proportions.

Left-Wing Democracy in the English Civil War by David W. Petegorsky, a young Canadian scholar, published in 1940, during the first year of the Second World War as "a choice" in Victor Gollancz's Left Book Club, is a landmark in that development. If Winstanley was already not quite "the forgotten radical" of Petegorsky's sub-title, after this full study the man and his ideology could never again be pushed back into obscurity, particularly as it was soon followed by G.H. Sabine's almost complete edition of *The Works* (1941) and a selection by L.D. Hamilton (1944), fruit of the enthusiasm of the Oxford University History Society, itself inspired by Christopher Hill. Since then there have been monographs in English from both sides of the Atlantic – American interest was set off by proponents of the scheme of "Single-Tax" Henry George early this century – and from France and Russia; numerous articles, including ones from the digging area itself; two novels and a compelling film. There is, it seems, a Winstanley for all seasons. Petegorsky's is one of them still.

The search for a settlement after Parliament's military defeat of Charles I in 1646 saw war pursued by other means, notably in print as successive régimes found it hard to maintain censorship. Professional grievances merging with aspirations for a share in the fruits of the victory it had won politicized the New Model Army at the same time as radical views about church and state, society and economics, proliferated among civilians, many drawn into an arena to which they had hitherto been denied access. Conservative men diagnosed a spreading gangrene, while optimists offered panaceas. Prominent in 1647 was a heterogeneous group, with enough in common to adhere to a loose programme, called by opponents Levellers, and dedicated particularly to the pursuit of the rights, constitutional and whatever, of smaller property-holders, with a feeling, among some of them, at least, for those who, in Oliver Cromwell's words, had "but the interest of breathing". Though, as Petegorsky puts it, they raised "in its most acute form the basic problem of all revolutions, the relationship of economic to political power and *vice versa*", the Levellers were not really revolutionary – *The Moderate* was the title of one of their newsheets – but they inserted the thin end of a wedge into the cracks of the existing system. In the years which saw a second civil war, the trial and execution of the King and the expedient establishment of a republic under the auspices of a purged single-chamber Parliament against a background of economic and social dislocation, the Levellers claimed a right of citizenship for reforming principles, which could be taken further and more broadly defined by other groupings critical of, and frustrated by, the existing régime. Notions can quickly become ideas in a revolutionary situation.

It was apt for Petegorsky to offer as a prelude to his examination of Winstanley a survey of the Levellers and their context. Even then much studied, the Levellers have continued under close investigation, with often controversial results. Additions to Petegorsky's bibliography indicate the main lines of the approaches of historians and political theorists, some not unconnected with the values of our own times.

"Every age tends to write history in its own image", says Petegorsky. No more than the scientist can the historian detach himself from his environment – nor perhaps should he, since the climate prompts fresh questions to carry enquiry forward. One may ask why was the theory of a general crisis in the mid-seventeenth century not adumbrated until the mid-twentieth? And, the answer lies in our own circumstances – the chequered progress of democracy, the impact of collectivism, the rise of fascism, the Great and later Depressions. Petegorsky's research was undertaken at the London School of Economics in the 1930s as the drift towards war accelerated. With its outbreak, inclusion of his work under a pointed title was imaginative but appropriate for the Left Book Club. Yet it was obvious at once – and time has reinforced it – that this was no ephemeral piece of leftist propaganda, but a work of scholarship, steeped in primary sources, abreast of historiography, hard thinking, well organized, clearly and vigorously expressed. The thrust of its argument is consistent, purposeful and persuasive, though, of course, it is not, nor could it be, the only story that can be made of Gerrard Winstanley.

For nearly three centuries Winstanley, though glimpsed from time to time, as Petegorsky indicates, remained a shadowy figure. References to him in those years are still being uncovered. For instance, we now know that Mrs Catharine Macaulay, the eighteenth-century republican historian, had copies of some of his tracts, and in the 1790s – that decade of revolution – his views were under discussion in a country parish near Swansea. More details of his life before and after the productive years have been collected, making him a very complex character, indeed. In the 1890s C.H. Firth, editing *The Clarke Papers*, a selection from the important Civil War archive at Worcester College, Oxford, mentioned the Diggers *en passant* as "a little band of socialists", and G.P. Gooch in *English Democratic Ideas of the Seventeenth Century* (1898 – later revised significantly by Petegorsky's supervisor, Harold Laski, 1927) – remarked how "almost alone of his contemporaries [Winstanley] recognised the well-being of the proletariate as constituting the criterion not only of political but of social conditions" and suggested that he had at length developed "a complete scheme of socialism". But echoing W. Comber (1678), L.S. Berens presented in 1906 an emphatically religious Winstanley sharing the outlook of early Quakers before George Fox had brought them within a discipline. Already the two chief approaches to the inwardness of the Digger's thought and action were signposted. Both start from the same point – the early indubitably spiritual tracts of 1648 – but soon move off in different directions, with side roads opening off the highways. (A third approach impatiently offered by Kevin Sharpe and A.L. Rowse – arsenic and old lace – takes pride in not wasting time upon the lunacies and trivialities of minor sects, "a distracted crack-brained people" charged by Rowse as moved by the politics of envy, a cardinal sin in the eyes of those comfortable enough not to be tempted by it.)

One main approach comes to a more or less materialist Winstanley – the other to a still emphatically, if not exclusively, spiritual advocate, developing less an ideology than an alternative theology, one brushing the margins of traditional Christianity, but still within them. Both allow for varieties of emphasis, even for some intermingling. Thus Sabine, while stressing a spiritual drift, offers glimpses of a more mundane thinker, aware that if religion pervaded all aspects of human life, notably economics and politics, there was a feed-back from them into religion. (It is surprising that since so much weight is placed by almost all commentators upon the very early mystical tracts they have not been reprinted since 1650. Sabine prints only abstracts and a few extracts and Hill in his *The Law of Freedom and Other Writings* only the Preface to Winstanley's own collected edition.) It has been argued that you cannot sift Winstanley's politics from his theological language and that there is "a profound dialectical relationship between his theology and his political views". If so, it cuts both ways.

Few of those who discern a degree of materialism in Winstanley's thinking have been as brusque as Edouard Bernstein, before Petegorsky, and George Juretic, after. A German revisionist marxist, Bernstein in the early 1900s (trans. into English, 1930) saw digging as essentially secular in motivation characterizing Winstanley's (and other associated) tracts as "couched in somewhat mystical phraseology, which manifestly serves to conceal the revolutionary designs of the authors". This surely precludes a serious analysis of the springs of his thought, yet it must be said that local landlords and the newsheets responded only to the dangers digging posed to public order and the Diggers' own letters underline the practical nature of what they were up to. Asserting that Winstanley was "no millenarian", George Juretic (1975) rejects any notion of a driving theology. For him *The True Levellers Standard Advanced* (dedication April 20 1649, only a couple of weeks after digging started at St. George's Hill), marked the birth of "an aspiring radicalism" concentrating on social reality, not "millenarian whimsy", and weaning Winstanley from social concepts "virtually devoid of socially substantive analysis". The language of the tracts leaves no impression on Juretic, who seems affronted by the notion that Winstanley may have walked for any length of time along a spiritual path. On the other hand W.S. Hudson (1943 and 1946), P. Elmen (1954), Lotte Mulligan and her La Trobe colleagues (1957) cannot contemplate that he may have moved into another. With variations of emphasis they assert or argue that his concern began, continued and ended as an urge for bringing in "a reign of righteousness", giving a persistent centrality to a mystical view of life in all its manifestations, consistent not only in its usage of a theological idiom but in a complete acceptance of its implications. Claiming to offer us Winstanley as "the man as he said he was", they put it that as a creature of his times he could hardly do otherwise. Established Christianity, it seems, could only be attacked through religious terminology. Their Winstanley uses an alternative theology – which one might feel he makes up as he goes along – capable of absorbing almost any past heresy and yet reflecting recognized forms of the Christian system. A. Badstock (1991) locates him in "that small vocal tradition which has continually posited . . . an alternative reading of the gospel harping on themes of protest against injustice and of hope for a radically new social order in the shape of the Kingdom or reign of God". But what is that shape? Elmen, for his part, claims in effect that without the millenarian theology the Digger episode would never have occurred, since otherwise Winstanley must have recognized the chimerical nature of what was attempted. This is an assumption. Parson Platt's victory over the Diggers and their innocent cows meant that turning the earth into a common treasury must be a slower process than at first hoped, but *The Law of Freedom* suggests that Winstanley still thought in 1652 it could be done, with or without the assistance of Oliver Cromwell. Badstock offers as "a most obvious point" that it is impossible to identify with any degree of certainty what the sources of Winstanley's thought really were yet insists on him attempting consistently to maintain "the essentials of the faith" – but what were they? Few historians are theologians enough to do more than observe that the man's thinking, developing rapidly over a period hardly longer than a first degree course, became complex. Perhaps it was also muddled.

The more materialist side of Winstanley has been most thoroughly explored by Christopher Hill. The Digger's character, works and doings run through all of Hill's writing, whether about puritanism, revolution, change and continuity, the experience of defeat, the role of the Bible, but his chief expositions are in his edition of *The Law of Freedom and Other Writings* and his *The Religion of Gerrard Winstanley* (1978). Like Mulligan's, his Winstanley is a man of his period – vitally 1640–1660, consistently characterized as revolutionary. Recognizing the peculiar significance of these two decades, Winstanley sees the times "going up like parchment in the fire". (The figure is well-found: parchment stood for the false learning of hireling priests, the formal records of lawyers and the state.) In the sense that many of his ideas can be found in other earlier and contemporary thinkers and activists, he was not an isolated individual. But he seems to have combined more of them than most, pushing

them harder, giving them a personal twist and relating them
closely to a unique ongoing analysis of the world he wanted
to turn upside down. This Winstanley comes at length to
abandon search for consolations elsewhere, after death.
Rather his philosophy works towards a design for living here
and now, with Reason – the Creator, less and less over the
canon of his tracts a transcendental God – prevailing over
evil to produce an equal society, at peace with itself, made
into "a oneness, making every creature the upholder of his
fellow". This is a doctrine of perfectability on earth with
men responding to "the Christ alive in us, not dead in
Jerusalem", rejecting external salvation, doing without a
God beyond the sky, heaven and hell. *Pace* Mulligan and
company, Hill's Winstanley rejects a personal God, not just
"the clergy's version . . . of a capricious arbitrary God", and
precludes "external saviours". There remains one saving
grace – communism, the earth a common treasury, there in
the earliest pamphlets, but made under the experience of
the power of the forces resisting it less theological, more,
much more, materialistic. St. George's Hill was not a
symbolic act but an experiment, a practical realization of an
image from a trance.

Advocates of an ethereal Winstanley stress the significance
of his language. So does Hill: "the way that he said it was
almost as important as what [he] said". Much of that
language is certainly theological – spiritual, chiliastic,
escatological, hylotheistic, millenarian, terms which historians
bandy about with (sometimes innocent) enthusiasm. Do we,
though, take the language literally and regard "the man and
his meaning as inextricable" from it, or should we, as Hill
suggests, go behind or beneath its surface? Perhaps we can
adapt George Herbert's metaphor:

> A man that looks on glass
> On it may stay his eye,
> Or if he pleaseth through it pass
> And then the heaven espy.

Most commentators find Winstanley an appealing figure. But not all. Distaste may be not unconnected with our own situation. It would be strange if current tensions had no impact upon attitudes towards the radicals of Interregnum England generally and Gerrard Winstanley in particular. For example, J.C. Davis (1976) no more approves of Winstanley than he does of Christopher Hill, whose work he criticizes, with a hint of a bias of his own, as politically motivated. Davis's Winstanley begins – as most do – by expressing a millenarianism, necessarily involving waiting upon the Lord (not yet Reason) with a passivity which can embrace St. George's Hill as a mere gesture. But in *The Law of Freedom* published in 1652 though written earlier, this has given way to a utopian reliance upon a dynamic secular state in the person of Oliver Cromwell, who not surprisingly failed to come up to expectations. Davis argues that Winstanley was never anti-authoritarian. Almost all his works contained some sort of appeal to established authorities or those he believed to be in command of power "to help him achieve his purpose". That sounds sinister. Davis sees totalitarianism in *The Law of Freedom*, a blue-print for a rigid utopian state. But it might also fairly be regarded as a basis for discussion. "Economic freedom" is, Davis says, "the only freedom that matters" for Winstanley. Why not? Freedom, "the man who will turn the word upside down", lies in the equal enjoyment of the earth, the basis of a genuine community. Davis deplores the restrictiveness of such a definition "based on economic necessity, not individual worth or dignity". But where, Winstanley might reply, is the dignity of the poor oppressed by the rich? Individual worth is recognized when a man does to another as he would have another do to him.

Winstanley's life before and after 1648–1652 has been assiduously raked over by R.T. Vann and J.D. Alsop in local archives. Vann shows Winstanley as coming from a lesser social standing and a less puritan background than hitherto supposed. He seems not displeased by this discovery and opines that "the radical is one who turns on a system in which he personally has failed". Alsop reinforces that by depicting the latter-day Winstanley as recovering from earlier economic failure, acquiring respectability and settling down into activities far removed from the communism of St. George's Hill. He more than hints at insincerity in the digger days, echoing Laurence Clarkson's charge of hypocrisy in *The Lost Sheep Found* (1660). Certainly there is a problem. G. Aylmer (1984) suggests a Winstanley 1 and a Winstanley 2 – surely there ought to be a 3 – each to be appraised separately. Hill sees a post-Restoration victim of the experience of defeat, withering into inaction. (William Walwyn, too, the most radical of the Levellers, who once spoke of endeavouring the abolition of private property, ended as a herbalist). The debate about this as about every other aspect of Winstanley continues.

Where does Petegorsky stand now after half a century of intensive historiography? His book was certainly a pioneer in the appraisal of the radicalism of the Interregnum. He saw the Civil War – the causes of which are still hotly debated – as "a challenge for power between social classes", but accepted that religion, notably "puritanism" played a vital part, though, anticipating C.H. George (1970), he grasped that "to embrace all the manifold phases of puritanism . . . into a single entity would stretch the concept so far that it would lose any historical utility". He is interested particularly in the way in which, abandoning stricter forms, such as Calvinism, some puritans claimed the right to determine their own religious observance. Since the established church generally went along with the policies of the state, critique of the one was critique of the other, opening up discussion of social and political topics hitherto proscribed. This process intensified as the war touched directly groups hitherto outside "the political nation" – a term unknown to Petegorsky. "Middling" and "meaner sorts of people" came to claim "contact with God" as not exclusive to the rich and mighty. The growth of sects sharing this sense was apparent even before war began –

Petegorsky cites a contemporary calculation that there were
29 in London alone in 1641. By 1646 Thomas Edwards
estimated in *Gangraena* some two hundred. Conservative
men were alarmed at "the rabble taking advantage of the
times". Parliament located all power inherently in "the
people", but it did not mean that lot. Who, indeed, were the
people? Petegorsky shows the Levellers providing some
answers, but charges them with putting faith too much in
political and legal reforms, failing to appreciate "the
fundamental nature" of economic relationships, and
adopting to the poor an attitude that was charitable rather
than radical.

For the latter we must turn to the true Levellers or the
Diggers, who through Winstanley provided the one genuine
transforming ideology that emerged from the war. Once
Petegorsky gets on to them the argument is developed with
vigour and incisiveness, drawing on a mass of primary,
particularly pamphlet, literature besides Winstanley's own
writings. Dating *The Saints Paradise* to late 1648, he notes,
along with the requirement to wait "with a humble spirit"
upon God to give deliverance, a note of social criticism
already sounding, since revelation will come not to the rich
and educated but to "the despised, the unlearned, the poor,
the nothings of this world (such as the world counts fools)".
The publication of *The Breaking of the Day of God* (May
1648) points even earlier to a Winstanley seeing history as "a
vital dynamic process", the story of a continuous conflict
between opposing forces. Though at this stage God will work
redemption within men rather than by men, there is a
growing stress on men's own experience which
"experimentally" – a key word with Winstanley – can lead to
action. Walking away from "imagination", "let Reason rule
the man and he will do as he would be done by". This golden
mean will knit every creature together into a oneness.
Recognizing the interdependence of human society and
nature, Winstanley is on the way to transferring his
philosophical and cosmological conceptions from religion

and morals to politics and economics and within the space of six or seven months has traversed a path from a chiliastic mysticism through a progressive rationality to a practical programme even though the language remains spiritual. Just how this has come about remains a puzzle for Petegorsky as it has for later commentators. The reader may take it from there.

No serious student of the Winstanley who has emerged over more than three centuries can profitably neglect Petegorsky's work – a pioneer that has become a classic. Petegorsky conveys the excitement which Gerrard Winstanley engendered on him – an excitement which survives for the reader after all the arguments that have followed. It may well be that the drift away from collectivism and the apparent triumph of individualism and the market have given even greater significance to the interpretation of the man and his message. Freedom, he said, was "the mark at which all men should aim" and by his writing showed where it was to be found.

Ivan Roots, 1995
Emeritus Professor of History, University of Exeter

Chapter One : THE BACKGROUND OF THE CIVIL WAR

" For wherefore is it that there is such wars and rumours of wars in the Nations of the Earth? And wherefore are men so mad as to destroy one another? But only to uphold Civil Propriety of Honor, Dominion and Riches one over another. . . . Propriety and single interest divides the people of a land and the whole world into parties and is the cause of all wars and bloodshed and contention everywhere."—*The True Levellers Standard Advanced* (1649).

Every age tends to write history in its own image; and when Victorian England came to record its version of the Civil War through the pen of S. R. Gardiner, it could see that conflict only as a magnificent operation of the special liberalism of its own period. A united nation suffering cruel tyranny and ruthless oppression had risen in its might and anger to strike down a despotic king and to preserve inviolate for future generations the priceless heritage of English liberty. Actually, however, the Civil War was a profound social struggle whose roots lie deep in the vast economic changes of the preceding century.

The most important of those changes, we may briefly note, was the accession to a position of increasing prominence and power of a class of men in the cities and towns whose importance derived not from their ownership of land, but from their possession of capital, and of those classes in the country who were revolutionizing the traditional scheme of agriculture and landholding. The effects of the rapid expansion of foreign and domestic trade, the remarkable development of capitalist industry, the establishment of an elaborate financial organization and the application of commercial methods to agriculture had been to achieve a radical alteration of the social structure and to re-define the social relationships feudalism had established; and from that redefinition there emerged the challenge that met and eventually broke the old concepts and sanctions that had governed those relationships.

If capitalism at the beginning of the seventeenth century

was yet in its infancy, it had already dealt a shattering blow to the old order. A society whose class divisions had been obscured and rationalized by the concept of status was dissolving into one that was undisguisedly based on the phenomenon of class. Wealth was disputing the claims of birth as the royal highway to social privilege. The impersonal relationships of an emergent capitalism were superseding the personal contacts that had been of the essence of feudalism. The supreme and all-embracing power of the Church had shrunk before the growing authority of the secular State. Expediency was replacing theological sanction as the bar before which social policy was being tried; and the stentorian tones of religious prescription were being modified by the pulsating and dynamic beat of the new economic realities.

As the seventeenth century opens, the middle classes are rapidly advancing to the fore of the new social order. The capitalist, everywhere, is emerging as society's most important, surely its most enterprising and ambitious, member. In the cities we meet him as the commercial financier eager to exploit the opportunities of speculation that have appeared on the ever-expanding economic horizon; or as the industrial capitalist embarking on an uncharted voyage of economic experiment; or as the sober tradesman industriously increasing his share of the local market. In the country we find him as the capitalist-farmer who regards his land solely as a business investment and agriculture purely as a commercial enterprise.

But the economic changes of the preceding century, in fashioning the development of a new middle class, produced at the same time another new social phenomenon—the antecedent of the modern proletariat. During the sixteenth century masses of peasants were permanently divorced from the soil by the process of enclosure. Where enclosure did not result directly in eviction, the pressure of other factors—the loss of common rights and its reaction on the peasants' income, the conversion of the demesne to pasture and the resultant diminution in the demand for labour, the deterioration of their legal status and the insecurity of their holdings— forced many more to abandon their holdings. Some were able to enter the service of their former landlords as hired labourers. Others betook themselves to the open-field villages. Many drifted to the towns, where nascent industry was unable to absorb the numbers who sought employment; and the corporations and statutory regulations barred their entrance into trades. Others—and their numbers were considerable—roamed the country as tramps and vagrants searching for employment that was seldom forthcoming. There thus advances for the first time to the forefront of the stage of English history a class of landless labourers, excluded from the ownership of the soil that had once been theirs and able to subsist only by the sale of their labour-power—when they could find purchasers.

The feudal structure of English society was therefore undergoing profound modification. England was still predominantly an agricultural country. The old nobility still possessed great estates; but they were being increasingly forced to break them up into smaller units and to adopt the newer, more efficient methods of management and cultivation of the gentry. The untitled gentry, recruited largely from the ranks of those whose fortune in trade had enabled them to acquire land or from those families who had shared in the spoliation of the monasteries, were growing in influence and number. The yeoman still tilled his own holding; and a new class of landless agricultural labourers had emerged.

In the cities and towns the commercial groups had become the dominating figures. Merchants and tradesmen were occupying increasingly important positions and their political power was growing daily. Despite the decline of the artisan guilds, the master-craftsmen still played an important rôle in economic life. The financial interests of the City of London already wielded an influence that was a portent of their future might. In the trades there was a large number of apprentices; and the development of manufacture and mining had created a considerable number of unorganized labourers.

The seventeenth century thus dawns on a dynamic society in which new forces have been unleashed and vast and glorious vistas revealed to man. Society has become aware of the fact that the world now affords limitless potentialities of development and exploitation. But, if men generally are becoming conscious that they stand on the threshold of a new era, the middle classes increasingly perceive that they alone wield the key to its entrance; for they alone could adequately exploit the opportunities that presented them-

selves. New enterprises demanded investment on which no
immediate return could be expected and which none but
they was prepared to venture. New machines and technical
processes required large capital outlay which only they could
supply. Speculation could be carried on only with ready
money which they alone possessed. Above all, the new age
demanded initiative and imagination which were to be found
only in those classes that were not shackled to the modes and
habits of the past. Society may have a promising future
before it; but it is already heavily mortgaged to the *bourgeoisie.* The realization that, while others must gaze help-
lessly from afar, the middle class alone will enter the Promised
Land imparts to its members a confidence that marks all
their efforts. They exhibit all the historical characteristics
of a class that is soon to challenge for supreme authority in
the State. They are aware of the peculiar interests which
unite them. They are conscious of their power and importance. They manifest a growing disregard of tradition and
authority. They are supremely, if quietly, confident of their
ultimate victory.

But that victory was neither easily nor quickly achieved.
Years of civil war were to bring to a climax, in blood and
slaughter, more than a century of conflict before England
was to be made safe for the new men of property. The
Tudors, it is true, in hastening the deterioration of the
nobility, were destroying the monarchy's principal ally and
thus ultimately enabling the middle class to reduce the
Crown to a position of splendid impotence. But at a time
when the *bourgeoisie,* though rising, had not yet risen, and
the aristocracy, though weakened, was still a factor of considerable importance, the monarchy, by holding the balance
of power between both, could play a dominant rôle; and
the Tudors and Stuarts were thus able to breathe some life
into a system already on the verge of collapse. That their
efforts should have been directed towards stabilizing the old
order rather than facilitating the transition to the new was a
natural consequence of the threat to their position they
sensed in the rising commercial classes. Through a system
of controls, the Tudors attempted to place themselves directly
athwart the driving economic forces of the period. In
practice, it is true, those controls functioned as a series of
irritating restrictions; in theory, at any rate, they implied

an attempt at complete regulation of economic activity. Land laws and enclosure regulations sought to curb the appetites of the capitalist-farmers and land merchants. In every phase of endeavour, State regulation attempted to impose, not altogether successfully, serious restrictions on the free development of economic enterprise; and the remnants of feudalism still operated to hamper and restrain commercial activity.[1] Where the sheer impact of economic change threatened to break through those barriers, conservatism was able to call to its assistance a body of morality inherited from the past, in whose name duties and obligations could be imposed whose performance clogged the wheels of the rapidly accelerating economic machine. For social concepts do not die an easy death; they linger long after the dynamic forces of social development have rendered them archaic. The sixteenth and early seventeenth centuries were still largely dominated by a philosophy that had been evolved to meet the needs of an earlier social order; and, because it belonged to an age that lay in the past, men felt that it impeded their advance to the future that stretched out before them. A mediaeval conception of stewardship as the essence of property attached a dragging weight to the feet of men engaged in a race in which free disposition of their resources was the ultimate condition of victory. The doctrine that individual ambition must be subordinated to social obligation may be an avenue to the Kingdom of Heaven; it sometimes loses one the good things of the earth. Mediaeval society may have been able to rationalize its class divisions by the theory that social harmony is maintained by the performance of occupational function because it was largely a static order with little social mobility. But that concept of status was unacceptable to a dynamic society in which men, through the acquisition of wealth, were constantly remaking the frontiers of class. Charity and a generous concern for the welfare of one's neighbour may be admirable ethical virtues—nay, duties; but they are hardly calculated to increase one's material capital. A concept of property as limited by communal responsibility, a functional view of social differences, a social evaluation of individual behaviour

---

[1] " Throughout almost all the social legislation of the Tudor period, we may see the England of the past erecting vain barriers against the England of the future."—G. Unwin, *Studies in Economic History* (1927), p. 315.

—these were the doctrines, the legacy of a former age, that the middle class encountered as obstructions to its expansion and development.

For many centuries a Church whose authority had been unquestioned and whose power was supreme had given those concepts concrete expression in the elaborate rules of behaviour it imposed and enforced on society. If the sixteenth century largely succeeded in destroying ecclesiastical supervision in the economic realm, it could not prevent the transfer of that control to the powerful state that breakdown served to create; and under the Tudors economic activity was as rigidly disciplined—albeit from a different motive—as it had formerly been by the ecclesiastical system. That it was accepted by the *bourgeoisie* was no doubt due to the fact that the monarchy still had its rôle to play in destroying the surviving vestiges of feudalism and in further reducing the feudal nobility; in part that acquiescence derived from a sober realization that to challenge its exercise would be to invite certain defeat. The order State regulation helped to maintain was, as well, the condition under which the middle class could strengthen its growing forces. More than a century was to elapse before the trend of development was securely to establish the claims of *laisser-faire*. But already the protest against interventionism was making itself heard. The protest of the House of Commons against Elizabethan monopolies is one of the earliest and most emphatic examples of that opposition.[1] " All free subjects ", asserted the House of Commons in 1604, " are born inheritable as to their land so also to the free exercise of their industry." [2] In the 1630's and the early years of the Civil War that protest swelled to new heights. " Tyranny may justly be esteemed the greatest calamity ", declares one anonymous pamphleteer,[3] " because it is in opposition to the chiefest felicity which lies in liberty and the free disposition of that which God and our own industry hath made ours." " In civil affaires ", urged Henry Robinson, " we see by experience that every man most commonly understands best his own businesse." [4] The chaotic events of the Interregnum, it is true, forced on the *bourgeoisie*

[1] Prothero, *Statutes and Constitutional Documents* (1913), p. 111.
[2] *Commons Journals*, May 21, 1604, Vol. I, p. 218.
[3] *A Brief Discourse on Tyrants and Tyranny* (1642), E. 127 (45).
[4] Henry Robinson, *Liberty of Conscience* (1644), E. 39 (1).

the adoption of a system of regulation more rigorous than that which it had fought to overthrow. But after the Restoration the current moves rapidly, and by the turn of the century the theoretical foundations of *laisser-faire* were already laid; State regulation has by that time lost its title to a coherent and valid social policy. What is significant to note, however, is the fact that as early as the closing decades of the sixteenth century men were learning, to their anger, because to their material loss, that the operation of State regulation was preventing them from reaping the harvest that lay before them. God had been ejected from the sphere that had come to be considered as rightfully Caesar's; the *bourgeoisie* was now to seek to render even Caesar powerless.

But what the middle class sought for itself it was anxious to deny to others. For itself it demanded freedom from restriction and interference; for the proletariat it wanted a discipline as rigorous as that from which the middle class itself was striving to escape. Capitalism required for its development a supply of free labour to man its growing enterprises, a labour army to wage its economic battles. That army was already in the process of creation; its recruiting-officers were those who were driving the English peasantry off the soil. But if it was to be an effective force in the service of capitalism, its members had to be at once submissive to authority and unquestioning of the purposes it would be utilized to achieve. It was therefore necessary to impose on the ever-increasing numbers of landless labourers both in town and country a discipline that would reduce them to a homogeneous mass and induce them to accept without question—or, at least, without effective protest—their rôle and status in the new order. They had to be disciplined to the ends of the new society.

By the early decades of the seventeenth century the *bourgeoisie* had begun to sense the tasks that lay before it. It had, first of all, to effect its release from the oppressive system of control the State attempted to enforce. But because that policy was rooted in a system of social concepts, the middle class had to complete the destruction of a body of social doctrine that economic development was already rendering obsolete and to substitute in its stead a system of thought that would hallow its ends and sanction its activities. Religion and philosophy had to be re-fashioned to serve

new masters and to fulfil new purposes. In giving freedom
to the middle classes the new modes of thought had to justify
its denial to the proletariat. And finally, if the *bourgeoisie*
was to continue its course without hindrance, the institutions
of power—the State—had to be captured from the aristocracy
that controlled them and re-dedicated to the service of the
conquerors.

It was therefore but a natural consequence that philosophic
thought generally and religious thought particularly should
undergo profound transformation during the sixteenth and
seventeenth centuries. Under the impact of economic development the authority of the Church had weakened; and
the social thought that was emerging from those changes was
becoming increasingly secular rather than theological in its
emphasis. Already, Calvinism, born and nurtured in an
environment in which the new forms of economic life were
facts to be accepted rather than innovations to be condemned,
constituted an important and radical departure from the
beaten path of religious theory and practice; and the form it
took in English Puritanism completed the process by which
theological precept was to adapt itself to the framework of the
new capitalist economy.[1]

No single formula, it must be emphasized, can serve as
an adequate definition of Puritanism. For, " besides the
Puritan in church policy ", Parker [2] asserts in protest against
the indiscriminate application of the term, " there were
Puritans in religion, Puritans in state and Puritans in
morality ".

> " There is a truer affinity of minde ", he declares, " be-
> tweene some which are Puritans and some which are not
> than betweene some Puritans and others of the contrary
> opinion and others."

There were within Puritanism itself many strains the profound
divergence of which the Civil War was so dramatically to
reveal. Nor, we must remember, was Puritanism ever a

---

[1] On the relationship of religious theory to social change in the sixteenth
and seventeenth centuries, and particularly on the rise of Puritanism, see
R. H. Tawney, *Religion and the Rise of Capitalism*, a book indispensable to
an understanding of the period. Cf. also H. J. Laski, *The Rise of European
Liberalism*, London (1936), Chaps. I and II.
[2] Henry Parker, *Discourse Concerning Puritans* (1641), E. 204 (3).

static entity. What might have been its characteristic features in the reign of Elizabeth had given way to new tendencies in that of James; and the character it bore after the Restoration would have rendered it difficult for us to recognize as its parent what passes for Puritanism on the eve of the Civil War. Those who helped to fashion Puritan thought would themselves have been the first to deny the body of social theory and practice that emerged as the implications of their teachings. To embrace all the manifold phases of Puritanism in a single unity would therefore require us to stretch our definition of the concept to a point at which it would lose its utility. But it is nevertheless true, that despite the transformation it underwent, there is a body of thought, an unmistakable attitude, a temperament, that we can identify as Puritanism; and in its development we can see the process—albeit unconscious—by which the middle class was shaping religious thought to its own needs and ends. For Puritanism, as Professor Tawney has so brilliantly shown, did not spread by itself or because of its inner beauty and consistency. It was adopted by the English middle classes because there was something in it that corresponded to the ethos of the period and because there was something in it they were able to use. What was the ethos?

It was, above all, a search for new sanctions for human behaviour, a quest for a rationale for the new modes of social conduct whose pattern-habit was tracing indelibly on English society. Men refused to obey the old precepts because their practical effect was a denial of those benefits which an expanding economy and their own ingenuity now made possible. The old Church could no longer provide a system to which even satisfactory lip-service could be paid because it was remote from the realities of daily life. The institutions that had once functioned as a complete setting for all of men's activities, and within whose framework all social values were given meaning and content, became merely one aspect of people's lives because they were increasingly ceasing to speak in the language men understood. Ethical and religious ideals no longer corresponded to the social reality they were intended to regulate; in the words of Tawney, " their practical ineffectiveness paved the way for their theoretical abandonment."

To the hand of the middle classes, however, there lay

the convenient doctrines of Calvinism. We do not intend to treat here of their early development in Geneva or of the practical expression they were given under the theocratic rule of Calvin and Beza.[1] But the central dogma of Calvinism was an all-embracing determinism, a doctrine of predestination, which asserted that all mankind was divided by God into the chosen few who were saved and the many who were damned, those who were to enjoy the eternal bliss of a heavenly Paradise and those who were to suffer the tortures of hell. That division had been determined by an incomprehensible act of the Divine Will, and no human effort could avail a whit to modify or avert that Divine decree. If no human act could bring grace, then the business of life was not to achieve salvation, but to glorify the name of God on earth; and that glorification was to be effected not primarily through prayer or religious worship, but in the daily routine of practical activity. The emphasis of religious teaching was thus shifted from the minutiæ of ceremonial observance to the practical conduct of everyday life. The responsibility of each individual to lead a life through which the Creator would be glorified became at least as fundamental as the duty of the Church to maintain those formal institutions through which that sanctification could be achieved. And the guide for all Christian conduct was no longer to be the authoritarian fiat of an ecclesiastical hierarchy, but the written word of the Scriptures in which God had eternally revealed Himself to man and whose interpretation was both each individual's responsibility and privilege. Perceptibly, let it be noted, a society already largely individualistic in practice was becoming increasingly individualistic in thought.

The appeal of these doctrines to late sixteenth- and seventeenth-century England was profound. In a theological system which insisted that mankind had already been divided into classes by the arbitrary decree of the Lord, the middle classes found their sanction for a class division that economic development was crystallizing; and through its emphasis on individual deportment as a means for the glorification of God, they were able to elevate to the lofty status of Christian virtues the social practices they had already adopted. God, they reasoned, who has already chosen those who are to enjoy

[1] See E. Choisy, *La Théocratie à Genève au temps de Calvin* (Geneva, 1897); *L'Etat Chrétien Calviniste à Genève au temps de Théodore de Bèze* (Geneva, 1902).

the blessings of Heaven, is unlikely to frown on His chosen while they still tread the earth.   And how else could He smile on the elect but by conferring on them the good things of life? A class consciousness bred of material success was purified by the cleansing waters of theological doctrine to become a conviction of innate superiority.   The poverty of the unfortunate became an indication of their moral failure. For if riches were proof of election, poverty was the yellow badge of damnation decreed by God and beyond any human power to revoke.   The destitute of yesterday whose lot society had been obligated to ease became the wicked of to-day whose distress no one need alleviate.   Poverty and suffering, once an eloquent reproach to the luxury of the wealthy and a powerful prick to their conscience, became merely confirmation of their own righteousness and a justification for the denial of their social responsibilities.

> ". . . the rich artificiall theeves doe rob the poore and that under a fained show of justice and a seeming holinesse," bitterly declares the author of that remarkable pamphlet, *Tyranipocrit*,[1] " and when they have done it most impiously they say and affirm that God's providence hath made them rich and those which they have robbed poore; for they say that God's providence maketh rich and poore."

If success was proof of election, it was thus but a logical inference that those practices which led to economic advancement were Christian virtues by whose exercise God was being glorified.   Those who strive for wealth need no longer be accused of being tainted of the Devil, for not riches themselves, but the manner in which they were gained and the ends to which they are dedicated are the criteria by which men are judged; not the mere possession of money, but the vices of luxury and extravagance and indulgence that it may encourage are to be shunned and condemned.   " It is generally maintained by many worldly wise men that riches, if men doe not set their hearts on them, cannot hinder godlinesse."[2]

The advantages to the *bourgeoisie* of a system that tended

---

[1] *Tyranipocrit discovered with all his wiles wherewith he vanquisheth* (1649), E. 569 (5), p. 16.
[2] Ibid., p. 17.

to equate social station with moral worth and to interpret social status as the expression of Divine Will need little emphasis. The more fortunate were confirmed both in the positions they held and in the practices by which those positions had been achieved. The less fortunate were told that attempts to transcend one's social class were not only futile, because pre-ordained, but constituted a protest against the immutable decree of the Lord. Everyone must therefore accept his station in the new order, however lowly; but within that station he must conduct himself in a manner that will exalt the name of his Maker. And the cardinal virtues became those practices on which society was now placing the seal of moral approval because they were conducive to material success—industry, thrift, diligence, sobriety, moderation. In Puritanism the middle class found both the sanction and the rationale it was seeking for its own activities and the discipline it was anxious to impose on the masses.

Nor was the appeal of Calvinism to the individual conscience rather than to an authoritarian hierarchy less attractive than its doctrine of predestination to the mood of those to whom the exercise of authority spelled on the one hand religious persecution, and on the other the retardation of economic progress. Its revolt against the ecclesiastical organization found eager support among those who saw in the Church's support of the monarchy one of the strongest bulwarks of the old order, and in its extravagance and mismanagement a criminal waste of valuable resources and— what was in their eyes still worse—a deliberate neglect of economic opportunity.

To summarize the complex development of Puritanism in so bald and mechanical a fashion, it must be emphasized, is to present an extreme over-simplification of the manner in which it both moulded and was shaped by its environment. It stresses, too, simply the process by which religious thought was adapting itself to the realities of the new order. But Puritanism, it must be pointed out, played a major rôle in the development of English liberalism. For if democracy and toleration were not of the essence of Puritanism, they were certainly its most important by-products. I say not of its essence because there was nothing inherent in Puritan thought that should have made it such a powerful factor in the promotion of the democratic ideal. Few sixteenth-century

Puritans doubted the wisdom and necessity of uniformity of religious worship or questioned that it was the duty of the civil authorities to enforce the true discipline. Nor would many early Puritans have ventured to suggest that religion depart from its principle of organization in a national Church. Puritanism in substituting for the infallible authority of the Church the infallible authority of the Scriptures had no intention of denying the necessity of a nationally-organized Church. It was simply protesting that the Church, in its existing form, could not claim to be divinely sanctioned. Puritanism, it is true, foundered when it attempted to determine the proper external form for the reformed Church; but that was a fact due not to its rejection of the principle, but to the nature of the various groups it had enrolled under its banners.

But the Puritans were driven to enunciate the principles of democratic control and religious liberty not by the inherent logic of their doctrines, but because of the experience they encountered. As a religious minority, they found themselves persecuted and suppressed; they were therefore forced to demand for themselves with increasing urgency the right to the free expression of their views. When that demand was reinforced by a general realization of the economic cost of religious persecution, the acceptance of the principle of religious toleration became an accomplished fact. When it became clear that they could find no place within the established Church, they were obliged to claim for each congregation the right to determine its own form of religious observance. When they realized how slight were their chances of reforming the Church by political action, they had to insist on the existence and authority of fundamental divine law that the hierarchy dare not contravene. Freedom for the expression of minority opinion, toleration of religious differences, the right of groups to determine their own forms of organization and procedure and the existence of a fundamental law by which authority must consider itself bound were principles that flowed not from the nature of Puritan doctrine, but from the realities of Puritan experience.

The influence of Puritanism on all sections of English society was far-reaching and profound. But its strength was largely concentrated in the rising industrial and commercial classes and the gentry in the country. Long before the Civil

War, the identification of these classes with religious dissent was becoming more apparent. Professor Usher's estimate of the distribution of Puritan ministers during the first decade of the seventeenth century suggests that the majority were located in the commercial and manufacturing areas of England.[1] Large numbers of young men were being encouraged to enter the ministry by the *nouveaux-riches* ; and the dedicatory prefaces of theological works no less than the funeral eulogies afford ample testimony of the degree to which Puritan preachers and students were dependent on the monied classes.[2]

> " They are men ", wrote Harris [3] of the Puritans, impressed by the fact that they were so largely to be found among the business elements, " which respect their profits above their consciences."

That it was these groups everywhere who formed the backbone of the resistance both to the Stuart regime and the Laudian Church during the Civil War, few contemporary observers fail to emphasize. Baxter's testimony needs no repetition.[4] Equally striking is the evidence of Sedgwick. Two factions, he asserts,[5] are fighting the war,

> " . . . the Court and Royall and Episcopall Party " and " the country people and the Puritan party ".
> " To the King goes men of honour as the nobility and the Gentry, such whose honour is predominate over their reason and religion . . . men of implicit faith whose conscience is much regulated by their superiors. . . . To the Parliament, men of a lower state and expressing their own reasons in religion, zealous and well-affected people, men of industry and labour that love freedom and to be something themselves; men whose consciences are their owne and so strict in them; cities, corporations, bodies . . ."

[1] R. G. Usher, *Reconstruction of the English Church* (1910), Vol. I, pp. 249–50.
[2] Wm. Haller, *The Rise of Puritanism* (1938), pp. 39–40 ; also Chap. I, note 45.
[3] John Harris, *The Puritan's Impuritie* (1641), E. 173 (8).
[4] Baxter, *Reliquiae Baxterianae* (1696), p. 30.
[5] Wm. Sedgwick, *The Leaves of the Tree of Life for the Healing of the Nations* (1648), E. 460 (10).

The Venetian Ambassador, reporting the overwhelming loyalty of London to the Parliamentary cause, wrote [1] that

> " the merchants who profess Calvinism and the lower classes among the inhabitants of this city pursue the promptings of their violent passions without reflection rather than their real interests ".

> " The common people here who are followers of the dogmas of Calvin ", he wrote a few months later, " detest monarchy." [2]

This union of religious dissent with the classes in the van of economic progress was no mere coincidence. Nor was it simply political exigency that forged the bonds of alliance between the middle class and the opponents of the Anglican Church. Opposition to Stuart rule and dissatisfaction with the ecclesiastical organization were alike the reaction to the existing system of a class of men whose minds and temperaments and needs had been fashioned by the new order.

Ecclesiastical, constitutional, legal and political issues are so inextricably entangled in the decades before the Civil War that their separation becomes an almost wholly impossible adventure. One thing, however, is clear—that all these developments must be set against the background that is fundamental to an understanding of the period: the growth of the middle class in numbers and strength, its struggle for political power, the reaction of the old order, their clash in armed conflict. Not for a moment would we deny that the religious or constitutional struggles had an independent reality of their own; the ecclesiastical differences, particularly, imparted to the struggle an acerbity that might otherwise not have been present. What we are simply emphasizing is the fact that these conflicts must be seen as parts of a much larger whole—as the expressions of a general revolt against a system which men felt was limiting their activities and hampering their development. The *bourgeoisie* rebelled against the old order because it was burdensome and oppressive. They felt themselves caught in the grip of a huge octopus from whose clutches they sought to escape. They had to deny a body of social thought that sanctioned the

---

[1] *Calendar of State Papers, Venetian, 1642-43*, June 27, 1642, p. 83.
[2] Ibid., August 22, 1642, p. 130.

practices against which they protested. They had to counter
the constitutional theory that claimed for the King the rights
they were anxious to abrogate. They had to oppose a legal
system that crystallized the relationships they were in the
process of transforming. They had to destroy a church that
was so antithetical to their own temper and which acted
vigorously to enforce its dictates. Above all, they had to
capture political power in order to abolish the engines of
repression and to establish in their stead the institutions
that would give effect to their own purposes and ambitions.
The middle class was advancing on many fronts; but those
fronts were simply sectors of one large battlefield.

Constitutionally, the debate resolved itself into a dispute
as to the incidence of sovereign power in the State. Under
the influence of Bodin, seventeenth-century thinkers were
increasingly concerned with the problem of sovereignty;
but not until its exercise was challenged did Englishmen
move to a consideration of its nature. Until the incisive
mind of Hobbes put the discussion in a more adequate
perspective, men were concerned simply with the practical
problem of its location. Did sovereignty rest solely with the
King or with the King-in-Parliament? Was its exercise
limited by any fundamental law? Did the King under the
claim of emergency powers have the right to disregard the
law? Were the Ministers who advised the Crown answerable
to Parliament for their actions?

The legal conflict was largely expressed in the struggle
of the common law for supremacy over the public and private
law of the State and in the attempts of the common lawyers
to deny the jurisdiction of the ecclesiastical courts. With the
development of trade and commerce, with the entrance of
the *bourgeoisie* to the universities and academies of learning,
an important class of common lawyers, united by their
special interests and their common ambitions, had emerged.
Jealous for power, eager for privilege, they attempted at every
point to extend their influence in the State; and their efforts
to deny the claims of the ecclesiastical courts and to extend
their own powers by curtailing the judicial competence and
rights of the Church figure prominently in the history of the
early decades of the seventeenth century. The denunciation
of the lawyers in which the popular literature of the Civil
War period abounds is probably the best index to the nature

of the methods and tactics they employed in furthering those ambitions.

The religious controversy is, of course, a dominant theme of the period. Generally, that controversy concerned the problems of internal reform on the one hand and the relationship of the Church to the secular authorities on the other. The general temper of Puritanism, with its emphasis on the individual conscience as the final guide to religious practice, was incompatible with a Church which vested religious direction in the arbitrary decree of an authoritarian hierarchy. The rapid growth of the High-Church tendency evoked the determined hostility of the House of Commons. There was the profound anti-clericalism that continued to increase in intensity during the reign of the Stuarts. Many currents contributed to that powerful anti-clerical tide. With the rise of an educated laity, the moral and spiritual authority of the clergy decreased; and as the ignorance of so many religious leaders was increasingly revealed, that loss of authority passed into disrespect and contempt. The excessive claims of Convocation to exclusive authority on problems of religious belief and discipline were indignantly challenged by men who had begun to feel, in growing measure, the vital need for a greater share in shaping the conditions under which they have to live. There was the profound suspicion and fear of the influence of Roman Catholicism. There was the antagonism the middle classes felt towards the Church as they grew to see in it the most important support of the monarchy, which was, after all, their chief enemy. And, above all else, there was the constant and irritating interference of the Church in secular and economic affairs. A Church already odious to men because it was the embodiment of a theoretical system they were endeavouring to remake now incurred their wrath because of its continual intrusion into their daily affairs.

That anti-clericalism and antagonism to the Church reached their height during Charles' reign, and particularly during Laud's tenure of office as Archbishop of Canterbury. For to Laud religion was still a totality embracing within its scope every aspect of corporate, no less than of individual, existence. Society was for him essentially a hierarchy of functions and duties, an organic unity whose harmony was complete when every one of its members diligently discharged his function. Unity was the essential condition of social harmony; and to Laud the price of unity was rigid uniformity. Economic individualism and religious nonconformity were equally destructive of social stability; for both impaired that uniformity that was a condition of its maintenance. " Unity cannot long continue in the Church where uniformity is shut out at the church door " [1] was a principle Laud applied equally to the State. Every aspect of human behaviour had therefore to be subjected to a rigid discipline; and Church and State were simply different agencies that operated to render that supervision effective. The economic practices of the mart and the liturgy of the Church, the money-exchange no less than the altar were subject to the same eternal law of God. And in an age when Mammon was challenging the claims of God to the allegiance of men that discipline had to be enforced with an unrelenting severity.

To his passionate pursuit of uniformity, Laud coupled an inability to compromise on details when such accommodation would have preserved what was essential. His attempts to enforce uniformity of worship and ritual evoked profound opposition. Through the Court of High Commission and the Metropolitical Visitation he enforced the rules he laid down for the maintenance of order. But the repressive nature of his rule has been considerably over-exaggerated. The punishments inflicted for deviations from his regulations or for defiance of his authority were, it is true, severe and frequently savage. The treatment of Bastwick, Prynne and Burton can be cited; and the £3000 fine imposed on Lodovick Bowyer for libelling Laud can be instanced to indicate how jealously Laud guarded his prestige and authority.[2] But these few cases have been remembered where countless others have been forgotten:

> " Few things impress the students of the records of the Commission ", declares Usher [3] in his study of the High Commission, " more than the superabundance of evidence testifying to the consistent care and effort shown by the Commissioners that their powers be exercised with equity, moderation and absolute fairness and that their procedure should be free from undue delay, expense and vexation."

[1] Laud, *Works* (1842), Vol. IV, p. 60.
[2] Rushworth, *Historical Collections*, Appendix to Vol. III, p. 65.
[3] R. G. Usher, *The Rise and Fall of the High Commission* (1913), p. 267.

" Not only did the Commission seek to secure the equity and justice of its own proceedings but it was ready to aid those oppressed elsewhere." [1]

" The indirect evidence of the popularity of the Court of High Commission under Laud's regime as well as in the previous four decades is overwhelming." [2]

Nor was the direct exercise of Laud's ecclesiastical authority generally repressive in its nature :

" For when shall the common people have leave to exercise ", read the declaration reintroducing the [3] Book of Sports in 1633, " if not upon the Sundays and Holy-Days, seeing they must apply their labour and win their living in all working-days? "

His suppression of Puritanism, however, was rigorous and did much to incur the deep enmity of the middle classes among whom Puritanism flourished.

But it was Laud's continued interference in secular affairs that more than anything else aroused the hostility of the *bourgeoisie* and eventually cost him his head. " This last yeares famin was made by man and not by God," he asserted [4] at Archer's trial; and he consistently brought that attitude to bear on his treatment of economic affairs. His hatred of enclosure, for example, was intense; and his activity on the Commission for Depopulation led Clarendon to observe that much of Laud's unpopularity derived from the fact that " he did a little too much countenance the Commission for Depopulation ".[5]   As one of the most powerful members of a commission to control all English colonies, he came into conflict with powerful merchant groups by refusing to sanction practices they wanted to adopt.[6]   His membership of the Treasury Commission brought him into similar conflict with the financial interests. His activity and prominence in the Court of Star Chamber were fiercely resented; and because of his influence, his power in affecting decision was formidable. The increase of ecclesiastical representation on

[1] R. G. Usher, *The Rise and Fall of the High Commission* (1913), p. 270.
[2] Ibid., p. 323.
[3] Gardiner, *Documents*, p. 101.
[4] *Reports of Cases in Star Chamber* (Camden Society), ed. Gardiner, p. 46.
[5] Clarendon, *History of the Rebellion*, Book I, par. 204.
[6] C. E. Wade, *John Pym* (1912), pp. 163–71.

the bench of the Court was widely attacked.[1] The economic effects of Laud's rule were the subject of many petitions and complaints on the eve of the Civil War. The strict observance of Saints' Days had, it was claimed, been very costly in economic terms; and his intolerance and persecution of the Puritans had acted as a serious deterrent to economic development by driving thousands of enterprising tradesmen from the country.[2]

The most important struggle of the middle classes, however, was with the Crown; for the monarchy was the very centre of the system by which they felt themselves oppressed. I have already referred briefly to the efforts of the Tudors to preserve the old order against the challenge of the new; and that policy was continued by the Stuarts. As with the Tudors, State regulation, if intended to govern all forms of economic life, became in practice a series of bothersome restrictions on the activity of the *bourgeoisie*. It is unnecessary to discuss that system of regulation at length. It found expression in the land laws, in the excise and custom regulations, in the grants of patents and monopolies and in innumerable petty orders and regulations. There was, for example, that survival of feudalism, the Court of Wards, which was used by the Stuarts as a source of revenue and whose abolition the gentry were continually demanding, for the farming out of land and wardships and the obligations such tenure imposed reduced the price and value of considerable areas of land. There were limitations on trading and restrictions on the freedom of markets imposed by the Crown. There were the sporadic efforts of the Stuarts to protect the peasantry by enforcing the statutes against enclosure, although after the depression of 1622 the gentry were given the opportunity to recoup their fortunes by the suspension of the laws. It is highly interesting to observe that as long as London maintained its prosperity, the City remained staunchly Royalist. After the depression of the 1620's, the London merchants became increasingly hostile to the Crown.

But it is important to note that before the Civil War, at any rate, there does not emerge from all of those conflicts

---

[1] During 1630-40 three bishops were permitted to sit as judges; cf. Phillips, " The Last Years of the Court of Star Chamber ", *Transactions Royal Historical Society*, 4th series (1938), p. 114.
[2] Gardiner, *Documents*, " Root and Branch Petition ", pp. 137–44.

B

any well-defined, consistent body of thought.   Theories were simply weapons with which the struggle was waged; and those weapons had to be adapted to the changing fortunes of battle.   As new positions were captured, new theoretical defences were erected; and retreats were generally covered with thick smoke-screens of legal and constitutional verbiage. The main theme of political thought during the decades before the Civil War [1] is the limitation of the powers of the monarchy and the attempt to transfer effective legislative power to Parliament.   But neither side had as yet clearly perceived the broad outlines of their struggle; and their differences found expression, until 1629, in a series of con-flicts over particular issues.   The will to power among the middle classes, however, was unmistakable.   By 1628 the House of Commons had already established itself as the senior partner in Parliament; contemporary observers declared that the wealth of the members of the House of Commons of that year was at least three times as great as that represented in the House of Lords.   Already the Commons were grasping at political power; and that fact was clearly recognized by Charles, who dissolved Parliament in 1629 because it sought " to erect an universal and overswaying power to themselves which belongs only to us and not to them ".[2]

We can therefore readily understand why the controversies over taxation and finance bulk so large in the political history of the period; to a considerable degree, in fact, they are the key to the political developments of the time.   For the roots of those struggles went much deeper than the demand of those who now paid the major share of taxes and duties for a greater measure of control in the administration of funds and a more authoritative voice in determining the purposes for which they should be spent.   Parliament, we must re-member, was endeavouring to bind the King to its will; the success of the monarchy in maintaining the old order was to depend largely on its ability to render itself independent of Parliament.   State finance still operated on the principle that the King, defraying peace-time expenses from his own revenues, could seek assistance from Parliament only for pur-

---

[1] For an analysis of the literature of the period, cf. J. W. Allen, *English Political Thought, 1603–60*, Vol. I (1603–44) (1938), *passim*.
[2] Gardiner, *Documents*, p. 95.

poses of war. Despite the efforts of Elizabeth and the Stuarts to avoid the complications of foreign adventure, they were continually becoming involved in 'Continental wars; and the Tudors and the Stuarts were constantly forced to seek Parliamentary grants. The spoliation of the Church lands considerably enhanced monarchical revenues; but costly wars, particularly the invasion of Ireland, and the depreciation of the value of money added heavy burdens to the Exchequer, and recourse was had to every device by means of which revenue might be increased. Elizabeth began the practice—and it was continued by James and Charles—of selling rather than leasing Crown lands, in an effort to realize ready money. Although the immediate effect of that policy was an increase in Crown revenue, it told in the long run on the permanent income. The costly and ill-advised foreign ventures of the Stuarts and an extravagance in their domestic affairs aggravated a financial plight already acute; and because of their heavy sale of Crown lands, their income remained stationary at a time when their needs and commitments had sharply increased. In every instance the attempts of both James and Charles to rule without Parliament foundered on the rocks of financial necessity. Parliament's grip on the purse-strings was its chief defence against the perpetuation of personal rule; to loosen those strings would have meant to release the only bond that held the Crown to Parliament. If the latter seems at times to have pressed its advantage unduly, its action served to emphasize that the King, in the final analysis, was dependent on his popular assembly.[1]

The struggle reached its climax during the period of Charles' personal rule from 1629 to 1640. For during those years the old order displayed a toughness that few had imagined it to possess. Investigation has forced historians to abandon the old conception of those years as a period of tyranny and oppression. Actually, the period was one of growing prosperity and considerable administrative efficiency. Whatever Charles' faults may have been—and no doubt they were many—he had a deep sense of justice. Financial necessity forced him to adopt many of the expedients to which he resorted; but his policy was at least equally actuated by a sincere concern for the welfare of the poorer

[1] On taxation and finance under the Tudors and the Stuarts, cf. F. C. Dietz, *English Public Finance, 1558–1641* (1932), *passim*.

of his subjects. At the same time that he was ordering the imposition of ship-money we find him insisting in his orders to the collectors

> "that no persons be assessed unto the same unless they be known to have Estates in Mony or Goods or other means to live by over and above their daily Labour; and where you find such persons to be taxed you are to take off what shall be set upon them and lay it upon those that are better able to bear it." [1]

Charles himself may have lacked the ability to give practical expression to his social ideals; but he had the able assistance of Laud and Strafford, whose subsequent fate at the hands of the Long Parliament is the most eloquent tribute to their success during the years of personal government.

We have already discussed Laud's rôle during that period; the needs of Charles' purse fortunately harmonized with the dictates of Laud's conscience. If Strafford lacked the intensity of Laud's religious convictions, he shared his passion for order and authority. An administrator rather than a thinker, practical rather than theoretic, Strafford was primarily concerned with the effective maintenance of strong government. For years a staunch opponent of the royal party, he had become convinced that no popular body could adequately control public affairs. Only a powerful central government deriving its authority from the King and administered by men zealous for the common welfare could achieve the efficiency he set as his ideal. Indifferent alike to the protests of friends and the abuse of enemies, he consistently gave effect, first as Lord President of the Council of the North and later as Lord Deputy of Ireland, to the policy he later summarized on the scaffold:

> "I had not any intention in my heart but what did aim at the joint and individual prosperity of the King and his people." [2]

Together, Charles, Laud and Strafford gave England for a decade a Government which attempted to subdue personal

---

[1] Rushworth, op. cit., Part II, Vol. I, p. 261.
[2] Rushworth, *The Tryal of the Earl of Strafford* (1700), p. 763.

ambition to the demands of the corporate well-being.   There was no sphere of economic activity into which the Government hesitated to venture.   Financial necessity drove it to the adoption of many unpopular measures; and sordid and pecuniary motives often lurk behind a policy that at first sight impresses us by its social idealism.   But the concern of the regime for the welfare of the poor and the protection of the less fortunate was nevertheless genuine and real.   We need but turn the pages of the *Calendars of State Papers* for the period to see how intense was the preoccupation of the Government with the regulation of economic affairs and how continuous was its intervention on behalf of the oppressed and the poverty-stricken:

> " The most characteristic feature of the economic policy of the Stuarts and of the Tudors ", one recent writer has declared, " was the continual endeavour to aid the new classes of society who suffered from the new capitalist development, above all the weavers and the artisans generally against the entrepreneurs and managers of industry and commerce, and also the agricultural population oppressed by the enclosures and sheep-rearing." [1]

One or two examples may suffice to indicate the measure of the social paternalism of the Government.   Particular energy was displayed in dealing with the land problem; [2] and landlords anxious to enclose ofttimes found themselves thwarted by the restraining hand of the Government or punished for defiance of its orders.   In 1630, for example, the justices of five Midland counties were instructed to remove all enclosures of the previous two years because they had resulted in depopulation. [3]   Commissions of investigation were appointed in 1632, 1635 and 1636, and special instructions issued to the Justices of Assize to enforce the Statutes against enclosure. [3]   Heavy fines were levied against offenders; one Roper, for example, was fined over £4000 and confined to the Fleet for enclosing his land, converting it to pasture

---

[1] Heckscher, *Mercantilism* (1935), Vol. I, p. 257.
[2] Cf. R. H. Tawney, *The Agrarian Problem in the Sixteenth Century* (1912), pp. 371–7.
[3] Leonard, " The Inclosure of the Common Fields in the Seventeenth Century ", *Transactions Royal Historical Society*, New Series, Vol. XIX, p. 128.

and evicting his tenants.[1]   Rushworth records that the commissions sent to Oxford, Cambridge, Warwick and Nottingham alone brought into the Exchequer over £30,000 in
fines.[2]

The dearth of corn and the consequent rise in prices in
1629–31 produced a very considerable burst of governmental
activity; the State Papers for the years following the shortage
are particularly full of the reports of the Justices of the Peace
on their measures to ease the hardships the dearth created.
Engrossers were heavily fined, seven Norfolk hoarders, for
example, being assessed £100 each for the practice.[3]   The
capitalist-farmers, eager to seize the profits a shortage of
commodities would normally have made possible, were particularly angered by the strenuous efforts of the Government
to reduce and to stabilize the prices of foodstuffs and to
provide the poor with food.

The regulation of wages, similarly, occupied much of the
Government's attention; and the Privy Council was frequently
intervening to protect employees from wage reductions.[4]
And no phase of governmental activity of the period is more
noteworthy than the efficiency that was achieved in the
administration of the Poor Law.[5]

Strafford, during his period of service both in the North
and in Ireland, was the ruthless and implacable foe of corruption, bribery and inefficiency. He made strenuous
efforts to revive trade and to relieve the poor; and his strict
enforcement of the laws for the regulation of the cloth trade
was bitterly resented by the clothiers.[6]   His persistent refusal
to favour one set of interests over another earned him the
deep enmity of the landlords and the commercial groups.

A benevolent paternalism, however, was but one aspect of
the economic policy of the Crown.   Charles' desperate efforts
to augment his revenue form a much less creditable phase of
its activities.   His determination to achieve that end without

---

[1] Rushworth, *Historical Collections*, Part II, Vol. I, p. 268.
[2] Ibid., p. 333.
[3] *Reports of Cases in the Courts of Star Chamber*, etc., p. 88.
[4] e.g. *C.S.P. Dom., 1631–33*, p. 22; E. Lipson, *Economic History of England*, Vol. III, p. 255; Rushworth, op. cit., p. 333.
[5] From 1631 to 1640, declares Miss Leonard, " we have had more poor
relief in England than we have ever had before or since." Leonard,
English Poor Relief (1900), p. 256; cf. Leonard, *passim* for the administration of poor relief during this period.
[6] R. R. Reid, *The Council of the North* (1920), pp. 412 ff.

recourse to Parliament forced him to tap every possible source of income; forced loans, ship-money, monopoly patents—among other measures—were the direct results of that effort.

The fines usually imposed on offenders no doubt added considerable zest to the social idealism of the Crown. Some of the prosecutions against enclosure, for example, do not seem to have been altogether free of ulterior motive. Monopoly grants,[1] one of the most important sources of royal revenue, to cite another instance, were ostensibly intended to encourage native industry by protecting it from foreign competition, to protect the small master and artisan from the domination of the capitalist and to assure the consumer an adequate supply of commodities at fair prices. In many instances monopoly undoubtedly worked to those ends; the commercial monopolies, particularly, were valuable factors in developing new areas. For the greater part, however, the industrial monopolies were little more than a device for raising money without the consent of Parliament. The income from this source was considerable. It has been claimed that towards the end of the decade the wine and soap monopolies were each yielding an annual income of £30,000 and tobacco the sum of £13,000 yearly.[2] A number of industries were actually in the hands of the Crown; gold and silver wire-drawing, pin-making, the manufacture of playing-cards and alum were all at one time or another royal monopolies. Charles made strenuous efforts to exact money from the coal trade from the North of England, and, failing that, vainly endeavoured to convert it into a royal monopoly.[3]

Although the granting of monopoly patents split middle-class opposition to the monarchy to a certain degree by creating powerful groups who had a vested interest in its preservation, the policy nevertheless united even more firmly the industrial elements already hostile to the Crown. The tendency to erect corporations on a narrow and exclusive basis and, by granting them wide powers, to place an entire

[1] On monopolies under the Stuarts, cf. G. Unwin, *Industrial Organization in the Sixteenth and Seventeenth Centuries* (1907), and *Gilds and Companies of London* (1938), Chap. XVII; and W. H. Price, *The English Patents of Monopoly* (1906), Chaps. III and XI.

[2] Price, op. cit., p. 42.

[3] J. U. Nef, *The Rise of the British Coal Industry* (1932), Vol. I, pp. 267-84.

industry under the control of a few people drove into opposition those who had been excluded from the privileges that had been conferred.   By the promulgation of proclamations in the support of monopolies, the Crown frequently brought those who infringed the patents before the hated Star Chamber for contempt of the royal prerogative.   Nor were the general economic effects of the monopolies very salutary ones. Economic progress was restricted; for, by affording a single concern protection against competition, the monopolies largely destroyed all incentive or stimulus to expansion.   In the soap monopoly, for example, the most hated of all, workmen and masters were forced out of employment.   To the protest of the industrialist was added the equally bitter complaint of the consumer.   Prices were generally raised far beyond the amount that had to be paid to the Exchequer; the quality of products frequently deteriorated.   Sir John Culpepper's speech to Parliament is but the most famous of the many speeches and petitions that voice the protest of the consumer against the operation of the monopolies.[1]

The extortion of direct taxation was even more unpopular than the grants of monopoly patents.   Whatever forms the legal or constitutional issues may have taken—and generally Charles was within his rights—the opposition of the middle classes to subsidies, to tonnage and poundage, to ship-money, derived from their realization that to grant the King power to levy direct taxation without the consent of Parliament would have been to abdicate whatever political power they possessed.   Hampden's case was fundamental in much more than the constitutional sense that has generally been stressed. Had the King been able effectively to establish the right conferred on him by the decision of the judges to levy taxation when he deemed an emergency existed, the annual income of £200,000 it was hoped the levy would assure would have rendered him permanently independent of Parliament.   The Venetian Ambassador, with that admirable insight into

---

[1] " These like the frogs of Egypt have gotten possession of our dwellings and have scarce a room free from them.   They sup in our cup, they dip in our fish, they sit by our fire, we find them in the dye-vat, wash-house and pandering tub, they share with the butler in his box, they have marked and scalded us from head to foot."   Speech of Sir John Culpepper, 1640. Quoted in M. James, *Social Problems and Policy during the Puritan Revolution* (1930), pp. 364–5; cf. also e.g., " Speech Delivered in Parliament by a Worthy Member Thereof Concerning the Grievances of the Kingdom, by I. P. Esquire " (1642).

English affairs that characterizes all the Venetian envoys in England during the period, clearly recognized the implications of the ship-money issue for the middle class.

> " If the people submit to this present prejudice ", he wrote, after the judges had rendered their preliminary opinion, " they are submitting to an eternal yoke and burying their past liberties which will remain a memory only." [1]

The propertied classes were thus continually encountering the Government as the enemy of property. Church and State were uniting to deny them the opportunity of exploring the new economic vistas that had opened up before them. The landlord anxious to enclose found himself baulked by the Commission for Depopulation. The manufacturer seeking to maximize profits by reducing wages was thwarted by an Order-in-Council. Merchant and industrialist alike found the highways of economic expansion blocked by the monopolies the Crown had created. At a time when men were endeavouring to establish as absolute the right of an individual in his own property, the State was insisting that that right was limited by social obligation and the fiscal needs of the Crown. Social policy was being administered not in the interests of wealth, but in accord with a conception of social justice which was felt to be mediaeval and antiquated. Poor-rates and ship-money were resented not merely because they made demands on men's purses, but because those who paid them were denied a voice in the determination of the ends to which they should be dedicated. And through the prerogative courts and other institutions, the Government was enforcing its will on those who attempted to evade its decrees.

But it must be emphasized that opposition to the paternal policy of the Crown had not yet become a full-blooded demand for a system of *laisser-faire*. That demand, it is true, was being voiced, as we have already seen, with increasing emphasis. But the protest that emerges before the Civil War is not primarily directed against the idea of State control as such; it is a dissatisfaction with the particular kind of control the State is enforcing.

> " While everyone feels himself injured by the present form of contributions ", the Earl of Danby told Charles in a letter

[1] *C.S.P., Venetian, 1636–39*, Feb. 27, 1637, p. 153.

B 2

of protest against ship-money, " no one will object to the contributions in themselves if they are levied in the proper manner." [1]

" Ship-money they judged of not according to the sum ", observed Baxter, " but they thought that propriety was thereby destroyed." [2]

The *bourgeoisie* rebelled against the monarchy because they considered its policy a challenge to the security of private property and because it was a bar to the economic development of which they felt themselves capable. That their opposition would force them to remake the very foundations of the State was a fact which, before t : Civil War at any rate, they did not appreciate. What they sought was simply a limitation of the power of the Crown and a dominating voice in the determination of public policy so that they could shape the legislative activity of the State to their own particular ends.

What is notable in the decade preceding the Civil War is the fact that the volume of active protest against Charles' Government seems to have been remarkably limited. The revival of trade in the 'thirties which followed on the slump of the preceding years ushered in a period of general prosperity which was maintained until 1638 or 1639. Governmental activity evidently checked for a time the progress of the en- closure movement, and the period is remarkably free of agrarian unrest. Little indication can be found in the liter- ature of the decade of any considerable dissatisfaction with the Government on the part of either the peasants or the town labourers and craftsmen ; on the contrary, there is ample evidence that the Government's policy evoked the approval of these groups. The middle classes, to be sure, were chafing under the yoke which they felt bore so heavily on them. The imposition of ship-money aroused considerable, if sporadic, opposition ; and the Venetian Ambassador, Correr, observed that " although few are bold enough to speak and object, yet a dull murmur is heard which ought to make them reflect ".[3] There can be no doubt that the groups that were so eager to curb the power of the Crown were endeavouring to rally their forces to challenge its authority.

---

[1] *C.S.P., Venetian, 1636–39,* Dec. 12, 1636, p. 110.
[2] Baxter, *Reliquiae Baxterianae* (1696), p. 37.
[3] *C.S.P., Venetian, 1636–39,* March 20, 1637, p. 167.

" It now seems ", wrote Correr in 1637, " that many of the leading men of the realm are determined to make a final effort to bring the forms of government back to their former state. They hold secret meetings for the purpose of achieving this result." [1]

A few weeks later he wrote of the

" frequent meetings which are held in many parts of the realm about making some acceptable proposals to the King for the assembling of Parliament ".[2]

The immediate emergence of Pym and his group as the nucleus around which the oppositionist elements rallied as soon as Parliament was convened was hardly an accidental occurrence ; it was, no doubt, the result of careful and deliberate preparation. But it is nevertheless remarkable that, during a period soon to be denounced as the most oppressive and tyrannical England had ever endured, there are so few signs of widespread discontent, certainly none of organized resistance.

It is therefore doubtful whether the opposition of the middle classes to the economic policy of the Crown could have achieved, of itself, the ends they desired to effect or have created the measure of popular dissatisfaction that enabled them to challenge the monarchy in war. It is at this point that the religious issue plays a rôle of such importance in the immediate political developments, for the close union of Church and State enabled the *bourgeoisie* to turn opposition to the former into revolt against the latter. Occasionally sincerely urged, as often as not skilfully and deliberately manipulated, the appeal to men's religious convictions obscured and distorted—for some years, at any rate—the fundamental issues in conflict. Large sections of the population whose material interests should have allied them with the Crown were to rally to Parliament because they thought it was struggling to exorcise the devils the former had introduced into England.

Flushed with his successes in England, Laud attempted in 1637 to impose the service of the Anglican Church in Presbyterian Scotland. The spirited resistance of the Scots—encouraged, no doubt, by Charles' opponents in England, confronted Charles with the alternatives of admitting failure or subduing Scotland by force of arms ; and because both

[1] *C.S.P., Venetian, 1636–39*, Jan. 16, 1637, p. 125.
[2] Ibid., Feb. 6, 1637, p. 136.

Laud and Charles were incapable of graceful retreat, they decided on military measures. It was an impossible affair for Charles to raise an army in his straitened financial circumstances, and he was forced to recall Strafford from Ireland to organize his campaign. The latter advised the summoning of Parliament in the spring of 1640 in the hope that the King's plea that he was assembling an army for the defence of the kingdom would evoke a favourable response. But Strafford misjudged the temper of Parliament. By 1640 the division into the groups who were to fight the Civil War had not yet emerged, and the King did not have the active support of any section in Parliament. With the exception of the spiritual peers, all classes represented in Parliament were united in their resistance to the arbitrary exercise of the royal prerogative, for it had borne as heavily on the nobility and the great landlords as on the capitalist-gentry and the merchants. Accordingly, when the Short Parliament began its session there was immediate unanimity in brushing aside the plea of national emergency and in an insistence that popular grievances receive prior consideration. Grimstone's opening speech clearly reflected the mood of Parliament.

" I am very much mistaken if there be not a case here at home ", he declared, " of as great a danger as that which is already put." [1]

Property had waited eleven years to assert its claims; it was in no mood to countenance a postponement of their discussion. By refusing to vote money until the question of arbitrary taxation had been discussed, Parliament placed the issue squarely before Charles. Intelligent compromise might have temporarily solved the impasse. The Lords had already expressed their readiness to give Charles' demands precedence over other business; and the vote in the Commons for a second conference with the Lords indicated that he had substantial support in the Lower House as well. But his unwillingness to make adequate concessions and his fear that Parliament was about to come to terms with the Scots impelled him to dissolve the session.

His appeal to the people was equally fruitless. The City refused to advance him any money. The Scots took advantage of his weakened position to invade England once again; and at

[1] Rushworth, op. cit., Part II, Vol. II, p. 1128.

Ripon, Charles was forced to surrender. The treaty, involving the immediate payment of considerable sums to the Scots, left him with no alternative but to summon Parliament again.

Meanwhile his opponents were preparing for the struggle by effectively turning the tide of religious dissatisfaction against the Crown. Several currents, we have already seen contributed to that stream. There was the general Puritan opposition to the High-Church spirit. A more immediate factor was the profound anti-clericalism that had become increasingly intensified after 1629. Largely, that anti-clerical sentiment was, as I have indicated, the expression of the resentment of the middle classes against the interference of the Church with economic life, their hatred of the bishops for their support of the Crown and their anxiety to weaken the power of the Church by destroying the elaborate ecclesiastical organization that rendered it so effective. Their opposition was stimulated as well, we can be certain, by their desire to bring on the market and to make available for development the rich lands still held by the Church.

Intimately associated with anti-clericalism, and to some extent its cause, was the widespread fear of Roman Catholicism. Long an undertone in English affairs, anti-Catholicism rose to a dominant pitch in the years directly prior to the Civil War. No one who has read the contemporary literature can deny that the fear of " popery " during those years, though unjustified in fact, was real and profound. That Laud ever contemplated a revival of Catholicism is absurd to assume. One writer, insisting in 1644 that religious differences had not been the prime cause of the Civil War, defended Laud against the accusation of popery.

> " Most of them have professed ", he declares, " that the Puritans did not so farre nor fundamentally dissent from their opinions as the Papists did; But it is true that the Puritans did go more crosse to their temporall ends, pompe and revenue than the Papists would have done. So that extremity of hatred against the Puritan though he were nearer to them in matters of religion caused them to make these approaches towards the Papist as being not so great an enemy to their temporall promotion." [1]

[1] *A Paradox; That Design Upon Religion was not the Cause of State Misgovernment but an effect of it* (London, 1644). (McAlpin Collection, Union Theological Seminary, New York.)

Zonga, the Venetian Secretary in London, asserted in 1638 that there was no basis to the charge of Roman Catholicism levied against Laud

> " because those who best know the more recondite aims of the Archbishop of Canterbury . . . know full well that he has only tolerated the liberty which the Catholics enjoy with the view of first reducing the Calvinists, or Puritans as they are called here, to a ready obedience to the King in matters of consequence also, so that once that party is under control, and it is very powerful, he can safely destroy the Catholic one as well by the arm of the laws ".[1]

But minds already poisoned against Laud and the system he enforced were fertile ground for suspicions of his active sympathy with Rome; and his behaviour did much to heighten those suspicions. The condition of the Catholics was improving steadily during the period of personal rule.[2] Laud's suppression of Puritanism was regarded as inspired by his desire to reintroduce Roman Catholicism into England. His fetish of ceremony and external forms in religious worship bore much closer kinship to the religion of Rome than it did to Protestant faith; and the entire ecclesiastical hierarchy smacked too much of papacy. The rapid growth and intensity of anti-Catholic sentiment may therefore have been, in the circumstances, a perfectly natural development. But it is clear that the fear was fostered and aggravated by those opposed to the Crown in order to win the support of groups, particularly the peasants and labourers, who might otherwise have rallied behind the monarchy. The bogey of papism is the seventeenth-century version of the modern red scare. Its success may be seen in the extent of the popular outcry against the alleged Catholic plots and sympathies of the Government during 1640–3.

> " This is the most powerful weapon ", wrote Correr of the charges of Catholicism made against the King, " with which they are able to hold the interests and tranquility of this good King seriously prejudiced ".[3]

What really enabled the religious issue to be used so effec-

---

[1] *C.S.P., Venetian, 1636–39,* Jan. 22, 1638, p. 358.
[2] W. K. Jordan, *Development of Religious Toleration in England, 1603–40,* pp. 184–6.
[3] *C.S.P., Venetian, 1642–43,* April 4, 1642, p. 30.

tively in arousing active opposition to the monarchy was the fact that in 1640, the year both the Short and Long Parliaments met, England entered a period of acute economic depression. In part, that depression was the natural result of a financial system, based, as was that of Charles, on indirect taxation of commodities.[1] Political unrest aggravated the situation, and Charles' seizure of the bullion created a serious financial dislocation whose repercussions on industry and commerce were profound. The depression of 1640 saw no exception to the normal tendency to blame economic distress on the Government of the day; and from 1640 a large number of petitions complaining of the acute economic crisis poured in on Parliament. Tradesmen, manufacturers, labourers, seamen, apprentices, people from every branch of the economic life of the country bitterly protested against the economic breakdown.[2] Although the peasantry, with its traditional inarticulateness, contributed few of these petitions, widespread agrarian riots testify to a considerable revival of enclosure.[3] We shall have occasion to consider in subsequent chapters how the people, looking to Parliament for amelioration of their economic distress, regarded the struggle being waged against the King as an effort to free themselves from the tyranny of poverty; from their disillusionment with Parliament was born the movement of protest and revolt that found expression first in the army and later in the agitation of the Levellers, the Diggers and kindred groups. What we are concerned with at the moment is the manner in which the economic plight of the people was fused with their religious grievances—real and fancied—in a general avalanche of protest against the monarchy.

During 1640 and 1641 anti-clericalism is the most prominent feature of the petitions, and all the ills of the country are laid at the door of the bishops. In 1642 anti-Catholicism has become the driving force of the protests, and Papists are seen lurking everywhere in the Kingdom to destroy religion and liberty. Among the

". . . manifold evils, pressures and grievances caused, practised and occasioned by the prelates", asserts the

---

[1] W. R. Scott, *Joint Stock Companies to 1720*, Vol. I, pp. 216–17.
[2] James, op. cit., *passim*; For typical petitions see B.M. 669, f. 4 (17), (50), (54), (55), (57), (60), etc.
[3] Ibid., pp. 90–4.

Root and Branch Petition of 1640, are " the multitudes of monopolies and patents, drawing with them innumerable perjuries; the large increase of customs with impositions upon commodities, the ship-money and many other great burthens upon the Commonwealth under which all groan ".[1]

The apprentices of London resent the intrusion of religion in economic life and

". . . the insulting domination of the Lordly Bishop of Canterbury and some others who triumph with too much arrogante insolence over us ".[2]

" The great decay and deadnesse in the trade of the said city ", the Council of Exeter complains, are due to the distractions in London, " which are occasioned by the infringing of the rights and priviledges of Parliament and the just liberty of the subject and by the opposition and hindrances which the Bishops and the Popish party have laid in the way of the proceedings of your Honourable Assembly." [3]

The silk trade has been ruined by " the distractions stirred up by the Prelates and Popish Lords," and the petitioners urge that

" Prelacy may be totally abolished . . . so that the malignant party may be disabled any longer to obstruct your most worthy and pious endeavours in reforming the church and composing so great and weighty affaires of these Kingdomes; which the petitioners humbly conceive will be the only meanes to give life and subsistance to trade and to prevent England's ruine to arise from its own inhabitants ".[4]

The anti-clerical sentiment and the fear of Catholicism were thus exploited to create popular opposition to the Royalists and merged with economic dissatisfaction to rally support to Parliament. There is probably considerable point to the accusation made by an anonymous pamphleteer in 1648.

[1] Gardiner, *Documents*, pp. 137–44.
[2] " The Apprentices of London's Petition," E. 180 (18).
[3] Petition of the Mayor, Aldermen and Common-Council of the City of Exeter, 1642, B.M. 669, f. 4 (58).
[4] Petition of the Master-Wardens and the Commonalty of the Mistery or Trade of the Silk-Throsters of London, B.M. 669, f. 4 (60).

" Though at first when the war was commenc'd ", he
asserts, " Master Hampden being asked by a minister why
religion was made a cause of it gave this account, that the
people would not stir else." [1]

The misrepresentation of the character and the aims of the
Royalists undoubtedly strengthened the Parliamentary party
in 1641 and 1642. In the end it only injured the latter's
position. For the people whom the misrepresentation had
deluded were soon to learn that the Presbyterians who advanced to the leadership of the Parliamentary forces were no
more interested in the alleviation of economic distress or the
establishment of religious liberty than those whom they had
deposed.

When the Long Parliament assembled in November it
was clear that its members had conceived no constructive
programme. They were simply interested in rectifying the
grievances they had protested. To free those who had
suffered from the arbitrary decrees of the Courts, to punish
those whose advice had been responsible for the measures
they opposed, to render it impossible for the King to rule
without their consent by erecting safeguards against the
absolute exercise of the royal prerogative, above all, to remove
all challenges to the security of private property were the
immediate objectives with which they were concerned.
Leighton, Burton, Bastwick and Lilburne were soon released
and compensated. Strafford was impeached and confined
to the Tower within eight days of the meeting of Parliament;
and Laud followed him five weeks later. In a series of statutes
Parliament struck at the bastions of the Stuart regime. The
Triennial Act provided that not more than three years could
elapse without summoning Parliament. By the Act of May 10,
1641, Parliament declared that it could be dissolved only by
its own consent. The Tonnage and Poundage Act prohibited
any further impositions without the consent of Parliament;
and together with the nullification of the ship-money decision,
it guaranteed the King's future financial dependence on
Parliament and removed the fear of arbitrary taxation. The
Courts of Star Chamber, of High Commission, of the North
and of Wales were swept away. The limits and boundaries
of the Royal Forests were restored and the exaction of knight-

---

[1] *The Regall Apology* (1648), E. 436 (5).

hood fines prohibited.[1] Parliament thus ensured that the King could not act without its consent; it had not yet asserted its claim to act independently of the sovereign.

On this programme Parliament displayed complete agree-ment. All men of property were united on the measures they had to take to limit the discretionary powers of the King, to admit the representatives of wealth to a greater share in the determination of public policy and to abolish those institutions that had obstructed their activities. But it is extremely doubtful whether, during 1640, many Parliamentarians realized the revolutionary implications of their measures and how far they would be driven to defend the positions they had assumed. During 1640 and the greater part of 1641 Parliament was content with countering the King's claim to absolutism by enunciating the principle that there existed a fundamental law by which the King must consider himself bound. It had not yet considered who was to be the final judge, in the event of disagreement between King and Parliament, of what fundamental law really was.

By the summer of 1641 distrust of the King and suspicion of his intrigues led the majority in the Commons to the realization that, as long as Charles retained control of the Executive, the value of the safeguards by which they tried to limit his power would remain extremely dubious. Accordingly, they endeavoured to secure a measure of control over the executive by demanding in June that the King remove those advisers to whom Parliament objected and replace them by those who had its approval.[2] That the divisions between the contending factions in the war had not yet crystallized can be seen in the fact that the Ten Propositions elaborating that demand were unanimously passed by the Commons and without serious opposition by the Lords.

But it was becoming increasingly clear to many that the ultimate implications of granting the demands of the majority in the Commons would be to cede to the latter supreme political power. As early as May, the Venetian Ambassador was writing that the sole aim of the Puritans in Parliament was

" to sweep away every kind of superior power together with the control of the monarchy ".[3]

---

[1] For the text of all these statutes see Gardiner, *Documents*, pp. 144 ff.
[2] Gardiner, *Documents*, " The Ten Propositions," p. 163.
[3] *C.S.P., Venetian, 1640–42*, May 24, 1641, p. 152.

The aristocracy began to perceive the threat to its privileges that the ascendancy of the middle classes implied. Already, for a century, the pressure of the new middle classes had seriously weakened the strength and prestige of the landed nobility. To permit the *bourgeoisie* to secure effective control of public policy, the aristocracy now realized, would seriously undermine the position of the latter. The recognition that the maintenance of their position demanded that they support the Crown against the middle classes began consciously to determine the policy of the members of the aristocracy. As the aims of the Commons became clearer and more explicit, party divisions quickly widened. By the time the Grand Remonstrance was voted, the nobility had largely taken up its position behind the King.

The earlier division over the Root and Branch Bill was, as Professor Allen has pointed out,[1] more superficial than real. The Bill was introduced, no doubt, for many reasons: the confiscation of the property attached to the bishoprics and the cathedral chapters would help pay the debts Parliament had incurred; denial to the King of the right to appoint bishops would deprive him of a powerful medium of propaganda by removing the pulpit from his control; excluding the bishops from Parliament would eliminate a large group of his most consistent supporters. But all parties in the Commons were agreed that Parliament must establish control over the Church. The division was simply on the question whether to abolish episcopacy altogether or to retain it as an instrument of the secular authorities. The Lords refused to consent to the exclusion of the bishops from the Upper House because they resented having the constitution of their body changed by the Commons. In part, their refusal derived from a reluctance to weaken the position of the King too greatly by removing his staunchest supporters. But these differences in themselves would never have led to civil war. What produced the sharp and final cleavage in Parliament was the realization of the nobility that to grant the full demands of the Commons would be seriously to weaken their own position. In self-defence they rallied to the support of the Crown.

To outline the emergence of the parties in this fashion is to summarize with deceptive simplicity a development that was

[1] Allen, op. cit., p. 346, f. 373.

really more complex in its nature. Many cast in their lot
with the monarchy because they sincerely feared that the
attacks on the Church would destroy all true religion. Others
shrank from the anarchy they were certain the sovereign
rule of a popular assembly would create. Others, like the
Catholics, saw in the monarchy their sole protection from the
persecution they feared would be unleashed against them in
the event of its defeat. But what more than anything else
permeates the groups who formed the bulwark of the Royalist
party is the sense that the victory of those who now constituted
the Parliamentary majority would be fatal to the kind of
privilege they had been accustomed to enjoy. That realization
drove them into armed support of the monarchy.

Whatever hopes the majority in the Commons may have
entertained for compromise with the King were rapidly fading
by November 1641. The demand for control of the Executive
had been rejected. There were indications that popular
opinion was beginning to react against Parliament:

> " The demands for fresh payments have been repeated
> in this city and in all the provinces," wrote Giustinian
> in September, " but the people fatigued by the multiplicity
> of so many extraordinary taxes do not show that prompti-
> tude that the occasion demands and Parliament is losing
> the great credit which it enjoyed universally since it appears
> that instead of relief, it has brought expenses and dis-
> comforts to the people." [1]

Parliament's claim to arbitrary authority in ecclesiastical
matters alarmed and alienated many of its supporters. The
Parliamentary leaders were quick to sense the subtle change
in the political atmosphere. They probably welcomed the
Irish Rebellion, for, apart from the fact that the control of the
army whose creation it made necessary became the direct
issue over which they made their assertion of sovereignty,
it afforded them an opportunity of carrying on effective
propaganda against the Royalists. Strenuous attempts were
made to win popular support by intensifying the campaign
to foist on the people the belief that the King was the tool, of a
" papist and malignant party ". The Grand Remonstrance,
introduced when division had already crystallized and the

---

[1] *C.S.P., Venetian, 1640–42*, Sept. 20, 1641, p. 215.

impossibility of peaceful compromise apparent, was essentially an appeal to the nation for support in a struggle which Parliamentary leaders were certain was imminent.

Subsequent events—the increase of violence in London, the attempted seizure of the five Members of the House of Commons, the attempt to secure the magazine at Hull—simply aggravated a situation already intensely acute. It was impossible for either side to retreat from the positions they had assumed; and the next few months simply represented a jockeying for advantage. The controversy over the control of the armed forces was fundamental to the entire conflict and had to lead directly to war. For control of the militia meant effectively the power to coerce; and that power, then as now, conferred the ability to determine public policy. In the Nineteen Propositions submitted to the King on June 1, 1642, Parliament formally demanded supreme political power by asking for control of the Executive and the militia and the right to determine the forms of the ecclesiastical settlement.[1] By the Declaration of June 6 in defence of the Militia Ordinance, Parliament announced that it was assuming supreme sovereignty in the state.[2]

In 1640 Parliament had asserted the existence of fundamental law that the King could not contravene. In 1642 it declared that, in the event of conflict as to the interpretation of the law, it alone was the final judge. Between both parties there could be no arbitrament but that of force. For, as Warr correctly saw

" the great men of the world being invested with the power thereof cannot be imagined to eclipse themselves or their own pomp unless by the violent interposition of the people's spirits who are most sensible of their own burdens and most forward in seeking reliefe ".[3]

On August 22 Charles raised his standard at Nottingham.

[1] Gardiner, *Documents*, p. 249.
[2] Ibid., p. 254.
[3] John Warr, *The Corruption and Deficiency of the Lawes of England Soberly Discovered* (1649), E. 559 (10).

CHAPTER TWO : THE DEVELOPMENT
OF RADICAL POLITICAL
THOUGHT DURING THE CIVIL
WAR

" This is the fruit of War from the beginning, for it removes Propriety
out of a weaker into a stronger hand but still upholds the curse of
bondage."—Winstanley, *A New Yeers Gift for the Parliament and Army*
(1650).

THE history of the early years of the Civil War is the story
of an indecisive military struggle irresolutely waged by both
parties, the control of both Parliament and its army by the
rich merchants of the City of London and those sections of
the landed aristocracy that opposed the King and the growing dissatisfaction with their leadership that rapidly developed.

The indecisiveness of the early stages of the war was in a
large measure the result of inefficient military organization
and faulty strategy; but it was at least equally due to the
fact that most of the Parliamentary leaders, particularly the
generals themselves members of the titled nobility, were
ardently seeking a compromise with the King. They
wavered in their prosecution of the war because they feared
that a shattering victory over the King would create an
irreparable breach in the old order of things that would
ultimately be fatal to their own position. They were worried
by the restlessness of the common people at least as much as
by the military threat of the Royalists:

" Is this the Liberty which we claim to vindicate by
shedding our blood? " Essex asked his colleagues in an
impassioned outburst. " This will be the reward of all
our labours and our posterity will say that to deliver them
from the yoke of the King we have subjected them to that
of the common people. If we do this the finger of scorn
will be pointed at us and so I am determined to devote
my life to repressing the audacity of the common people." [1]

[1] *C.S.P., Venetian, 1643–47*, Dec. 16, 1644, p. 162.

From the very beginning of the war much effective authority was passing from the capitalist-gentry who had led the opposition to Charles in Parliament to the financial interests of the City of London; for, as the Venetian envoy astutely observed:

". . . since the city pays the money for the war, they also claim the right to direct it." [1]

Together with the landed gentry, they continued the work they had begun before the outbreak of war of refashioning the State to give effect to their own purposes. On the one hand, they sought to destroy the power of the aristocracy; on the other, they attempted to suppress the threat of the common people. Parliament, for example, orders the convocation of an Assembly to design the ecclesiastical structure of the kingdom. The Assembly overwhelmingly favours a rigid Presbyterian centralism not only because its establishment will buy the vital military aid of the Scots, but because it will enable the dominant groups, through control of the elderships, to maintain that iron discipline that is so essential if they are to direct social activity to the ends they desire.[2] The Printing Ordinance of June 1643 is designed not merely to curb Royalist propaganda, but to suppress the sects through which the discontented are beginning to utter their inchoate but unmistakable protests [3] in an effort to silence the aggressive and irrepressible spokesmen of the poor. Unordained ministers are forbidden to preach. At the same time, Parliament continues its attack on the old order. The estates of delinquents are sequestered not merely because their income will help to finance the war, but because their ultimate confiscation will destroy the economic basis of the power of their owners. The abolition of the Court of Wards and other feudal survivals sweeps away—for the gentry, at any rate—the last vestiges of a restraining feudalism. The insistence on the payment of tithes is intended not only to place the ecclesiastical establishment on a stable foundation,

[1] C.S.P., Venetian, 1643–47, Aug. 28, 1643, p. 11.
[2] Presbyterianism, even Gardiner admits, was adopted by the wealthy merchants and tradesmen of the City, for " by filling the elderships those very merchants and tradesmen constituted the Church for purposes of jurisdiction. Whatever ecclesiastical tyranny there was would be exercised by themselves." Gardiner, Civil War, Vol. III, p. 79.
[3] Infra, pp. 87 ff.

but to win for the regime now in power the support of the clergy by giving them a vested interest in its maintenance. The ordinance for the abolition of archbishops and bishops and for the confiscation of their lands not merely seals the fate of the hated Laudian prelacy, but makes available for development and exploitation the rich and coveted estates of the Church.[1]

But opposition to the leadership of the financial circles of the City and of the wealthier gentry, who formed the core of the Presbyterian party, developed rapidly. We shall treat at length the general indifference and opposition to the war that were widespread among the common people. But, as an appreciation of the rigid rule the domination of the Presbyterians implied spread throughout the country, as suspicion of their negotiations with the King deepened in many quarters and as dissatisfaction with their half-hearted prosecution of the war grew rife, the squirearchy and lesser gentry in the country and the manufacturers and merchants of the cities and towns began a campaign of active opposition to Presbyterian leadership, insisting on a more vigorous and determined conduct of hostilities. That this opposition came so prominently to the fore in the Assembly on the question of religious toleration must not be taken to indicate that its roots were primarily in the soil of ecclesiastical conviction. Ecclesiastical reconstruction as the first major practical problem to whose solution Parliament addressed itself naturally threw the religious differences of both groups into sharp relief. But those differences were but one aspect of their respective schemes of social values; and those values were largely a function of their respective class positions. Religion to the seventeenth-century Englishman meant much more than the formalities of worship: it was essentially that set of values which sanctioned his social practices. Religion was still too intimately bound up with the social fabric to permit of its consideration independently of the social system of which it was a part. The struggle for freedom of conscience during the Civil War is therefore nothing less than a struggle for freedom of speech and expression. Religious freedom implied the opportunity to question the assumptions of the existing social order; and to criticize the ecclesiastical

[1] For the text of all these ordinances see Firth and Rait, *Acts and Ordinances of the Interregnum*, Vol. I.

organization was effectively to undermine the social system it buttressed. We cannot understand the vital rôle of the struggle for religious freedom during the Civil War and the passionate earnestness with which it was debated unless we clearly grasp its significance as the ability to criticize the social order that was being established.

Through the Five Dissenting Brethren, themselves victims of a persecuting Church, and hence apprehensive of the centralized power the Presbyterian system conferred, the Independents began that struggle in the Assembly.[1] Originally claiming no more than tolerance for their own doctrines, they were soon forced to champion a programme of complete religious liberty; for in defending their claims to a particular freedom of expression they were obliged to argue a theoretical justification of the general principle of religious tolerance. As the broader and more fundamental social implications of the struggle were perceived, considerable sections of the more progressive groups in Parliament and in the army and the multifarious sects rallied to the support of the Independents; and the pressure of allies more progressive than themselves forced the latter to abandon their original limited position and to take their stand on a much broader platform. When, by 1645, the opposition to Presbyterianism had become more coherent and unified, Parliament hastened to approve by ordinance the Assembly's directory for the establishment of Presbyterian forms of worship throughout the country.[2]

But in the army, at any rate, the Presbyterians were being ousted from leadership. Angered by the failure of the Generals to press home advantages gained in the campaign of the autumn of 1644, Cromwell succeeded in forcing through Parliament early in 1645 the ordinance for the organization of the New Model Army under the command of Fairfax and the Self-Denying Ordinance whose intention and effect were to force the resignation of the Presbyterian generals from their military commands. The Self-Denying

[1] For the history of the Westminster Assembly and accounts of its debates see W. K. Jordan, *The Development of Religious Toleration in England, 1640–60* (1932, etc.), *passim*.

[2] Firth and Rait, Vol. I, Jan. 4, 1645, p. 582. English Presbyterianism was always strongly Erastian, for it was intended that a Parliament dominated by the propertied groups should control the ecclesiastical organization, and not that the Church should dominate the State.

Ordinance which took the control of the Army out of the hands of the Lords was opposed, significantly enough, by the Upper House.

With the organization of the New Model and the accession of Cromwell to military leadership, the King was soon reduced to military impotence; and after the Battle of Naseby the Royalists presented no effective threat to Parliamentary supremacy. From that point the history of the Civil War is no longer the record of the struggle between the Royalists and Parliament, but of the conflicts between the various classes that had composed the Parliamentary front. Until each class or group achieved power, it played a progressive rôle in the struggle for the enfranchisement of the emerging capitalism; then, like the Presbyterians in 1647 and the Independents in 1649, it became a reactionary and counter-revolutionary force.

But it must be emphasized that the Civil War was from its very outset never more than a war of minorities. The traditional picture of a united nation rising spiritedly in defence of Protestantism and freedom, or of two inspired armies battling passionately in what they conceived to be the service of the Lord, is largely an exercise in imagination of the liberal historians, and bears little relationship to historical fact.

The squirearchy and the commercial groups who had formed the core of the Parliamentary resistance to Charles and the landed aristocracy who had rallied to his support readily responded to the call to battle. But the apprentices and artisans of London, and the peasants and the agricultural labourers of the Midlands who formed the bulk of the Parliamentary army, and the peasantry of the North who largely comprised the Royalist forces fought only when conscripted. At the very beginning of the war there was, it is true, no lack of volunteers on either side. But by 1643 voluntary service proved inadequate to meet the stern demands of warfare and both sides were forced to resort to impressment. Parliament, particularly, was seriously confronted with the problem of man-power. Initial disillusionment with Parliament was spreading; the flood of volunteers dwindled to a mere trickle and then dried up completely; desertion during 1643 and 1644 depleted the ranks considerably; very large numbers of men refused to serve beyond the borders of their respective counties.   In 1642 Parliament had attempted to induce the apprentices to enlist for service by guaranteeing them against the forfeiture of their indentures and discrimination on demobilizaton.[1]   But persuasion proved inadequate to cope with the situation and a determined campaign of impressment was begun.

> " All this week ", reported the Venetian secretary in 1643, " they have been pressing men with so much inhumanity that many of the objectors have been injured and five killed not without serious riots in one part or another of this confused, divided and wretched city." [2]

As the number of desertions increased and as the riots against impressment grew more serious, Parliament was forced to intensify the drastic nature of its methods.

> " They are busy recruiting everywhere and also pressing all sorts of persons with barbarous violence." [3]

The tactics employed by Parliament in recruiting its army had momentous consequences.   They alienated the sympathy of vast numbers throughout the country.

> " The violence which is used to persons of every description to force them to serve in the army ", noted Agostini in 1645, " is having a great effect in cooling off the favour of the common people on which alone Parliament subsists." [4]

More important, they sowed the seeds for the development of the rank and file as a revolutionary force.   Anger at the manner in which they had been forced to serve gave the ranks a common sympathy that led to a deeper unity on more fundamental problems; and when dissatisfaction with their irregular and inadequate pay had deepened, the insistence that forced service be forever outlawed became a minimum demand on which all groups could unite in developing a common programme.

During the early years of the war, Parliament made strenuous efforts to arouse a greater degree of enthusiasm

---

[1] Firth and Rait, Vol. I, p. 37.
[2] *C.S.P.*, *Venetian, 1643–47*, Sept. 4, 1643, p. 11.
[3] Ibid., May 6, 1644, p. 94.
[4] Ibid., May 12, 1645, p. 190.   Even half the men in the New Model Army were pressed.

among the troops for the struggle in which they were engaged. Preachers trained the heavy artillery of Scriptural quotation on them to urge that they were nothing less than the soldiers of God in a crusade against the idolatrous heathen.　Pamphlets told them that they were striving to recapture the citadels of liberty from those who were undermining their foundations.[1] But the zeal these efforts instilled in the rank and file was superficial.　Experience proved to be much more effective than exhortation in shaping the attitude and views of the army.

Nor was Parliament's definition of its " war aims " more successful in enlisting popular support throughout the country at large.　Its assertion that it took up arms against the King to preserve " the true religion, the laws, liberty and peace of the kingdome " failed to impress; for the Royalists were equally claiming to be fighting for those ends.　Certainly there was no common agreement among the various groups that composed the Parliamentary front as to what really constituted the " true religion, the laws, liberty and peace of the Kingdome ".　" Liberty " and " freedom " may function admirably as vague ethical concepts or as political

---

[1] One example of the propaganda circulated to the troops deserves to be quoted at length.　It is *The Souldiers Catechisme*, which was used as a handbook by the Parliamentary army.　Its several editions testify to the wide circulation it enjoyed:

" 1. I fight to recover the King out of the hands of a Popish Malignant Company.

2. I fight for the Lawes and Liberties of my Country which are now in danger to be overthrown by them that have long laboured to bring into this Kingdome an Arbitrary and Tyrannical Government. . . .

3. I fight for the preservation of our Parliament. . . .

4. I fight in the defence and maintenance of the True Protestant Religion which is now violently opposed and will be utterly supprest in this Kingdome. . . . (pp. 2–3).

What from the quality of your enemies?

We may conclude that God will not prosper them.

1. Because they are for the most part Papists and Atheists.

2. Because they are for the most part inhumane, barbarous and cruell. . . .

3. Because they are generally the most horrible cursers and blasphemers in the world.

4. Because they are enemies to God and the power of goodnesse and therefore the Lord will scatter them " (pp. 11–12).

(*The Souldiers Catechisme*, " Composed for the Parliament's Armie ". Robert Ram (1644), E. 1186 (1).

It was republished in 1684 to " satisfie tender consciences in the ground upon which the late thorough Reformation proceeded ".　(Copy in the McAlpin Collection, Union Theological Seminary, New York City.)

shibboleths; but they can have no concrete meaning for people who are asked to sacrifice for their achievement save in terms of the experience and environment in which they are immersed and the problems by which they are confronted. To the large-scale capitalist-farmer freedom meant unrestricted opportunity to enclose and evict; to the peasant it meant, on the contrary, effective restraint on such activity. Liberty to the labourer or petty freeholder implied a release from the haunting fear of insecurity and the grinding yoke of poverty; to the rising merchant or manufacturer it represented the ability to continue unchallenged his subjection of those groups so that on their exploitation he could build his own material prosperity. For the propertied classes the true laws of England were those which respected the absolute rights of private property; to the artisan, the petty tradesman, the peasant or the agricultural labourer they were those which protected him from the arbitrary exercise of those privileges. Nor, as we have already noted, was there any greater degree of unanimity on the religious issue. At the outset of the war, it is true, all groups enrolled under the Parliamentary banner were united by their general hatred of clericalism and their fears of Catholicism. But when the grounds for their fears had been removed by the destruction of prelacy and they were forced to give positive expression to their convictions in a system of ecclesiastical government, they were riven by profound differences that would admit of no compromise. Whatever purely religious considerations might have been involved, the rich merchants of the City had no intentions of relaxing an ecclesiastical discipline that enabled them to control effectively the classes they wanted to exploit and to prevent the propagation of ideas they considered dangerous or subversive. The lesser gentry, the smaller merchants, the tradesmen, frightened by the avenues of oppression a system of central control opened up and aware of the drastic limitation on social criticism Presbyterianism imposed, insisted on a broader freedom than those who dominated Parliament were prepared to extend.

From 1640 to 1642 Parliament's manipulation of the religious issue had aroused considerable opposition to the Royalists. Parliament was able to unite diverse classes in its support by the original enunciation of the ideals for which it was fighting because the vagueness in which those ideals

were stated enabled each class to lend to them its own interpretation—an interpretation, we should emphasize, that was
fashioned by the needs and ambitions of its members.   But
as the war dragged on indecisively, as the ultimate intentions
of Parliament were revealed by the legislation it enacted,
increasing numbers throughout the country became aware
of the fact that the ends they were being utilized to achieve
were not those for which they had imagined themselves to
be fighting.

What drove home to the common people more effectively
than anything else the realization that, whatever the outcome
of the war, they stood to gain nothing from it was the rapid
and serious deterioration of their economic position.   We
have already discussed briefly the beginnings of the economic
depression in 1639 and 1640.   The political instability of
1641 and 1642 rendered conditions much more acute than
they would normally have been; and the outbreak of hostilities
brought about a general collapse of the economic life of the
country.   It was but natural under these conditions that the
people should identify the struggle that was being waged
against the King for freedom and liberty as an effort to
restore economic normalcy, and that the alleviation of their
distress became the measuring-rod by which they gauged
both the sincerity of Parliament's assertions and the success
of its efforts.   But conditions grew steadily worse.   The
normal functioning of trade and agriculture over large areas
was ended by military occupation.

> " The tradesman hath not nowe halfe that employment
> as in former times," reported one pamphleteer in 1642.
> " Tenants in the country have their rents so raised through
> scarcitie of money and so many levies to the King and
> country that they can hardly subsist to helpe themselves
> or relieve the poore in their parish, hence beggarie is
> become an Epidemicall disease raigning over the whole
> land." [1]

The troops of both armies freely plundered the country.
The inability of both sides to supply their forces adequately
gave rise to the practice of free-quarter, that inflicted intolerable hardship on the people throughout the country

---

[1] *A Caution to Keepe Money ; Shewing the Miserie of the Want Thereof* (1642),
E. 146 (21).

and aroused bitter and sustained protest. The tremendous burden of taxation and levies imposed to finance the war bore heavily on the populace at a time when the prices of foodstuffs and other vital commodities were rising steeply.

> " It is now impossible ", observed the Venetian Ambassador as early as January 1643, " for the poor to live in this Kingdom." [1]

The breakdown of communications, both internal and external, seriously hampered trade and commerce; and large amounts of capital were withdrawn from the country, particularly by foreign merchants. Landowners took advantage of the prevailing chaos and the breakdown of effective and interested authority to indulge in their favourite pastime of enclosure. During 1642 a large number of petitions poured in on Parliament complaining of acute distress; and if their frequency and vehemence decreased somewhat in 1643, it was not because the situation had become less serious, but because the people were becoming habituated to the misery they were enduring.

The early years of the war were, thus, for the common people of England a period of bewildering confusion and deepening misery, of eager hopes and, then, of a gradual and crushing disillusionment. An England in which, as far as they were aware, " every man ", in the words of Warwick, " sat·quiet under his own vine tree and the fountain of justice ran clear and current " had suddenly been plunged into fratricidal strife. Parliament, by its promises, roused their hopes, and then, by its behaviour, shattered the dreams it had inspired. They were years of restlessness and stirring, of questioning and seeking. Unable as yet to give expression to their aspirations in secular or political terms or to voice their moods and attitudes in the language of daily affairs, profoundly conscious of their overwhelming need to escape from the misery that encompassed them, but uncertain of the ways in which that escape was to be achieved, disappointed in the Parliament in which they had centred their hopes, yet not quite prepared to repudiate it finally, they expressed themselves in the only terms in which they had been trained and habituated to think—in the language and forms of religion and spirituality. Prevailing Puritan concepts proved empty and devoid of meaning for them largely because

[1] C.S.P., Venetian, 1643–47, Jan. 16, 1643, p. 230.

those concepts had been fashioned to fulfil the purposes of a rising middle class and not the needs of the oppressed. The latter found their expression in religious mysticism. The widespread growth of sectarian activity and mystical enthusiasm after 1640 is the unmistakable beginnings of a class consciousness that later took more definite form in revolutionary political action. When their needs had crystal-lized in their own minds into practical demands for social reform, when their disillusionment with Parliament had become final and when their experience in the army had imparted to them a sense of their corporate unity, the people passed to more practical action than the spinning of visions; then they sought to drag down the millennium they had been anticipating from the ethereal realms of heaven to the reality of daily life.

There had always been in England strains of mystical religion; the Lollard Movement, certainly, is one of the outstanding examples of what might be termed the religion of the common people. During the sixteenth century those strains had no doubt been encouraged by the growth of Anabaptism and its short-lived triumph at Munster, and by the work of such writers as Denk and Franck, of Schwenck-feld and Boehme. German refugees, fleeing from persecution in their native land, brought to England much of the spirit of those Continental mystics. But the soil in which it thrived, like that in which it first took root, was that which had been turned by the furrow of social unrest and watered by the tears of poverty and the hope of amelioration. For, whatever accidental differences of doctrine may have distinguished the innumerable sects from each other, there are common to all of them a protest against the existing order and their status as individuals within it, an attempt to escape an un-pleasant and ever-present reality by identification with something that transcended their daily lives and the insistence on the imminence of a millennium or salvation. The pro-found dissatisfaction of the oppressed with their condition impelled them to an effort to transcend their immediate selves and environment through a mystical union with God, to seek compensation for their suffering in a sense of nearness to their Maker. They gave expression to the hopes that the events of 1640–2 had aroused—hopes to which they clung all the more desperately as their plight grew worse—by affirming that the millennium, and with it their deliverance from suffering, was at hand. We can see something of that millenary fervour in the early years of the war in such writings as those of Archer and Hanserd Knollys.[1] Essentially, the sects were countering the inegalitarianism that was fundamental to Puritanism. Puritanism, by identifying worldly success with election, told the poor that they were damned of God because they were not of the Elect. The answer of those who were told that they were condemned to abject poverty in this world and to eternal damnation in the next was to assert the essential equality of all human beings before God by denying the doctrine of predestination and affirming, in its stead, that the key to salvation was revelation. Puritanism had insisted that knowledge of God could come only through study and understanding of the Bible. By substituting the written word of the Scriptures for the hierarchy as the final authority in religious life, it took the effective direction of religious affairs from the hands of the prelates only to make it the monopoly of a literate, educated class. The reply of the poor—and hence, the illiterate and uneducated—was that not formal learning but an inner spiritual experience and inspiration were the true source of religious knowledge, that contact with God was not the exclusive privilege of a superior class, but could be attained by any man however humble his station. On the contrary, that inner spiritual experience by which alone men could be saved was far more likely to occur in those whom suffering had rendered meek and humble than in those whose wealth had made them haughty and proud. Salvation, they therefore affirmed in proclaiming the spiritual equality of mankind, was not a monopoly of a Chosen Elect, but possible for everyone; for every human being had within him a spark of divinity, an Inner Light that might at any moment be kindled.

The result was a tremendous outburst after 1640 of sectarian activity and the remarkable spread of mystical religion.[2] Sects

[1] John Archer, *The Personall Raigne of Christ Upon Earth* (1641), E. 180 (13); Hanserd Knollys, *A Glimpse of Sion's Glory* (1641), E. 175 (5). On Knollys' authorship of this tract see Haller, *The Rise of Puritanism*, Chap. VII, note 32.

[2] For brief accounts of the sects see Haller, op. cit., Chap. VII, and W. Y. Tindall, *John Bunyan, Mechanick Preacher*, Chap. IV. R. M. Jones in his several works on the mysticism of this period—e.g., *Mysticism and Democracy* (1932) and *Studies in Mystical Religion* (1909)—has not adequately appreciated the social basis of the movements he seeks to describe.

C

bred and multiplied and seemed to fill the earth. No doubt, orthodox churchmen, alarmed by the sudden appearance of such widespread " heresy " in those classes whose claim to thought and expression they considered an inexcusable pre-sumption, were haunted by their fear of the sects until they saw a heresy in every utterance and the emergence of a sect from every gathering. Certainly, we find it difficult to-day to credit the existence of some of the sects hysterical pamphleteers were constantly discovering.[1] But, if hyper-sensitive consciences tended to exaggerate the degree to which this mystical enthusiasm was given formal organization, there can be no doubt of the powerful appeal it made to the oppressed classes during the entire course of the Civil War.

What was a much more offensive and dangerous sin in the eyes of the pious was the activity of the " mechanick " preachers and the manner in which ordinary tradesmen and labourers took it upon themselves to tell their fellows of their spiritual experiences. Brewer and baker, cooper and cobbler, tinker and tailor, all inspired by the light of revelation that burned within them, mounted pulpit and platform to spread their message to their fellow-oppressed and downtrodden.

> " These kind of Vermin swarm like Caterpillars
> And hold Conventicles in Barnes and Sellars
> Some preach (or prate) in Woods, in fields, in stables
> In hollow trees, in tubs, on tops of tables,"

one none-too-sympathetic observer wrote of their activities.[2] The professional preacher, alarmed by the wholesale invasion of his field by these upstart amateurs, joined with the devout

[1] e.g., the author of *A Discovery of 29 Sects here in London all of which except the first are divelish and damnable* (1641), E. 168 (7), lists the Adamites, Brightanists, Thessalonians, Chaldeans, Electrians, Donatists, Panonians, Junonians, Damasians, Saturnians, Bacchanalians, etc. Pagitt, in his *Heresiography : or a Description of the Heretickes and Sectaries of these latter times* (1645), E. 282 (5), has an even more interesting roster of over thirty sects, which includes the Pueris Similes, Liberi, Libertians, Semper-Orantes, Deo-Relicti, Hethringtonians, Traskites, Muncerians, Hutites, Bewkeldians, Castilians, Monasterienses, Servetians, Johnsonians, Wilkin-sonians, Scattered Flock, Grindletonians, etc. *Religion's Enemies ; with a relation as by Anabaptists, Brownists, Papists, Familists, Atheists, and Follists saucily presuming to tosse Religion in a blanquet* (1641), E. 176 (7), adds the Etticheans, Montanists, Pelagians, Nonatians, Marcianists and Nicolatians. Edwards in his *Gangraena*, writing in 1646 during a renewed wave of sectarian activity estimates that there were 199 sects in England at the time.

[2] *A Swarme of Sectaries and Schismatiques ; wherein is discovered the strange preaching (or prating) of such as are by their trades Coblers, Tinkers, Pedlers, Weavers, Sow-Gelders and Chymney-Sweepers.* John Taylor (1641), E. 158 (1).

cleric who feared for the future of religion in pouring a burning stream of scorn and ridicule on the sects and their spokesmen.[1] They were not ordained. They were illiterate and ignorant. They were mad and insane. They were merely tradesmen and husbandmen and labourers. They were destroying all true faith in the Kingdom.

" But whence come they now," asks Pagitt, " from the schooles of the Prophets? No, many of them from mechannicke trades as one from a stable from currying his horses: another from a stall from cobbling his shoes: and these sit down in Moses chaire to mend all as Embassadours of Jesus Christ, as Heralds of the Most High God: these take upon them to reveale their secrets of almighty God, to open and shut heaven, to save soules." [2]

But the sects merely thrived on persecution; and martyrdom served but to add fuel to the inner light that animated their preachers. Against the shafts of the orthodox they were armed with the arguments of cobbler How [3] and horserubber Spencer,[4] who had denied that learning was an avenue to the understanding of God and had asserted the right of the humble to offer spiritual food to the people; and the championing of their claim to the free expression of their views by respectable citizens like Brooke and Walwyn encouraged them to further defiance of the conventional.

If the theological heresies of the sects shocked the pious churchmen, the social implications of their teachings frightened the men of property. There is little in the preachments

[1] For the early years of the war see, e.g., in addition to the Tracts already mentioned, *Religion's Loterie or the Churches Amazement wherein is declared how many sorts of Religions there is crept into the very bowels of this Kingdom* (1642), E. 176 (7); *The Divisions of the Church of England crept in at severall doores* (1642), E. 180 (10); *A Short History of the Anabaptists* (1642), E. 148 (5); *The Brownists Synagogue* (1641), E. 172 (32); *New Preachers New* (1641), E. 180 (26); *A Nest of Serpents* (1641), E. 168 (12); *A Curb for Sectaries and Bold Propheciers* (1641), E. 176 (17); *A Description of the Family of Love* (1642), E. 168 (2), etc. Dexter in his Bibliography lists over forty such attacks between 1640 and 1642 alone. *Congregationalism* (1880).

[2] *Heresiography* (1645), E. 282 (5).

[3] Samuel How, *The Sufficiencie of the Spirit's Teaching Without Humane Learning or a Treatise tending to prove Humane-learning to be no helpe to the Spiritual Understanding of the Word of God* (1645), E. 25 (16). Although How died in 1640, his pamphlet was reprinted several times. The copy in the McAlpin Collection was published in 1640.

[4] John Spencer, *A Short Treatise Concerning the Lawfulnesse of Every Man's Exercising his Gift as God shall call him thereunto* (1641), E. 172 (4).

of the sects in those early years that constitutes either a conscious demand for social equality or the suggestion of a programme of social reform; and it is doubtful whether many recognized in the first outburst of mystical religion the manifestations of an awakening class-consciousness among the oppressed.   But the emphasis of the itinerant preachers on the essential equality of all human beings, their denial that wealth constituted a passport to salvation and their conviction of the imminence of the millennium were profoundly disturbing to those who were filling their coffers with the good things of the earth.   For the belief that all men are created spiritually equal has a habit of translating itself into an insistence that material inequality is a sin before the Lord because it is a perversion of His divine scheme; and the conviction that one is about to inherit the Kingdom of Heaven often leads to a demand for a commensurate share of the earth.   Certainly, it is not difficult to imagine the preacher who audaciously ventured to ascend the pulpit inveighing, in the manner of his soap-box cousin of to-day, against a system that flagrantly violated the equality of all in the sight of the Lord by conferring luxury on the few and decreeing poverty for the rest; and his declamation no doubt formulated the implicit demand that men share their wealth and abdicate their privileges.   It is difficult to speak with confidence on the degree to which that demand was explicitly asserted, because we must largely depend for our knowledge of what the preachers said on those who ridiculed them—and the fears of the latter impelled them to wild exaggeration.   But this much is certain —that the early attacks on the sects were almost as much concerned with the social as with the religious aspects of their heresies.   Many writers warned England of the dangerous and subversive social tenets the sects were propagating:

"The Familists", warns one author, "would have all things common not onely goods and cattell but wife and children." [1]

The Anabaptists, the most feared of all sects, teach

"that a Christian may not with a safe conscience possesse anything proper to himselfe but whatsoever he hath he must make common".[2]

[1] *The Divisions of the Church of England* (1642), E. 180 (10).
[2] *Heresiography*, pp. 12–13.

THE DEVELOPMENT OF RADICAL POLITICAL THOUGHT 69

Another, recalling that Muenzer

> " preached that all goods must be common and all men free and of equall dignity ", warns that Anabaptism, " the gospel of licentiousness and rebellion . . ."

is rife in England and that its dangerous influence is rapidly spreading throughout the country.[1] Where those who so apprehensively watched the growth of the sects do not fear the direct implications of their teachings for property, they are deeply disturbed because of the anarchy their ideas seem to exalt:

> " They preach ", declares Richard Carter, " that all Christian liberty is lost if we obey anything that is imposed on us by man." [2]

Their fears, it must be granted, were certainly far from being groundless. If no organized challenge to the rights and security of property had as yet emerged from the sufferings of the common people, there was ample evidence that the misery into which they had been plunged would soon give shape and voice to that challenge. As early as 1640, South-wark and Lambeth, centres of working-class discontent and agitation throughout the entire war, were the scene of frequent " traitorous and rebellious assemblies " and of " base people tumultuously assembled " that the Council was forced to punish and repress.[3] Apprentices were rioting in London.[4] Many petitions of 1641 and 1642 express the fear—others the threat—that the dire need of the people would drive them to violent and desperate action.

> " Their cryes daily come to our eares for food ", wrote the clothiers of Suffolk and Essex describing the plight of the poor in their counties, " not without threatnings and some beginnings of mutinies." [5]
> " If these things be any longer suspended ", declared the

---

[1] *A Short History of the Anabaptists of High and Low Germany* (1642), E. 148 (5).
[2] Richard Carter, *The Schismatick Stigmatized* (1641), E. 179 (14).
[3] *C.S.P., Dom., 1640*, May 15, 1640, p. 167; also pp. 172, 250, etc.
[4] Ibid., May 16, 1640, p. 174.
[5] *To the King's Most Excellent Majesty, the Humble Petition of the Clothiers of Suffolk and Essex* (1641). Seligman Collection, Columbia University, New York.

working men of London in demanding that immediate measures be taken to revive trade, " they will force your petitioners to extremities not fit to be named." [1]

In January 1642 Pym warned the House of Lords against the dangers of " tumults and insurrections of the meaner sort of people ", adding " that what they cannot buy . . . they will take ".[2]

In the country there were widespread riots against enclosure. Peasants, everywhere, evidently inspired by the sentiment expressed by those who attacked the estates of the Earl of Suffolk in 1643 that

" if they took not Advantage of the Time, they shall never have the Opportunity again ",[3]

pulled down fences and levelled enclosures, dug up ditches that had been filled in and filled in ditches that had been dug up. Royal grounds in Cornwall, in the Forest of Dean, in West Durham, Roxham and Huntingdon and on Hounslow Heath were attacked and entered by irate peasants. So serious did the attacks on enclosures become that the Lords, moved by concern for their own estates, ordered in July 1641 that no enclosures that had been made up to the first day of the meeting of the Long Parliament could be interfered with, and where such enclosures were menaced the owners could enlist the assistance of the Justices of Peace in suppressing any disorder. But the attacks continued with little interruption during 1642–3. From many towns in Huntingdonshire, Somersetshire, Hertfordshire, Lincolnshire, Dorsetshire and Wiltshire came frequent complaints of enclosure riots.[4] The Lords in 1643, for example, were forced to pass an ordinance

" to suppress all Riotous and disorderly persons in and about Meere, Shaftesberry and Brome Selwood in the County of Sommerset, Dorset and Wilts " who " break open enclosures, throw down houses ".[5]

---

[1] *Pettition of 15,000 poore labouring men known by the name of Porters and the lowest members of the Citie of London* (1641), B.M. 669, f. 4 (55).
[2] *Lords' Journals*, Vol. IV, p. 541.
[3] Ibid., Vol. VI, p. 21.
[4] James, op. cit., pp. 90–4.
[5] Firth and Rait, Vol. I, May 3, 1643, p. 139.

In the riots and unrest in town and country, in the feverish surge of sectarian activity and in the tremendous volume of public discussion among the hitherto-inarticulate poorer classes,[1] we can discern the first expression of the revolutionary spirit that was to be crystallized by subsequent events into the radical movements of 1647–9. It is too early to see in them as yet the emergence of a proletarian, or even a democratic, ideology. But intellectual influences were already at work which, merged with the developments of the following years, helped to rescue the movement of discontent from the chiliastic mysticism and ineffectual sectarianism into which it threatened to dissipate and to convert it to secular and rational purposes and, for a time, to revolutionary activity. We can see some of those influences in the writings of the more advanced Parliamentary theorists like Parker and Rutherford, Herle and Burroughs: in their emphasis on natural law, on the people as the only source of all political power and consent as the only valid basis for the exercise of political authority. The Royalists, waging what was primarily a defensive struggle, could appeal to history or to Scripture to prove the lawfulness of their position. The apologists of Parliament, claiming for it rights it had never exercised, found the argument from the past inadequate for their purposes; and the more intelligent of them were forced to enunciate some theory of natural or fundamental law which men by the exercise of reason could apprehend and by which the exercise of authority was limited. Driven to justify their rebellion against established authority, they had to ascribe the origin of political power to the people, to assert the conditional nature of its exercise and the right of the people, either directly or through their representatives, to remove those to whom it has been entrusted when they have exceeded their trust or no longer command popular consent.

"Power is originally inherent in the people," declares Parker, "and it is nothing else but that might and vigour

[1] No account has been attempted here of the remarkable emergence of public opinion and discussion as a factor in the political developments of 1640–60, or of the vital rôle of the pamphlet and pulpit during the period in familiarizing the people in detailed manner with all the issues of the day. For some account of the vast pamphlet literature of the period see Fortescue's Introduction to his *Catalogue of the Thomason Collection* and Haller's Introduction to *Tracts on Liberty in the Puritan Revolution* (1934), 3 vols.

which such and such a society of men contains in itself. . . .
The people is the true efficient cause of power." [1]

It is unimportant that Parker equates Parliament with the
People and thus gives to it that absolute power he took from
the King. " Parliament is indeèd the State itself." [2] What
is significant in Parker and other Parliamentary writers is the
insistence on the conditional nature of political power, on
the origin of government in some sort of social contract and
on its limitation by some fundamental law of nature or reason
that each individual can discover. There is a growing
tendency to assert that the individual citizen's conscience must
be the final determinant or judge of the validity of law.[3]
There is the individualism that had always been latent in
Puritan thought, and in a large measure fundamental to it,
that through the Independents, and more particularly the
Levellers, was translated into the doctrine of the inalienable
rights of every individual which society must respect and
secure. There is the argument for toleration that emerged
out of the work of the Independents in the Westminster
Assembly and in the writings of Brooke and Walwyn and Roger
Williams, and which, if originally dictated by strategic and
political considerations, rapidly developed a much broader
significance and based itself on more purely rationalistic
premises.[4] There is the deepening recognition of the relative
rather than the absolute nature of knowledge and truth.[5]
There is a growing faith in the efficacy of education and
rational persuasion that is reflected during 1640-4 in the
writings and activity of Hartlib and Comenius, of Milton
and Harmar.[6] And there are the unmistakable, if crude,

[1] Parker, *Observations upon Some of His Majesties Late Answers and Expresses*
(1642), E. 153 (62), l. 2. Reprinted in Haller, *Tracts on Liberty in the
Puritan Revolution* (1934), Vol. II, p. 165.

[2] Ibid., p. 34.

[3] e.g., John Goodwin, *Anti-Cavalierisme* (1642), E. 123 (35). Reprinted
in Haller, Vol. II, p. 215.

[4] e.g., Goodwin, *Anti-Cavalierisme*; Walwyn, *The Power of Love* (1643),
E. 1206 (2) ; *Some Considerations tending to undeceiving those whose judgments are
misinformed* (1642) ; *The Compassionate Samaritan* (1644), E. 1202 (1) ;
Brooke, *A Discourse opening the Nature of that Episcopacie which is exercised in
England* (1641), E. 177 (22) ; Williams, *The Bloudy Tenent* (1644), E. 1 (2).

[5] e.g., Henry Robinson, *Liberty of Conscience* (1644), E. 39 (1).

[6] Hartlib, *A Description of the Famous Kingdom of Macaria* (1641),
E. 173 (28) ; *Considerations tending to the happy accomplishment of England's
Reformation* (1647), E. 389 (4) ; Comenius, *A Reformation of Schooles* (1642) ;
Milton, *Of Education* (1644) ; Harmar, *Vox Populi : or Gloucestersheres Desire*

beginnings of a scientific materialism that finds its most striking expression in Overton's pamphlet on immortality, which, if still playing deference to theological formulæ, is remarkable for its frankly materialistic arguments from psychological and biological analyses.[1] We shall discuss at a later stage how the Levellers, but to a much greater degree the Diggers, drew on these various currents of thought to fashion the theoretical basis of their claims and activities which, in the case of Winstanley at any rate, took final form as the one genuine proletarian ideology that the Civil War produced.

By 1645 the complaints of the common people were being voiced in much less confused and more categorical terms. It is not merely that as a result of the continually worsening economic situation petitions and pamphlets had become more bitter and determined in their tone, or that grievances and demands were being formulated in more concrete and definite form. What is more important is that their authors were beginning to perceive, however imperfectly, the true nature of the Civil War. It is too early to look for a reasoned statement of the class nature of the struggle; but there was already a growing recognition of the fact that the *bourgeoisie* dominating Parliament had been waging war for ends exclusively its own. Parliament is criticized not merely because it has proved itself ineffectual in relieving distress; it is condemned because it has deliberately deceived and wilfully lied to those it claimed to represent. It declared for liberty;

---

with the way to make a Kingdome happy by setting up of School-Masters in every parish (1642), E. 146 (2).

[1] Richard Overton, *Man's Mortalitie : or a Treatise wherein tis proved both Theologically and Philosophically that whole Man (as a rational Creature) is a compound wholly mortall contrary to that common distinction of soule and body and that the present going of the soule into Heaven or Hell is a meer Fiction* (1644), E. 29 (16) :

" Man is but a creature whose severall parts and members are endowed with proper natures or faculties each subservient to other to make him a living Rational Creature, whose degrees of excellences of naturall faculties make him in his kind more excellent than the Beasts. . . . It doth not follow that those faculties together are a Being of themselves immortal ; for as members cannot be perfect members without them, so they cannot be faculties without their members : and separation cannot be without the destruction of both : as attraction or heat is the propertie of fire which cannot be if fire cease. . . . If it be no unnaturall that seeing hearing etc. should be produced by an elementary operation as none deny in the propagation of Beasts : why is not the Rationall Facultie of man as naturall in Man and may as well be produced elementarily by man, as the other by Beasts and be as actually mortal? "

C 2

it has imposed greater tyranny. It promised to alleviate distress; it has wrought deeper misery.[1] That recognition, it must be admitted, had not yet become general in 1645; but it is met with increasing frequency during the year.

The developing rationalism was making its influence felt over a broad field. Economic and political discussion was being stripped of the theological camouflage in which it had hitherto invariably been cloaked. Pamphleteers were attempting, in increasing measure, a scientific and dispassionate analysis of the economic problems of the country. If they failed at any point to pierce through to the core of the phenomena they confronted, they indicate, at any rate, a more rational perception of the social needs and problems of the time and the formulation of a scientific approach to their solution.

Walwyn, Overton, Lilburne—among others—were rapidly moving to an enunciation of the theoretical argument on which the progressive forces both in London and the army were soon to take their stand. Walwyn was insisting that religious toleration was not an end in itself, but the prerequisite of a much more comprehensive liberty on which alone an adequate social order could be built:

" Who can live ", he asks, " where he hath not the free-dome of his minde and the exercise of his conscience? " [2]

[1] e.g., *The Generall Complaint of the Most Oppressed, Distressed Commons of England Complaining to and Crying Out Upon the Tyranny of the Perpetuall Parliament at Westminster* (1645), E. 300 (15) :

" Wee (as men) confident of your integrity did chuse you as our Proctors and Atturnies, the King's Majesty with his best councell and we (the poore Commons) entrusted you with all we had but we had no mistrust that you would deceive us of all we had. We trusted you to maintaine our peace, and not to embroile us in an universalle endlesse bloudye war. We trusted you with our estates and you have Rob'd, Plundered and Undon us ; we trusted you with our freedomes and you have loaden us with slavery and bondage, we trusted you with our lives and by you we are slaughtered and murther'd every day. . . . Thus we perceive that you pretend to fight for the Protestant religion and all the world may see and say, you have made a delicate dainty Directory, new religion of it. And you have fought for the King but it hath been to catch him and make him no King. You have fought for our liberties and you have taken them from us. You have fought for the Gospell and you have spoyl'd the Church, you have fought for our goods and you have em and you have fought to destroye the Kingdome and you have done it. . . ."

[2] Walwyn, *A Helpe to the Right Understanding of a Discourse Concerning Independency* (1645), E. 259 (2) ; also *England's Lamentable Slaverie* (1645), E. 304 (18). Both are reprinted in Haller, op. cit.

Overton was asserting the supremacy of reason in all human affairs and the fact that no compulsion can be valid against its dictates.   Lilburne had become acutely aware of the social problems of the common people and the conditions by which they were oppressed.   He still retained his faith in Parliament and in its ability to redress their grievances; but he was emphasizing that the law it promulgates must be governed by equity and that those who legislate must themselves be bound by the law they decree.   He had already left the army and had begun to dramatize in his own stormy and tempestuous experiences the larger issues around which the events of the next few years were to revolve.   In *England's Birth-Right Justified* he provided the petty tradesman, the artisan, the small merchant with a coherent statement of their grievances and the basis of a practical programme that could satisfy their needs.   There are the attack on the commercial monopolies, the most formidable enemy of the small business man, and the protest against the collapse of trade and the inadequacy of the measures that have been taken to revive business.   There is the complaint against the heavy burden of taxes and assessments.   There is the insistence that safeguards must be erected against the abuse of governmental power by provision for the election of annual Parliaments, by demanding an account of all those who handle public funds and by divesting Parliament of all its judicial functions.   He expresses popular resentment against the difficulty the people encounter in bringing their complaints to the attention of Parliament or the Council of London.   And fundamental to his entire argument is the insistence that positive law must be limited in its operation by the inalienable rights and liberties that every Englishman possesses and of which Magna Charta is the basis and guarantee.   The law, he therefore demanded, must be written in a language all men understand, so that they may know their rights and privileges.   There is already prominent in his utterances, let it be noted, that concern for the security of private property that was to make him essentially the spokesman of the small merchants and property-holders, of masters and apprentices themselves hoping to become masters, but that was to prevent him from developing like Winstanley, a real proletarian ideology:

" Yea, take away the declared, unrepealed Law and

then where is Meum and Tuum and Libertie and Propertie?'' [1]

But there is a frank recognition that only the common unity
of those classes for whom he speaks and mass pressure on those
in authority can achieve the ends he desires:

> "Therefore look about you betimes before it is too
> late," he earnestly appeals to the people, "and give not
> occasion to your children yet unborne to curse you, for
> making them slaves by your covetousness, cowardly basenesse
> and faint-heartednesse; therefore up as one man and in a
> just and legall way call those to account that endeavour
> to destroy and betray your Liberties and Freedomes." [1]

The year witnessed, as well, the first important organized
movement against the war—the armed rising of the Club-
Men in Dorsetshire and Wiltshire. Determined to end the
misery wrought by the war, fearful that their liberties would
disappear completely and alarmed by the threat to their lives
and property, thousands of the inhabitants of those counties
petitioned the King and Parliament to conclude an immediate
peace and armed themselves, in their own words,

> ". . . to joyne with and assist one another in the mutuall
> defence of our Liberties and Properties against all Plun-
> derers and all unlaefull violence whatsoever ". [2]

We should note with particular interest their resolution that
any of their number

> ". . . who will suffer in his person or estate in the execution
> of the premises, that shall be accounted as the suffering of
> the generality and reparation shall be made to the party
> suffering according to his damages; and in case losse of
> life, provision shall be made for his wife and children and
> that at the Countrey's charge ". [2]

The rising of the Club-Men was soon crushed by the army
Fairfax led against them; but their effort indicates how

---

[1] Lilburne, *England's Birth-Right Justified* (1645), E. 304 (17).
[2] *The Desires and Resolutions of the Club-Men of the Counties of Dorset and Wilts.* (July 12, 1645), E. 292 (24).

rapidly opposition to the war was developing into organized protest and rebellion.

Meanwhile, similar radical tendencies were manifesting themselves among the rank and file of the New Model. When the Independents succeeded in removing the Presbyterian Generals from leadership, they lost little time in impressing their doctrines on the army; and some of the most progressive preachers of the time, like Dell, Saltmarsh, Hugh Peters and William Sedgwick, were chaplains to the New Model during 1645–6. In the soldiery they found an audience eagerly receptive to their message; for to the common soldiers the domination of the Presbyterians implied the impressment that had forced them into the army, irregular and insufficient pay and the hardships the ravages of war had inflicted on their families. The debates in the Assembly were followed with keen interest by the army. The circulation of pamphlets was widespread; and there is abundant evidence that the fundamental issues they raised were heatedly discussed and argued. The pious Baxter, annoyed by his cold reception from Cromwell when he visited the army after the Battle of Naseby, can hardly be considered an objective and unprejudiced observer of its opinions; but his testimony nevertheless affords us an interesting picture of the ferment of ideas that was proceeding in the army at the time:

" But when I came to the army among Cromwell's soldiers ", he reports, " I found a new face of things I had never dreamt of; I heard the plotting heads very hot upon that which intimated their intention to subvert both Church and State. Independency and Anabaptistry were most prevalent. Antinomianism and Arminianism were equally distributed. . . . Abundance of the common troopers and many of the Officers I found to be honest, sober, Orthodox men and others tractable ready to hear the truth and of upright intentions. But a few proud, self-conceited, hot-headed sectaries had got into the highest places and were Cromwell's chief favourites, and by their very heat and activity bore down the rest or carried them along with them. . . . The greatest part of the common soldiers especially of the Foot were ignorant men of little religion." [1]

[1] Baxter, *Reliquiae Baxterianae* (1696), pp. 50, 53. Baxter's remark that he found little religion—i.e., his Presbyterianism—among the infantry is

By the end of 1645, that is to say, all the elements out of which a democratic and progressive movement could be formed were already present.   Both in London and in the army considerable numbers of the common people were beginning to question, and many to repudiate, the leadership of Parliament.   They were becoming aware that they, like their leaders, had peculiar interests which should unite them. Some of them, in fact, were beginning to act for a realization of those interests.   A sma .]group of thinkers and writers was developing the basic assumptions for a popular movement and was already interpreting the meaning of events to the people.   They were beginning to apply their principles to changing circumstances and to give direction to the radical movement.   And a vigorous, aggressive, popular leader was offering himself as a test of the issues that were being disputed.

The integration of those tendencies into a coherent political philosophy was forced on the radical wing of the Independents by the events of 1646.   The arrest of Lilburne, his clash with the Lords, Overton's imprisonment and the mass protests those incidents inspired brought forth a series of pamphlets and petitions in which the scattered elements of democratic thought were fused into a consistent doctrine that became the basis of the revolutionary movement of the following year.   The fact, too, that the Civil War had been temporarily brought to an end made it necessary for progressive thinkers to formulate their demands in concrete and specific terms;   and many pamphlets began to expand the suggestions that Lilburne and others had advanced into a comprehensive political programme that was rooted in the needs of the common people.

The political philosophy that emerges from the radical writings of 1646, however, had not yet become the intellectual equipment of a political party; for not until the latter part of 1647 did the Leveller Movement assume organized form. But it represents the body of principles in which politically conscious radicals were crystallizing the dissatisfaction of the people with the direction events were taking, the expression of those who protested to Parliament that

---

interesting, for the infantry was overwhelmingly drawn from the poorest classes, among whom Presbyterianism found little sympathy.   The cavalry, which was expected to supply its own horses and arms, was generally recruited from the gentry and nobility.

" yee are Rich and abound in goods and have need of
nothing; but the afflictions of the poore, your hunger-
starved brethren, ye have no compassion of ".[1]

It was the argument which those who were aware of the
needs of those classes were employing to sanction the demands
they were making and to justify the decreasing allegiance
they were rendering to Parliament. As the people and the
army were familiarized with those concepts through the work
of pamphleteers and propagandists and through their application and relevance to their own practical problems, they
served to integrate popular protest into a broad political
movement because the people recognized in them the expression of their own needs and aspirations.

Essentially, the argument that the progressives developed
in 1646 was that all political power emanates from the people
and that its exercise is valid only when it is based on their
free and common consent. The power of the Lords, Lilburne
therefore argued in denying their authority over him, was
entirely arbitrary, because it did not derive in any way from
the consent of the people. That no man may rule over
another against his will is generally held to be a self-evident
truth that is grounded in the very nature of society itself.
Occasionally, it may be argued, as with Lilburne, from
Creation. God created man in His image and gave him
dominion over the earth and all the things therein

". . . but made him not Lord nor gave him dominion over
the individuals of mankind no further than by their free
consent or agreement by giving up their power each to
other for their better being ".[2]

Government is created by a freely negotiated social contract
and is established by the people to enable them to order
their affairs more conveniently. Although the doctrine of
contract is fundamental to the Leveller argument, there is no
clear definition of its nature. There are occasional passages
in Lilburne which indicate the contract, in his view, to have
been one negotiated between the individuals who compose

[1] Overton, *A Remonstrance of Many Thousand Citizens* (June 1646),
E. 343 (11). Reprinted in Haller, op. cit., Vol. III, p. 365.
[2] Lilburne, *London's Liberty in Chains Discovered* (1646). Guildhall
Library.

society themselves for their mutual benefit; others suggest the agreement to have been one between the community and the rulers it creates. But the limits it sets to government are unmistakable.

> " The people's native right on which the social contract rests is to name and instruct rulers to do that which if it had been convenient the people might have done themselves." [1]

The power Government enjoys is therefore a purely delegated one that is revocable at will; and it can never claim rights and privileges the people themselves do not possess. If government is simply a trust, the people can cancel their grant of authority when those on whom it has been conferred no longer command their consent. When in 1647 and 1648 it became clear that the House of Commons would not adopt the programme the Levellers urged on it, Lilburne and his followers denied its authority by claiming that since it had failed to give effect to the wishes of the people, the power with which it had been entrusted had been revoked and annulled. To recognize its legality would have been to sanction arbitrary and tyrannical rule. One meets with increasing frequency in the Leveller discussions of the origins of government during this period the reference to the Norman Conquest that was so popular with all writers during the Civil War. But with the Levellers the Conquest was adduced not as an appeal to pre-Norman precedent, but to enable them to answer in historical terms how a free people, living under a government it had established by common consent, came to find itself under arbitrary domination. To the Levellers, the introduction of that arbitrary rule in England dated from the Norman Conquest.

Their entire argument was based on their doctrine of natural rights. Every individual, they asserted, was endowed with certain inalienable rights of which he could never be deprived. There is some confusion in Leveller writings of 1646, and in their subsequent utterances as well, as to the origin or nature of those rights. Occasionally they are derived, as with Overton, from the fact that since all men are equally born the children of God, they should therefore enjoy equal rights.

[1] Overton, *Remonstrance*, op. cit.

" For by natural birth all men are equally and alike borne to like propriety, liberty and freedome." [1]

More frequently, these rights are held to be self-evident because they are dictated by reason. Lilburne, when occasion rendered it convenient, could identify fundamental or natural law with reason, precedent, Magna Charta, Acts of Parliament or the Word of God. But, on the whole, there is a consistent identification of natural law with reason and an insistence that those laws and rights are natural which reason enables us to discover.

" Nothing which is against Reason is lawfull, it is a sure maxim, for Reason is the Life of the Law." [2]

The specific content of those natural rights was to vary with political exigency; and the doctrine of natural law was to be used, as Ireton later protested, to sanction every demand the progressives found it necessary or expedient to make. Already, indeed, it is being employed to give authority to the appeals of many classes and interests. One pamphleteer, for example, urging the introduction of a system of *laisser-faire*, claims that monopolies and the control of commerce by the wealthy merchants of London are against the Law of Nature:

". . . it is irrationall, reason being the foundation of all honest laws gives to every man propriety of interest, freedom of enjoyment and improvement to his own advantage ".[3]

Another pleads for freedom of trade:

". . . it being the birthright of every man to be alike free to transport that or any commodity into what parts beyond the seas seemeth most advantageous to him ".[4]

But however those rights may have been interpreted, the Levellers were emphatic that the end and purpose of social organization was to guarantee them to every individual and

[1] Overton, *An Arrow against all Tyrants and Tyranny* (1646), E. 356 (14).
[2] Overton, *A Defiance against all Arbitrary Usurpations or Encroachments* (Sept. 1646), E. 353 (17).
[3] Thomas Johnson, *A Plea for Free-Mens Liberties* (1646), E. 319 (1).
[4] *The Golden-Fleece Defended, or Reasons against the Company of Merchant Adventurers* (March 1647), E. 381 (10).

to render them, through appropriate legislative action, an effective reality.

A particularly significant feature of the democratic argument of 1646 is the degree to which political theory has been divorced from theological sanction. It is of course true, as Professor Woodhouse has recently emphasized, that the terms in which the Puritan of the Civil War viewed his world were primarily religious terms.[1] But, if progressive thinkers were still employing the forms and language of theological argument in elaborating the democratic ideology, the burden of their emphasis was in an increasing measure a wholly secular one. Political principle may frequently be couched in the language of theology or argued by analogy from Scriptural evidence; but the structure of radical political theory already rests on a foundation that is essentially secular in its nature. At no fundamental point does it require reference to theological sanction for its validity.

It must be pointed out, however, that there is little in the formal principles the democrats were advancing during 1646 that is strikingly new or original. Essentially, they were attempting to bind Parliament with principles Parliamentary writers had already used to bind the King. That all political power originates in the people, that government is a trust based on a social contract that is revocable at will and that there exists a fundamental law that guarantees the rights of all Englishmen were arguments Parliamentary theorists had been making from the very beginning of the war and with the first two of which, at any rate, English thinkers had been familiarized through the " Vindiciae ". Parliamentary writers, too, would have had little difficulty in assenting to the proposition that law must conform to reason, for many of them were already identifying the fundamental law of which they spoke with reason; the tendency to base political theory on a secular foundation and to find a rational rather than a supernatural sanction for human rightness was certainly not limited to the radicals.

What is of vital importance, however, is the fact that the progressives attempted to apply those principles in order to

[1] A. S. P. Woodhouse, *Puritanism and Liberty* (1938), Introduction, p. 39. Professor Woodhouse, however, has failed to emphasize that the interpretation the Puritan lent to those terms was profoundly conditioned by the social changes of the century and by the impact of political and economic development on traditional concepts. See *supra*, Chap. I, pp. 20–8.

place effective sovereignty in the hands of the common people. The apologists of Parliament had utilized the concepts of contract and fundamental law simply to justify their rebellion against the King, to provide the financial groups and the gentry with a rationale for their seizure of power. And they had been careful to circumscribe the areas in which those concepts operated in order to justify the exercise of absolute power by a Parliament dominated by the upper *bourgeoisie*. Government, they may claim, is above all else, a trust; but only Parliament, representing the dominant economic interests of the country, is to define the breach of that trust. Law, it may be admitted, must conform to reason; but the reason it embodies must be that of the *bourgeoisie*. And when, with the attainment of power by the *bourgeoisie*, those concepts had served their purpose, they could be discarded or repudiated—as with Ireton in the Army Debates—when they were being effectively employed to challenge the autocratic power the dominant classes were endeavouring to exercise.

In the hands of the progressive groups, however, those principles became the basis of a political programme that sought to vest power with the people. Governments function solely as representatives of the people; the latter must therefore at all times remain superior to their agents, and it is they who must ultimately determine when those they have chosen no longer merit their trust. Fundamental law, the radicals insisted, must represent not a body of privileges of an economically ascendant minority, but the interests of all the individuals in the nation. The Levellers, it is true, in interpreting those interests equated them with the needs of the tradesmen and artisans and peasants they represented. But their major importance for political theory lies in their attempts to set up constitutional machinery that would render the sovereignty of the people effective by limiting the practical operation of government. It is from those efforts that there emerged in 1647 the idea of a written constitution whose acceptance by the entire people would make the processes of consent an actual fact rather than an historical fiction and whose provisions would guarantee each individual his inalienable and natural rights by defining the boundaries of governmental activity.

But we must note the absence in Leveller theory, from

its very beginnings, of any realistic analysis of social power or a conception of historical development. As early as 1645 and 1646 the radicals saw clearly that no social organization could be justified which perpetuated social inequality and which operated simply to make the rich richer and to keep the poor destitute; and their demands for social and economic reform constitute a programme that was far in advance of the age. But they never lost the conviction that informs their early writings that the reforms they demanded could be effected merely by devising the appropriate constitutional mechanisms. There was no serious effort to analyse in realistic terms the roots of the power of those against whose tyranny they protested or the historical development of their supremacy. Overton, alone, in 1646 seems to have had some conception of the significance of class division and of the problems emerging from that division that the radical movement would have to confront.

> " Such hath been the misterious subtilty from genera-
> tion to generation of those cunning usurpers whereby
> they have driven on their wicked designes of tyranny
> and arbitrary domination under the fair, specious, deceitfull
> pretences of Liberty and Freedom that the poore deceived
> people are even (in a manner) bestiallized in their under-
> standings, become so stupid and grossly ignorant of them-
> selves and of their own naturall immunities and strength
> wherewith God by nature hath enriched them that they
> are even degenerated from being men . . ." [1]

While the theoretical basis of the radical movement was being formulated and the general ferment of ideas was agitating the army, the mass protests that the arrests of Lilburne and Overton aroused in London point to the beginnings of the organization of discontent among the London populace. There is little to indicate that the principles the radicals were urging had yet penetrated to the peasantry in the country; the writings of 1646 certainly do not indicate that the progressives had at any point made contact with the agrarian problem. But there was a renewed and more intense outburst of sectarian activity throughout the country that would seem to have been the expression of the deepening class

---

[1] Overton, *A Defiance against all Arbitrary Usurpations or Encroachments* (1646), E. 353 (17).

consciousness of the oppressed. During 1646 and 1647 an increasing number of " heresy inventories " flowed from the Press; and there is in them a much more acute awareness of the sources and roots of those " heresies " than had been manifested during the first wave of mystical enthusiasm. Edwards,[1] the most hysterical of the many cataloguers of heresy, could devote, in 1646, the first two parts of his *Gangraena* almost exclusively to what seemed to him to be the purely religious errors of the sects. By the time he had published the third part six months later, however, he was profoundly agitated by the realization that those whose doctrines he had been examining were defying civil as well as ecclesiastical authority; and this section was primarily dedicated to an account of their social and political doctrines. And that tendency became more and more general among those who were attacking the sects. To a considerable degree those attacks aided the sects in attaining political maturity. For as the tirades against them became increasingly secular and political in their emphasis, the sects were driven to carry on the argument in similar terms; and the process by which they translated their chiliastic visions into social and political concepts and transformed their inchoate revolutionary impulses into purposeful action was thereby accelerated.

If we cannot accept the highly prejudiced analyses of the " cataloguers " as a completely accurate account of what some of the sects were actually preaching, we can gather from them a vivid impression of the impact their activities were making on their contemporaries. Thus, the author of that comparatively sober pamphlet, *Mercurius Rusticus*, after asserting that Chelmsford in Essex was being governed by a tinker, two tailors, two cobblers, two pedlars, etc., gives an interesting account of their doctrines. They teach, among other things, he declares,

" . . . that the relation of master and servant hath no ground or warrant in the New Testament but rather the contrary . . . that one man should have a thousand pounds a yeere and another not one pound perhaps not

[1] Edwards, *Gangraena or a Catalogue and Discovery of Many of the Errours, Heresies, Blasphemies and Pernicious Practices of the Sectaries of this Time*, Part I, Feb. 1646; Part II, May 1646; Part III, Dec. 1646. See also Clement Walker, *History of Independency* (May 1648), E. 445 (1); (Sept. 1648), E. 413 (19).

as much but must live by the sweat of his browes and labour before he eate, hath no ground neither in Nature or in Scripture. . . . That the common people heretofore kept under blindnesse and ignorance have a long time yeelded themselves servants, nay slaves to the nobility and gentry; but God hath now opened their eyes and discovered unto them their Christian liberty; and therefore it is now fit that the Nobility and Gentry should serve their servants or at least worke for their owne maintenance; and if they will not worke, they ought not to eate." [1]

The author of another blast against the sects illustrating his attack on the " mechanick " preachers with pictures of a confectioner, a smith, a shoemaker, a tailor, a sadler, a porter, a box-maker, a soap-boiler, a glover, a meat-man, a chicken-man and a button-maker, all of whom are preaching in and about London, protests against the spreading of a materialism that teaches that the Scriptures are to be obeyed only when they conform to reason, that the immortality of the soul is a fiction and " that all the Heaven there is is here on Earth " [2]

How seriously Parliament viewed this renewed outburst of sectarian enthusiasm can be seen from the introduction in Parliament in September 1646 of the infamous ordinance against heresy [3] and the Ordinance of both Houses of February 4, 1647:

" concerning the growth and spreading of Errors, Heresies, and Blasphemies and for setting aside a day of Publike Humiliation to seeke God's assistance for the suppressing and preventing the same ", because of " the perillous condition that this Kingdome is in through the abominable blasphemies and damnable heresies vented and spread abroad therein ".[4]

In 1647 the dissatisfaction of the common people was transformed into a revolutionary movement that for several years seriously challenged the foundations on which the middle classes were endeavouring to stabilize the State. That movement developed simultaneously in the army, in

[1] *Mercurius Rusticus or the Countries Complaint of the barbarous outrages Committed by the Sectaries of this late flourishing Kingdome* (1646), E. 1099 (1).
[2] *A Discovery of the Most Dangerous and Damnable Tenets that have been spread within this few yeares* (April 1647), 669, f. 11 (6).
[3] Gardiner, *Civil War*, Vol. III, p. 139.
[4] Firth and Rait, Vol. I, p. 913.

London and in many sections throughout the country. It was rooted in each instance in the particular complaints of the rank and file of the soldiery, of the artisans and petty tradesmen and of the peasantry and small freeholders. It was aided by the crisis that developed among the ruling classes when the Presbyterian majority attempted to impose its " peace terms " on the country. And it was marked by an increasing determination in the oppressed classes to resort to independent mass action in furthering their demands.

The army, never regularly or adequately paid, demanded the payment of its arrears, adequate security for future payments, effective guarantees of indemnity and the prohibition of impressment for military service.[1] The tradesmen and apprentices had been impoverished by the complete collapse of trade, by unemployment and, in the cloth and woollen industries particularly, by the crushing pressure of the Merchant Adventurers. The peasants were oppressed by the insecurity of their tenures, by excessive fines and rents, by unrestrained enclosure and by the loss of their markets in the cities. Successive years of bad harvests had further aggravated their desperate situation. Everywhere, rising prices, taxes, levies, assessments, tithes, impositions, free-quarter, added unbearable burdens to an already distressed populace. The breakdown of local administration and of the judicial system rendered an appeal to the law in case of even the most flagrant abuses well-nigh impossible.[2] Largely as a result of Leveller activity, those streams of discontent soon burrowed deeper and broader channels ; and before long they had been converted into a vigorous movement for fundamental social change that threatened to push the revolution to a point far beyond that at which its original makers were endeavouring to arrest its progress.

For Parliament during 1647 was still dominated by the financial and commercial groups of the City and the landed gentry. Its temper was considerably more conservative than it had been during the previous year. The removal of the threat of the Scotch army had restored to the Presbyterians the support of many whom that fear had previously alienated ;

[1] By March 1647 the foot soldiers were eighteen weeks and the horse dragoons forty-three weeks in arrears. Total arrears amounted to £331,000 (*C.J.*, V, 126).
[2] From the autumn of 1642 to the autumn of 1648 no judges went the circuits. F. A. Inderwick, *The Interregnum*, p. 173.

and growing alarm at the swelling tide of discontent fostered a general insistence that effective measures be taken for the restoration of order. For by the beginning of 1647 the classes now in power had achieved practically everything for which they had plunged the country into war. The institutions that had thwarted and hampered economic progress had been swept away. Trade and commerce had been liberated from the arbitrary interference of the monarchy. Land and capital had been released for development and exploitation through the expropriation of estates, the abolition of feudal survivals and the removal of restraint on enclosure. The royal bureaucracy had been shattered. The Church was being stripped of the independent financial and judicial powers it had hitherto exercised; and the confiscation of its lands had destroyed the economic basis of its strength. The monarchy had been defeated in the field; and whatever power it might wield in the future it would exercise solely at the pleasure of its conquerors. State power was now in the hands of the *bourgeoisie*; and the latter, having attained its ends, now sought to consolidate the positions it had won.

At this point, however, it found itself confronted with the dilemma that has generally faced the victors of all *bourgeois* revolutions in modern history. It was faced with the army it had created to effect its victory—an army of peasants and labourers, of artisans and apprentices, with deep-seated grievances whose satisfaction it was urgently demanding and with a profound sense of its corporate unity. The *bourgeoisie* was confronted, as well, with those classes in town and country who had suffered such acute distress during the war, whose free-quarter and taxes and excise had financed the victory and in whom Parliament's promises had aroused profound expectations of social improvement. The army and the common people now demanded their share of the fruits of the victory their sacrifice had rendered possible. Parliament refused to satisfy those demands because their effect would have been to limit and, ultimately, to abrogate the exclusive privileges of the now-dominant *bourgeoisie*. Instead, it attempted to remove the most serious threat to its position by disbanding the army and sending several regiments for service to Ireland. That effort gave unity and coherence to the radical movements in the army and throughout the entire country because it made clear to the people more effectively than anything else that the victory that had been achieved was not their victory.

Those radical movements, as we have already indicated, were growing long before Parliament's efforts to rid itself of its victorious army. They had manifested themselves in the current of opposition to the war that had flowed ceaselessly since 1643, in the popular activity of the sects and in the riots and disturbances throughout the country. London had seen the organized beginnings of revolutionary protest in the mass demonstrations against the arrest of Lilburne and Overton in 1646; it had witnessed, too, the maturation of the political consciousness of those who were to give leadership to the movement. By the beginning of 1647 that political consciousness had begun to permeate wide sections of the people. We can see it in the demands of the London apprentices for monthly holidays which they claim

"... after so successful and voluntary hazard of their lives for Religion, Laws and Liberties. . . ." [1]

or in the assertion of the thousands of unemployed young men that

"... although the meanest members of this great Commonwealth ", they have nevertheless " by birth a right of subsistence here ".[2]

There is, for example, a firm and impressive statement from the inhabitants of Buckinghamshire and Hertfordshire that indicates that the country people, too, were becoming politically articulate.[3]

[1] *Two Petitions of the Apprentices of London and parts Adjacent for Lawfull Recreations* (Feb. 9 and 11, 1647), E. 375 (1).
[2] *The Humble Petition of Many Thousands of Young Men and Apprentices of the City of London* (March 1, 1647), E. 378 (15).
[3] *The Humble Petition of the Inhabitants of Buckinghamshire and Hertfordshire*, 669, f. 10 (115). Presented in Feb. 1647.
After describing the manner in which they had been denied their just liberties before the war and their expectation that Parliament would release them from tyranny and oppression, they declare:

"We for our better weal and happiness chose and betrusted your Honours for the same end and purpose; and to that end we have elected, invested and betrusted you with our indubitable and naturall power and Birth-Rights, for the just and legall removal of our Nationall Evils; In the expectation whereof we have waited ever since your first sitting continually and cheerfully assisting you with our lives, person, estates, being much encouraged thereto by the severall protestations and

In London the radical movement began to assume more
definite form in the support of a series of petitions addressed
to the House of Commons as " The Supreme Authority of this
Nation ", urging the enactment of a series of constitutional
and social reforms.   When the Petition, after having been
prematurely brought before the House on March 15, was
formally submitted in May, the House ordered it to be burned
by the common hangman.   Those petitions were as yet comparatively mild in their tone, though their recognition of the
House of Commons as the supreme authority in the nation
was considered a grave affront to Parliament.   They grate-
fully acknowledge the achievements of Parliament in having
suppressed episcopacy and in having abolished Star-Chamber
and other prerogative institutions.

> " But such is our misery ", they complain, " that after
> the expense of so much precious time, of blood and treasure
> and the ruine of so many thousands of honest families in
> recovering our Liberties, wee still finde this Nation oppressed
> with grievances of the same destructive nature as formerly." [1]

They urge constitutional changes, legal reforms, the prohibition of impressment and imprisonment for debt and complete
freedom of religious worship and opinion.   There is a special
protest against the Merchant Adventurers Company and a
demand for its immediate liquidation because it operates

> " to the extream prejudice of all such industrious people
> as to depend on clothing and woollen manufacture . . . and
> to the great discouragement and disadvantage of all sorts
> of Tradesmen, sea-faring men and hindrance of shipping
> and navigation ".[1]

---

declarations wherein you have solemnly protested before the Great God
of Heaven and Earth and to the whole world have declared your upright and wel-grounded resolutions to vindicate the just liberties of every
Free-Born Englishman without exception."

They voiced their profound disappointment that Parliament has failed
them in their hopes and warn it to heed " the slavish condition that we
the free people of England are yet subject unto by reason of those Arbitrary
practices that are still continued. . . ."

[1] Sept. 1648, E. 464 (19) : On the identity of this pamphlet with " the
Large Petition " see T. C. Pease, *The Leveller Movement*, p. 158, n. 1.

Parliament's attitude to the claims of the common people is strikingly revealed in the draft of the answer rejecting the petition that was prepared by the Commons:

> "We wish you would keep within the bounds of obedience", it declares, "and not presume to anticipate our counsels and prevent our proceedings by telling us what you expect our resolutions to be. We are contented to receive your grievances but not be schooled by you." [1]

Parliament's action in rejecting the petitions convinced the Levellers that they could not hope to effect their ends through its medium. Asserting that the House of Commons by failing to act in accordance with the wishes of the people had broken its trust and forfeited its authority, they declared the kingdom to have reverted to a state of nature in which no constituted authority existed and turned to the army.

For by this time the rank and file of the army was rapidly emerging as the most powerful revolutionary force in the land. In February and March Parliament passed a series of votes to disband the army and to crush the threat its presence embodied by sending large numbers to Ireland. The terms of disbandment were utterly inacceptable, for they failed at any point to meet the demands of the soldiers. With remarkable speed the rank and file proceeded to create its own democratic organs of expression and representation by the election of Agitators representing every troop and company, who evidently functioned jointly as company and regimental committees and from which the representatives who comprised the Council of Agitators were drawn. From protest against disbandment in terms of their particular grievances they rapidly moved to a general attack on Parliament on broader and more fundamental issues. As early as May they appealed to Fairfax and their officers that the attempt to send them to Ireland was

> "but a meere cloake for some who have lately tasted of soveraignty; and being lifted beyond their ordinary sphaere of servants seek to become masters and degenerate into tyrants ".[2]

---

[1] *C.S.P., Dom., 1645–47*, pp. 558–9.
[2] *The Apology of the Common Soldiers of his Excellency Thos. Fairfaxes Army* (May 3, 1647), E. 385 (18).

They had hoped by their victory, they declare, to establish a system of justice which

> ". . . the meanest subject should freely enjoy his right, liberty and properties in all things. . . . Upon this ground of hope we have gone through all difficulties and dangers that wee might purchase to the people of this land and ourselves a plentifull crop and harvest of Libertie and Peace but instead of it, to the great griefe and sadning of our hearts wee see that oppression is as great as ever if not greater. . . ."[1]

Innumerable petitions protesting against the attempt to disband the army were addressed to Parliament from all parts of the country; and many pamphlets were directed to the army urging it to remain firm in its resistance. These pamphlets are remarkable for the clarity with which their authors perceive the motives that inspire Parliament; they equally recognize that the army now constitutes the last bastion of the people in their struggle for liberty and a better social order:

> " It was very requisite and wisely done that they should vote this army", wrote one pamphleteer immediately after the vote for disbandment had been passed, " because it is the onely block and stumbling-stone to their designe of Presbytery and Lordly predominancy and that it may not be a refuge pillar for the oppressed and distressed commons of England where on to leane in claiming of justice and their just rights and liberties." [2]
> " It is apparent ", declares another, " that the disbanding or otherwise dissolving of this army is the only plenary expedient to render us Vassals and slaves to the will of our enemies and to bring upon us the worst of miseries." [3]

As the revolutionary consciousness of the common soldiery deepened, class divisions both in Parliament and the army emerged in sharper outline. In Parliament the Independents were becoming alarmed by the strength of Presbyterian reaction and by the fear that the intrigues of the King might yet succeed in restoring power to the monarchy and the

---

[1] *The Apology of the Common Soldiers of his Excellency Thos. Fairfaxes Army* (May 3, 1647), E. 385 (18).
[2] *A Warning for all the Counties of England to Awake Spedily Out of their Dreames and apply themselves to all Just Meanes for the Recovery and Preservation of their Liberties* (March 1647), E. 381 (13).
[3] *A New Found Stratagem* (April 1647), E. 384 (11).

nobility, and thus undo the work of the revolution.   In the army the gulf that separated the rank and file from their officers widened daily.   The officers, generally recruited from the gentry and the commercial classes, allied themselves on the whole with the Independent faction in Parliament.   Some were prepared to accept Parliament's terms and to agree to immediate disbandment.[1]   Others, like Cromwell, sought to compromise with the Presbyterian majority.   When they discovered the intransigeance of the latter, they threw in their lot with the army—not because of sympathy with its revolutionary aspirations, but because they hoped to use it in coercing Parliament into compromise.

We must not make too much of that breach between the Independents in Parliament and in the army now led by Cromwell and the wealthy Presbyterians, important though their difference may have proved to be in subsequent political development.   The former are as solicitous as anyone in the country for the interests of property.   They are no less profoundly disturbed than the Presbyterians by the threat to those interests that is shaping itself throughout the land.   They are prepared—and for a time, anxious—to restore the King.   They are even willing, in return for a limited toleration for themselves, to acquiesce in the establishment of Presbyterianism:

". . . though the leaders of each party seem to maintain a hot opposition ", wrote one author in a penetrating recognition of the fundamental identity of interest of both groups, " yet when any profit or preferment is to be reached at it is to be observed that a powerful Independent especially moves for a Presbyterian; or a leading Presbyterian for an Independent: and seldome doth one oppose or speake against another (in such cases) unless something of particular spleene or competition come between which cause them to breake the common rule. . . . By this artifice the Grandees of each side share the Commonwealth between them." [2]

[1] *C.S.P., Dom., 1645–47* (March 22, 1647), p. 541 : " Engagement signed by the officers who drew off from the army at the conclusion of the war ", in which the twenty-nine signatories express their readiness to disband or to go to Ireland, confident that Parliament will give them satisfaction re arrears and indemnity, etc.

[2] *The Mystery of the Two Juntos, Presbyterian and Independent or the Serpent in the Bosom Unfolded* (June 1647), E. 393 (28).   Pease ascribes the pamphlet to Clement Walker.

But where the wealthy commercial and financial groups and the landed aristocracy in the Presbyterian ranks wanted to vest absolute power in Parliament or to share it with the King, the merchants, the squirearchy, the industrialists, aware of the tyranny such a Parliament might at some time exercise, were anxious to create certain checks on its activity which they themselves could operate. The hostility between both groups was due less to any fundamental irreconcilability of end and purpose than to the fact that the mutual suspicion aroused by the intrigues of the one with the King and the manipulation of the army by the other led the Independents to fear a complete negation of the revolution and the Presbyterians its extension. Those fears drove a considerable number of the Presbyterians into alliance with the Royalists in the second Civil War and pushed the Independents into closer collaboration with the radicals until the execution of the King.

But if Cromwell and the Independents determined to support the army in its demands on the Presbyterian Parliament, they spared no effort to curb its enthusiastic radicalism. They sought to climb to power on its shoulders; but at no point did they share its fundamental aspirations. If the rank and file organized its Councils of Agitators, Cromwell and Ireton were quick to minimize its influence by absorbing it into a General Council of the Army that they " packed " with officers. In the struggle between the Army and Parliament in the summer of 1647 for control of the City, the proposals of the Agitators for decisive action by the army were vetoed by the officers; and the demands and suggested programmes of the rank and file were being continually tempered and modified by the conservatism of those officers. When, largely as a result of Leveller influence, the Army Council in November favoured the Agreement of the People and the scheduled general rendezvous at Ware seemed destined to witness its acceptance by the entire army, Cromwell, by a supreme effort, thwarted its ratification. He quickly suppressed the mutiny that arose among some of the more radical regiments; and those soldiers who had been most active in promoting the Agreement, among them one Will Everard, were arrested and later cashiered from the army.

The fundamental class interests that so sharply rent the army are strikingly. and frankly revealed during the course of the Army Debates at Putney during October and November.

Cromwell, Ireton and the officers are exclusively concerned to make England safe for the men of property they represent; and all social policy must be judged in terms of its consequences for property. That is the burden of Ireton's impassioned appeal:

" All the main thing I speak for, is because I would have an eye to property." [1]

They are vitally interested in order; but they are equally concerned that the order that is established shall be one that secures the sacred privileges of wealth. Every argument they advance, whether on the suffrage or the sanctity of contract or natural law, derives directly from that class position. The effective determination of public policy, they insist, must be entrusted to a Parliament in whose election only property-holders will be permitted to participate. Ireton is prepared to concede to the common people the right

" to air and place and ground and the freedom of the highways and other things, to live amongst us ",[2]

but the shaping of public policy must remain the exclusive privilege of

" the persons in whom all land lies and those in corporations in whom all trading lies ".[2]

For, he frankly confesses his fear, if

" you may have such men chosen or at least the major part of them (as have no local or permanent interest) why may not these men vote against all property? " [3]

If government is to be administered by a propertied minority solely in the interests of wealth, its decrees must not be challenged by the common people. Law must be obeyed and agreements honoured whatever their content; for law, Ireton argues, derives its claim to obedience simply because it emanates from a source formally competent to enact authority.

To the Levellers and the Agitators, on the other hand, the

---

[1] *Putney Debates*, Edited with an important introduction by Professor Woodhouse; *Puritanism and Liberty*, p. 57. The earlier edition in the Camden Society Publications, *Clarke Papers*, ed. Firth, New Series, Vols. XLIX, LIV, contains a valuable introduction by Professor Firth.

[2] Woodhouse, op. cit., p. 54.   [3] Ibid., p. 63.

only valid end of state activity is the general welfare of the common people and the protection of their rights; and to the achievement of those ends all claims of property and privilege must be subordinated, for everyone has an equal claim to share in the common good:

> " . . . the poorest he that is in England hath a life to live as the greatest he ".[1]
> " We have engaged in this Kingdom and ventured our lives ", Sexby declares bluntly, " to recover our birthrights and privileges as Englishmen. . . . There are many thousands of us soldiers that have ventured our lives; we have had little propriety in the kingdom as to our estates, yet we have had a birthright." [2]

And that birthright, he and his fellow-Agitators insist, is the claim of every Englishman to social equality and to share in the determination of the nature of the society in which he is to live and the laws by which he is to be governed. Effective sovereignty must therefore be vested not in a minority of property owners, but in the entire people; and that sovereignty is to be rendered an operative reality by a system of universal suffrage.

> ". . . every man born in England, cannot, ought not, either by the Law of God nor the Law of Nature to be exempted from the choice of those who are to make laws for him to live under and for him, for aught I know, to lose his life under ". [3]

If the purpose of social organization is to secure the well-being of the people, the validity of law cannot be determined by reference to its source of origin but must be measured purely by its consequences; and of those results the people themselves are to be the judges. Ireton was quick to protest that such an argument involved a state of contingent anarchy:

> ". . . for a man to infer that upon any particular issue you may dispute that authority by what is commanded whether it is just or unjust, this would be the end of all government ".[4]

---

[1] Woodhouse, op. cit., p. 53.   [2] Ibid., p. 69.
[3] Ibid., p. 56.   [4] Ibid., p. 29.

But the Levellers saw no less clearly that the acceptance of Ireton's view-point would mean the enslavement of the majority who were denied the opportunity to share in the making of policy to the tyranny of wealth and privilege.

There is a marked tendency in the early stages of the debate for the Levellers and the Agitators to shrink from pushing their arguments to their logical conclusions. Ireton recognizes more clearly than they the implications of their position. The argument from natural law, he urges, can lead to a denial of the right of property:

> " By that same right of nature (whatever it be) that you pretend by which you can say, one man hath an equall right with another to the choosing of him that shall govern him —by the same right of nature, he hath the same equall right in any goods he sees—meat, drink, clothes—to take and use them for his sustenance." [1]

Rainborough hastens to assure him that his party has no intentions of challenging the institution of property.

> " To say because a man pleads that every man hath a voice (by right of nature) that therefore it destroys by the same argument all property—this is to forget the Law of God. That there's a property, the Law of God says it; else why hath God made the law ' Thou shalt not steal ? ' " [2]

But, as the Levellers begin to appreciate the fundamental significance of Ireton's argument and his uncompromising class position, they are driven progressively leftward:

> " Sir, I see that it is impossible to have liberty but all property must be taken away ", Rainborough firmly tells Ireton. ". . . But I would fain know what the soldier hath fought for all this while? He hath fought to enslave himself, to give power to men of riches, men of estates, to make him a perpetual slave." [3]

Sexby, with his characteristic bluntness, expresses the disillusionment of the entire army:

> " I confess ", he declares, " many of us fought for those ends which, we since saw, were not those which caused us to go through difficulties and straits and to venture all in

---

[1] Woodhouse, op. cit., p. 58.   [2] Ibid., p. 59.   [3] Ibid., p. 71.

D

the ship with you.   It had been good in you to have adver-
tised us of it and I believe you would have had fewer under
your command to command." [1]

The irreconcilable class divisions the debates have revealed
are finely crystallized by Rainborough:

> " There is a great deal of difference between us two," he
> declares, turning to Ireton.   " If a man hath all he doth
> desire, he may wish to sit still; but if I think I have nothing
> at all of what I fought for, I do not think the argument
> holds that I must desist as well as he." [2]

Through him, the common people are announcing to the
bourgeoisie their determination to fight for the rights and
liberties the latter are attempting to deny them.

The revolutionary movement gathered momentum rapidly
during 1647.   It developed, as we have already indicated, in
the army, in London and throughout the country.   The
Army Agitators developed an elaborate organizational structure;   the New Model agitators were particularly active.
They maintained contact with the civilian populace, with the
armies in other parts of the country and with the navy;   they
organized meetings and demonstrations;   they conducted an
extensive correspondence;   they evidently operated a printing
press of their own.[3]

They were in constant contact with Lilburne, to whom they
turned for advice and guidance.   There is ample evidence of
considerable Leveller activity in the army in the early months
of the year.[4]

> " I made a vigorous and strong attempt upon the private
> Soldiery of your Army," Lilburne boasted to Fairfax, " and
> with abundance of study and paines, and the expense of
> some scores of pounds, I brought my just, honest and lawfull
> intentions by my agents, instruments and interest to a good
> ripeness." [5]

---

[1] Woodhouse, op. cit., p. 74.   [2] Ibid., p. 78.
[3] See, e.g., *Advertisements for Managing the Counsels of the Army* (May 4,
1647), *Letters to the Agitators.* · Reprinted in part in Woodhouse, op. cit.,
pp. 398–400.
[4] Gardiner, *Civil War*, Vol. III, pp. 237, 245, etc.
[5] Lilburne, *The Juglers Discovered* (Sept. 1647), E. 409 (22).

It was largely as a result of this advice that the soldiers chose new agitators to represent them in September.

" Suffer not one sort of men too long to remain adjutators ", he cautioned the soldiers, " lest they be corrupted by bribes of office or places of preferment; for standing waters though never so pure at first, in time putrifies." [1]

He impressed on them the importance of basing their agitation on the mass support of the people. To that end, he urged them

" to presse for moneys to pay your quarters, the want of which will speddily (by free quarter) destroy the army in the poore country people's affections, whose burthens are intolerable in paying excise for that very meat the Soldiers eate from them gratis and yet paying heavy taxation besides. . .". [1]

During the summer and autumn of 1647 the relationships between the civilian radicals and the army grew more intimate. There is evidence of a remarkable unity of feeling between the agitators and the London apprentices and a recognition of their common interests in the struggle:

" Your safety shall be equally before us with our own ", write the Agitators in thanking the apprentices for their petitions in behalf of the army.[2]

During the Army Debates the City Levellers came forth to join the Agitators in arguing the radical cause. We can see the results of their collaboration in the increasing effectiveness with which the revolutionary needs of the people are now stated in documents like the *Case of the Army* and the *Agreement of the People*. But we must never overlook the fact that, whatever direction the Leveller leaders may have given to the army, the revolutionary development of the latter was a spontaneous and mass phenomenon.

[1] Lilburne, " Advice to the Private Soldiers " (Aug. 21, 1647). Appended to *The Juglers Discovered*, op. cit.
[2] *The Petition of the Wel-Affected Young Men and Apprentices of London to Sir Thomas Fairfax, together with a Congratulatory Letter from the Agitators in the Army to the Apprentices* (July 1647), E. 399 (2). See also, e.g., *The Humble Acknowledgment and Congratulations of Many Thousands Young Men and Apprentices . . . to His Excellency Sir Thomas Fairfax* (Aug. 1647), E. 403 (1).

" Whereas you say the Agents did it ", an anonymous Agitator contradicted Ireton, " it was the soldiers did put the Agents upon these meetings. It was the dissatisfactions that were in the Army which provoked, which occasioned those meetings, which you suppose tends so much to dividings; and the reasons of such dissatisfactions are because those whom they had to trust to act for them were not true to them." [1]

The activity in the army was paralleled by agitation in London. Emissaries were sent by the London Levellers to carry on propagandist activity in all parts of the country. It is uncertain whether the Levellers developed any extensive organizational machinery in 1647 beyond that required for the publication and distribution of their pamphlets. But by the end of the year they had elaborated plans for a nationwide organization of their activities. We can see the results of their efforts in the fact that the people in giving expression to the class consciousness that was being so rapidly intensified among them spoke the language of the Leveller leaders. One could point to many magnificent examples of the depth of that feeling in 1647. There is, for example, that eloquent and powerful pamphlet, *The Antipodes*. When the Long Parliament first assembled, writes the author, England groaned under many evils—monopolies, favouritism before the law, imprisonment without just cause, burdensome taxation. Parliament promised to remedy those conditions, to restore the rule of law and the freedom of the individual. But Parliament has betrayed its trust:

" Heare oh Heavens and tremble oh Earth ", he passionately appeals. " Oh England, stand amazed. Many of your trustees have conceived wickedness. They promised liberty but behold slavery, they pretended justice but behold oppression; they pretended reformation but behold deformation; they pleaded law but have lost conscience; they pretended purity but behold hypocrisy. . . . Our condition is much worse than at the beginning, for then we knew our sicknesse and remedye but now such are our distempers that wee may more easily know them than cure them. 'Tis their privilege is our bondage, their power our

---

[1] Woodhouse, op. cit., p. 88.

pestilence, their rights our poverty, their wils our law, their smiles our safety, their frownes our ruine. . . ."

" And you poore Commons of England," he concludes in a stirring call to the people, " unlesse you seriously and suddainly lay your condition to heart and as one man rise up for the vindicating of yourselves against those which have abused and daily endeavoured to inslave you and if you doe not now take this opportunity in joyning with and assisting of this army . . . know assuredly that you doe hammer out a yoake for your own necks which will pierce the lives, liberties and estates of yourselves and posterities and when your sufferings bring you sorrow you may not happily find deliverers." [1]

There is, too, that even more remarkable pamphlet by " a friend of the inslaved communalty ", probably Lawrence Clarkson, that reveals a fundamental understanding of the nature and significance of class division that is found, among the Leveller leaders, only in Overton:

> . " Consider how impossible it is for those that oppresse you to ease and free you from oppressions; " he reasons. " For who are the oppressors but the Nobility and Gentry; and who are oppressed, is it not the Yeoman, the Farmer, the Tradesman and the Labourer? then consider have you not chosen oppressors to relieve you from oppression? . . . It is naturally inbred in the major part of the nobility and gentry to oppresse the persons of such that are not as rich and honourable as themselves, to judge the poore but fooles and them wise. . . . It is they that oppresse you, insomuch that your slavery is their liberty, your poverty is their prosperity." [2]

If organized agitation among the peasantry was not as intensive as it was either in London or in the army—and that fact is to be explained almost entirely in terms of the special difficulties the organization of activity in rural areas encountered—the dissatisfaction of the peasantry with Parliament was none the less profound. It is impossible to deter-

---

[1] *The Antipodes or Reformation with the Heeles Upward.* I.H. (July 1647), E. 399 (16).
[2] *A General Charge of Impeachment of High Treason in the Name of Justice-Equity against the Communalty* (Oct. 1647), E. 410 (9).

mine to what extent the petitions that emanated from the country were the spontaneous expression of the political consciousness of the agrarian population and to what degree they were the work of the Leveller emissaries. But there was certainly a widespread protest from the country against the attempt to disband the army that developed from the recognition of the rôle it had to play in securing freedom for the common people.[1] Spasmodic rioting continued during the year. The army petitions contain no reference to the agrarian problem or the demands of the peasantry. But there can be little doubt that these sections of the rank and file that had been recruited from the peasantry were more concerned with enclosures and tenures than with restrictions on trade and industry. By the middle of the year some of the Leveller leaders had become aware, in limited fashion, of the agrarian problem. Overton, appealing over the heads of Parliament to the people in July, includes in his programme for what seems to be the first time, the demand

> ". . . that all grounds which anciently lay in common for the poore and are now impropriate, inclosed and fenced in may forthwith (in whose hands soever they are) be cast out and laid open againe to the free and common use and benefit of the poore ".[2]

The demands of the peasantry subsequently became an integral part of Leveller programmes. But those demands, though manifesting a sincere solicitude for the state of the poor, were essentially limited, as we shall later see, to the needs of the peasantry and petty freeholders. Not until the end of 1648 did the impact of Leveller propaganda on the landless labourers translate itself into a plea for common ownership.

The political developments of 1647-9 can be summarized but briefly at this point. Their central theme is the struggle for power between the Independents and the army led by Cromwell and the Presbyterians. The latter tried to secure their position through accommodation with the Royalists;

---

[1] e.g., *Four Petitions to Fairfax from Essex, Norfolk and Sussex, Hertford and Buckinghamshire* (1647), E. 393 (7).

[2] Overton, *An Appeal from the Degenerate Representative Body the Commons of England Assembled at Westminster to the Body Represented, the Free People in General* (July 1647), E. 398 (28).

Cromwell bid for power through the pressure of the army. Cromwell may not have been a dissembling hypocrite; but he was certainly the supreme political opportunist of the period. To attain his end, there was no medium he was not prepared to utilize. He could intrigue with Charles and negotiate with the Levellers. He could, when necessary, purge Parliament and finally execute the King. But throughout he remained consistent in one thing—in his determination to suppress the threat of the common people by retaining absolute control of the army and by crushing whatever popular movements ventured to challenge his authority. It was essential to the purpose of the Independents that they retain the allegiance of all sections of the army; but they were careful, in so doing, to deny the radical elements any share in its control. During 1648, the alliance of considerable sections of the Presbyterians with the Royalists plunged the country into the counter-revolutionary second Civil War and placed the government in jeopardy. Confronted by a common danger, Parliament and the army temporarily shelved their struggle. But when the war had been brought to an end and the Parliamentary majority, but particularly the Lords, persisted in their negotiations with the King, the Independents were driven to the realization that they could guarantee the order they desired to establish only by the direct seizure of power by the army and the execution of the King. To maintain the unity that was vital to their purpose, they were forced to move closer to the policy of the Left. There was a series of negotiations and compromises that revealed that the conflict between the revolutionary aims of the Levellers and the essential conservatism of the army leaders was as fundamental as ever.[1] If anything, the army leaders, conscious that supreme power was within their grasp, already betrayed, as with Ireton in the Whitehall Debates, their reactionary intentions. But they remained sufficiently united in purpose to effect the unity they required. Ireton, by accepting the Leveller demand that the kingdom be settled through the medium of an Agreement of the People, secured their reluctant acquiescence in the immediate pro-

[1] " He (Cromwell) and the Levellers can as soon combine as fire and water", wrote a Royalist newspaper at the time, " . . . the Levellers aim being at pure democracy . . . and the design of Oliver and his grandees for an Oligarchy in the hands of himselfe." *Mercurius Pragmaticus* (Dec. 19-26, 1648), E. 477 (30).

gramme he suggested. Pride's Purge and the execution of the King installed the army in the seat of power.

With their accession to power, Cromwell and the Independents cast off the specious liberalism in which they had paraded. The vote of Jan. 4, 1649, which declared that " the people under God are the original of all power " and which established the House of Commons as the supreme authority in the land may superficially seem to have been a formal triumph for the Levellers. Actually, it was a hollow mockery. For, when that declaration was issued, supreme power in the State was already in the hands of a small minority whose authority rested solely on the army it commanded and who was to rule England ruthlessly by the naked power of the sword.

The suppression of the mutiny at Ware in November, 1647, and the subsequent purge of the army restored discipline in the ranks and seriously arrested revolutionary activity. Parliament's vote to make no further addresses to the King did much to heal the breach between the officers and the common soldiery; and when the Army Council adjourned for the last time in January, after expressing its satisfaction with Parliament's decision, the army leaders had largely regained the confidence of the soldiers. As the revolutionary fervour of the army temporarily cooled, the Levellers became a more purely civilian movement. The discovery of their plans by the Government early in 1648, the arrest of Lilburne and Wildman and the second Civil War checked organized Leveller activity until the autumn of the year. But as the movement tended to base itself more and more exclusively on the civilian populace and as its propaganda spread to the towns and country, its economic and social aspects became considerably more prominent than they had hitherto been. Where radical petitions of earlier years had generally revealed the hand of Leveller organizers, those of 1648 unmistakably reflect a genuine spontaneity. They are much more profoundly concerned with the acute economic distress of the signatories than with immediate political developments; and the demands for social reform are put forward with a much greater urgency than are those for constitutional change. They are suffused by a sense of desperation; and there runs through them the continual threat of violence to which the desperation of the people is driving them.[1] This spontaneous expression of the social dissatisfaction of the people reveals a more intense class consciousness, a more bitter protest against class division and an increasing determination to resort to independent mass action if Parliament continues to ignore the frantic appeals that are being made to it:

> " Its your taxes, Customs and Excise that compells the Countrey to raise the price of food and to buy nothing from us but meer absolute necessaries ", the starving tradesmen bitterly protest to the rich of the Kingdom, " and then you of the City that buy our work must have your Tables furnished and your Cups overflow; and therefore will give us little or nothing for our Work, even what you please because you know we must sell for moneys to set our Families on work or else famish; Thus our Flesh is whereupon you Rich Men live and wherewith you deck and adorn yourselves. Yee great men, is it not your plenty and abundance which begets you Pride and Riot? And do not your Pride beget ambition and your ambition faction and your faction these civil broils? what else but your ambition and faction continue our distractions and oppressions? Is not all the controversie whose slaves the poor shall be? "

With eloquent bitterness they contrast their extreme destitution with the luxury of the members of Parliament and the wealthy officers—a luxury that the latter enjoy only as a result of their shameful exploitation of the poor:

> " What then are your ruffling silkes and velvets and youre glittering gold and silver laces, are they not the

---

[1] Some conception of the situation in 1648 may be gleaned from an account by William Sedgwick that is more restrained and objective in its analysis than were most pamphlets of the period.

" Honest industry, quite discouraged being almost use-less ", he writes. " Most men that have estates betrayed by one side or other, plundered, sequestered. Trading (the life and substance of thousands) decaying, eaten up with taxes; your poor ready to famish or to rise and pull relief from the rich men's hands by violence; the heavens and earth jarring in unseasonable weather; and summer and winter invading each other's quarters; which threatens famine upon you. Squeezed by taxes, wrack'd with war, the anvill indeed of misery upon which all the stroakes of vengeance fall. A wofull nation! once the freest people in the world, now the veriest slaves."—William Sedgwick, *The Leaves of the Trees of Life for the Healing of the Nations* (1648), E. 460 (10).

D 2

sweat of our browes and the wants of our backs and bellies? "

They conclude with a frantic appeal to Parliament and to the army:

" Oh, Parliament men and soldiers! Necessity dissolves all law and government and hunger will break through stone walls. Tender mothers will sooner devour you than the fruit of their own womb and hunger regards no swords and cannons. . . . Oh hearke at our doors how our children cry ' bread, bread, bread ', and we how with bleeding hearts cry once more to you, pity an enslaved, oppressed people; carry our cries in the large petition to the Parliament and tell them if they still be deafe, the tears of the oppressed will wash away the foundations of their houses." [1]

There is, too, that equally eloquent protest of the " Plaine Men of England against the Rich and Mightie " for the intrigues of the Lords with the King, and their efforts to weaken the authority of the House of Commons by allying themselves with the rich men of the City and for encouraging division among the poor to prevent their unity:

" all proceedings ever since evidently demonstrating a con-federacy amongst the rich and mighty to impovish and so to enslave all the plaine and mean people throughout the land ".[2]
" Ye have by corruption in Government, by unjust and unequall lawes, by fraud, cousenage, tyranny and oppres-sion gotten most of the land of this distressed and enslaved nation into your ravenous clawes, ye have by monopolies, usuries and combinations engrossed all the wealth, monies and houses into your possessions! yea and enclosed our commons in most Counties. . . . How excessively and un-

---

[1] *The Mournfull Cryes of Many Thousand Poor Tradesmen who are ready to famish through decay of trade or The Warning Teares of the Oppressed* (Jan. 1648), 669, f. 11 (116). The Large Petition referred to is probably the Smithfield Petition drawn up in Jan. 1648. It is printed in Lilburne's *Impeachment of High Treason*, E. 508 (20).
[2] *England's Troublers Troubled or the Just Resolutions of the Plaine Men of England against the Rich and Mightie by whose pride, treachery and wilfulness they are brought into extream necessity and misery* (Aug. 1648), E. 459 (11).

conscionably have ye advanced your land rents in the Country and house and shop rents in the City within these fourty years? How many families have ye eaten out at doores and made beggars, some with racke rents and others with engrossing of leases and monopolizing of trades? . . . When with extreme care, rackt credit and hard labour, ourselves and servants have produced our manufactures, with what cruelty have ye wrought and still worke upon our necessities and enrich yourselves upon our extremities, offering yea frequently buying our work for lesse than (you know) the stuff whereof it was made cost us; by which and the like unconscionable meanes in grinding the faces of the poore and advancing yourselves on our ruins, most of you rich citizens come to your wealth without any kind of remorse or Christian compassion for your so undoing of poor families and pitifully eating the bread out of the young crying infants mouths." [1]

They warn the Lords that unless the latter cease to corrupt the House of Commons and to provoke the army and, instead, actively promote the restoration of trade, they will resort to economic action by refusing to pay rents or debts or taxes.

" Ye must hold us excused ", they declare, " for paying any of you either rents, debts or interest and all enclosures of fens and commons ye must expect to be layed open." [1]

We should observe, too, that they strike a note that, surprisingly enough, is seldom sounded in Leveller literature— a recognition of the potentialities of the expanding economy and the protest that the denial to anyone of his just share of those benefits is nothing less than an act of robbery:

" But these and many other enormities are parcells of the fruits of evile, corrupt and tyrannicale Government and of covetous, wicked and ambitious Governers, perverting most undutifully and unconscionably the end of God's creation who in all nations hath most wisely and liberally provided a sufficiency of necessaries for the Inhabitants and unto every particular or individuale person whereof a competency is due and which if witheld is in his

[1] *England's Troublers Troubled* (Aug. 1648), E., 459 (11).

sight no less than robbery and injustice. And therefore by all just governments ought to be carefully lookt unto and prevented, it being most unreasonable where God hath given enough that any should perish through want and penury. These things we have begun now more seriously to consider than at any time heretofore " is their concluding warning, " ye giving us more and more cause to do so." [1]

But as the social and economic aspects of the movement emerged in greater detail and with increasing emphasis, their limited character became more obvious. We hear in the protests and demands the voice of those classes of the *petit bourgeoisie* whom the new capitalist development in trade and industry and agriculture had most seriously affected. The petty tradesmen and manufacturers in the towns and the peasants in the country demand the abolition of the special privileges the law extended to the monopolist and the enclosing landlord. They seek equality of opportunity with the wealthier business enterprises and the larger unit of production that were becoming more important in the economic life of the country. They insist that all restrictions on trade and industry that operate to the prejudice of the small business men be removed and that protection and encouragement be extended them in the exercise of their trades and businesses. Taxes and excise should either be completely abolished or more equitably distributed in accordance with capacity to pay.

In 1648 the peasantry and smaller freeholders have become equally articulate. Like the tradesmen, they protest against the legally-supported privileges of the gentry and nobility. For the Ordinance of 1646,[2] while removing the feudal survivals that hampered the tenants-in-chief, did nothing to ease the burden of the smaller tenants. There is the continual demand from the latter in Leveller petitions for the abolition of copyhold tenures and their conversion to freehold :

" The Ancient and almost antiquated badge of slavery, viz. all bare Tenures by Copies, Oaths of Fealty, Homage,

---

[1] *England's Troublers Troubled* (Aug. 1648), 'E. 459 (11).
[2] Firth and Rait, op. cit., Vol. I, p. 833.

Fines at Will of Lord, etc. (being the Conquerors' marks on the people) may be taken away." [1]

demands one of their manifestos. Failing that, they suggest that after a fixed period all uncertain services and fines should be converted into fixed rents. Primogeniture is frequently attacked because it confers undue privileges; and there is, of course, the constant complaint against enclosure because it has resulted in the impoverishment of such considerable numbers of the peasantry.

But if the peasants and tradesmen had become fully aware of the nature of their struggle with the Right, they had become almost equally sensitive to the danger they conceived to be threatening them from the Left. There is no evidence during 1648 of any independent movement of the workers in the towns or of the landless labourers in the country. But there are indications, which we shall discuss in a later chapter, that these propertyless classes found the Leveller programme inadequate and, to a considerable measure, irrelevant to their situation; for restrictions on monopoly or the conversion of tenures bore little significance for those who had neither trades nor land. There is in all Leveller literature, it is true, a sincere and very generous solicitude for the welfare of the poor and the dispossessed. The various Leveller petitions and manifestos insist that poor relief be much more efficiently organized and administered, and that adequate measures be taken to prevent begging and destitution. All enclosed fens and commons, they repeatedly urged, should be opened for the benefit of the poor; and income from enclosures should be dedicated to their relief. But those suggestions were inspired by sympathy and charitable motives rather than by any deep concern with the problems of the propertyless classes. Wage-earners, in fact the Levellers agreed, were to be excluded from the scheme of universal suffrage they were advocating; and beyond adequate relief from destitution, they had little claim on the State.

In fact, while the tradesmen and peasants were demanding concessions from the commercial groups and the gentry, they had begun to emphasize their determined opposition to any fundamental revisions of the economic foundations of the State. During 1648 almost every Leveller petition

[1] *A New Engagement or Manifesto* (1648), 669, f. 12 (97).

included the demand that the Government pledge itself never to introduce legislation that might destroy or abrogate the rights of private property. In March, Lilburne repudiated the designation of his party as " The Levellers ", declaring of his followers that

"... they have been the truest and constantest asserters of liberty and propriety (which are quite opposite to communitie and levelling) that have been in the whole land ".[1]

He challenges anyone to adduce anything in their writings or declarations

" that doth in the least tend to the destruction of liberty and proprietie or to the setting up of Levelling by universal communitie or anything really and truly like it ".[1]

All Leveller petitions now listed, among the things they had been expecting of Parliament,

"... that you would have bound yourselves and all future Parliaments from abolishing propriety, levelling men's estates or making all things common ".[2]

The Second Agreement of the People of 1648 already included in the limitations on the power of governments

"... that no representative shall in any wise render up, or give, or take away any foundations of common right, liberty or safety contained in this Agreement, nor shall level men's estates, destroy propriety, or make all things common ".[3]

Walwyn, it is true, was reported to have declared on one occasion

"... that it was a sad and miserable thing that it should so continue and that it would never be well until all things were common ".[4]

---

[1] Lilburne, *A Whip for the Present House of Lords or the Levellers Levelled* (March 1648), E. 431 (1).
[2] *To the Right Honourable the Commons of England. . . . The Humble Petition of Thousands Well-Affected Persons* (Sept. 11, 1648), E. 464 (5).
[3] *The Second Agreement of the People*, printed in Lilburne's *Foundations of Freedom*, E. 476 (26).
[4] *Walwyn's Wiles or the Manifestators Manifestated* (1649), E. 554 (24).

But Walwyn was probably the most advanced of all the Levellers; and the particular statement, at any rate, was denied both by Walwyn [1] and his intimate acquaintances.[2]

Several factors undoubtedly impelled the Levellers to deny so emphatically their intention to introduce any form of communal ownership and to insist on the constitutional limitation they sought to impose on Parliament through the Agreement of the People against interference in fundamental fashion with the rights of private property. The constant attempts of their opponents to discredit the Levellers by accusing them of intending to abolish private property undoubtedly obliged the latter to protest their eminent respectability; and they spared no effort to prove the truth of that protestation. Then, as the radical movement became a more purely civilian affair and attracted in increasing measure the support of the peasantry and of the tradesmen, a more conservative factor was introduced into their activities. The peasants, with their traditional and deep-rooted fear of losing their lands, and the tradesmen, apprehensive lest they be deprived of their businesses, probably insisted that nothing in the Leveller programme implied an attack on private ownership. Yet, these factors in themselves would hardly have called forth from the Levellers such an emphatic avowal of their allegiance to the principle of private property. What probably contributed to evoking their denial of communistic intentions in greater measure than anything else, was the fact that even before Winstanley had begun to issue his tracts or the Diggers had made their appearance on St. George's Hill to begin their experiment in practical communism there was already a significant, though as yet inarticulate, current of opinion among the propertyless classes that the problems of economic oppression and class division the Levellers were attempting to confront could not be adequately solved until private property had been abolished and a system of common ownership established in its stead.

"I would not be mistaken as if I were an enemy to great estates," Cooke hastens to explain as early as January 1648 in setting forth his scheme for the alleviation of poverty, betraying an anxiety to dissociate himself from that

---

[1] Walwyn, *The Fountain of Slander Discovered* (May 1649), E. 557 (4).
[2] *The Charity of Church-Men or a Vindication of Mr. William Walwyn, Merchant.* By H. E. (May 1649), E. 556 (20).

current of opinion. " I am not of their opinion that drive at a parity, to have all men alike, tis but a Utopian fiction, the Scripture holds forth no such thing; the poore ye shall alwayes have with you. . . ." [1]

There was a renewed outburst of radical agitation in the autumn of 1648, when, with the end of the second Civil War, considerable sections of Parliament persisted in their negotiations with the King. Those efforts drew angry and threatening protests from the army, the country and the City radicals. Lilburne, alarmed that the Independents preparing to challenge for power would establish a regime as autocratic as that of the Presbyterians or of Charles, renewed his agitation for the acceptance of the Agreement as the only method that would guarantee freedom and security to the people. The negotiations and compromises between the Independents, the Army and the Levellers in the months that preceded the execution of Charles lessened overt revolutionary activity; but when, with the accession of Cromwell to power, the reactionary nature of the regime he proposed to establish was revealed there was an intense resurgence of revolutionary agitation, which we shall examine in a later chapter, that was brought to a climax by the revolts at Burford and Oxford. But, in Leveller theory at any rate, there were no further developments of fundamental importance; for the arguments they had advanced against the arbitrary rule of the Presbyterian Parliament were equally valid when directed against the Commonwealth.

There was, we should note, throughout the entire period of radical activity a consistent effort to crush the Leveller movement, to suppress all radical propaganda throughout the country and to eliminate the extreme elements in the army. The circulation and presentation of petitions, one of the most effective methods of crystallizing discontent and organizing mass demonstrations, were continually being rendered more difficult. When Parliament, for example, after considerable pressure from the apprentices, was forced to grant them a daily holiday every month,[2] its alarm at their growing class consciousness and its fear that they would take

---

[1] John Cooke, *Unum Necessarium or the Poor Man's Case* (Jan. 1648), E. 425 (1).
[2] *Supra*, p. 123.   Firth and Rait, June 8, 1647, Vol. I, p. 954.

advantage of their free day to engage in political discussion and activity impelled it to issue an ordinance three weeks later giving the justices the right to imprison any apprentices

". . . who cause any riotous or tumultuous assembly to the disturbance of the peace on such day of recreation ";[1]

and "disturbance of the peace", then, as now, afforded a convenient pretext for the suppression of undesirable political activity. Meetings were continually interfered with and dispersed.[2] "Poore Wise-Man" accurately forewarned the "plaine people" of the tactics that would be employed by those in power to discredit all progressive movements:

"The bait they will use", he wrote, "will be the suppression of Hereticks and Schismaticks which henceforth ye shall finde to be but nicknames for any that oppose tyrants and oppressors by which they have endeavoured to make those odious to the rude multitude whose honestie and conscience could not otherwise be blemished."[3]

Libel and defamation, it is true, were the normal and accepted political weapons of the day; but they were excessively employed to bring the Levellers and other radical writers into disrepute. They were denounced as godless and blasphemous. They were atheists and libertines. The notorious blasphemy ordinance of May 1648, ostensibly directed against the heretical activities of the sects, was in reality a deadly political

[1] Firth and Rait, June 28, 1647, Vol. I, p. 985.
[2] Thus, for example, the Committee of both Houses writes to the Committee of the Militia of London, Westminster, Tower Hamlets and Southwark in February 1648, concerning the "scandalous and seditious pamphlets" of Lilburne and his associates "tending to stir up and move the people to disobedience and to employ force against the Parliament. Among these are papers called the Agreement of the People, the Earnest Petition of Many Free-Born People of England, the Cries of Many Poor Tradesmen, etc. We are certainly informed that there are frequent and set meetings within the City and places adjacent held for promoting and carrying out the ends advocated by these papers, and in some of these meetings things have been contrived and enacted tending to the raising of new troubles and for disturbance of the quiet of the kingdom. We have thought it necessary to give you this intimation thereof and desire you to use your industry and the best means in your power to find out and disperse all such meetings and put down all attempts to act upon these recommendations so that no prejudice or inconvenience may come to the peace of the kingdom thereby which business we recommend to your best and most effectual care." *C.S.P., Dom., 1648–49* (Feb. 5, 1648), pp. 14–15.
[3] *The Poore Wise-Man's Admonition Unto all the Plaine People of London* (June 1647), E. 392 (4).

weapon by which the Government could strike down any activity they chose to consider subversive; for it covered such a multitude of sins that none but the most rigidly dogmatic Presbyterian could feel himself secure from its threat.[1] No accusation is met with more frequently than the charge that the Levellers planned to abolish private property and to impose social equality by force. Their very name was fastened on them by their opponents to convey the impression that the essence of their programme was their intention to " level all estates and to make all things common ", a charge which was consistently denied by the Levellers as categorically as it was asserted. The Ordinance of Sept. 30, 1647 " against unlicensed or scandalous pamphlets and for the better Regulating of Printing " attempted to impose a rigid Press censorship.[2]

Both Parliament and the army leaders were continually attempting to break the radical movement by the arrests of its most active leaders. We have already referred to the arrests and purge in the army after the mutiny at Ware. Five leading City Levellers were imprisoned in the autumn of 1647; and Lilburne and Wildman suffered a similar fate early in the New Year. In March 1649 Lilburne, Overton, Walwyn and Prince were confined to the Tower. The campaign of repression, we shall later see, was greatly intensified after the establishment of the Commonwealth. Lilburne describes the tactics used by Parliament to suppress Leveller activity in a passage that reveals their striking similarity to the technique of our own day:

"... their only fears remain upon our Discoveries ", he wrote of the Parliamentary and army leade , " to prevent which they use means that either we might not have the opportunity to lay open their treacheries and

[1] The blasphemies for which one was liable to punishment under the ordinance literally embraced every popular principle the sects and progressive thinkers were preaching. Included in the list are the denial of immortality or that the Scriptures represented the literal word of God, the assertion that "all men shall be saved", that "man is bound to believe no more than by his reason he can comprehend", that "Revelations or the workings of the Spirit are a rule of Faith or Christian Life though diverse from or contrary to the Written Word of God", that "Church Government by Presbytery is Anti-Christian or unlawfull", or that "Magistracy or the power of the Civil Magistrate by law established in England is unlawful."—Firth and Rait, May 2, 1648, Vol. I, p. 1133.

[2] Firth and Rait, Vol. I, p. 1021.

Hypocrisies or not to be believed if we did it. In order to the first. They strictly stop the Presse. In order to the second: They blast us with all the scandals and false reports their wit or malice could invent against us: and so monstrously have prized into all our actions and made use of all our friendly intimacies. . . . By these arts are they now fastened in their powers." [1]

This determined campaign of suppression had two major results. Considerable numbers of the Levellers and the army radicals, finally convinced of the impossibility of accomplishing their ends through political action, determined to act in more direct fashion and to make a bid for the forceful seizure of power. The sustained riots of 1649 and the mutinies in the army at Burford and Oxford were the results of that resolution. On the other hand, there were many who, discouraged by the overwhelming resistance they encountered, despaired of realizing social change through their own efforts and began, in increasing measure, to invoke the assistance of the Almighty to accomplish what political agitation had failed to achieve. There is thus an important revival from 1648 onwards of mystical religion and sectarian enthusiasm; [2] it is to this period that the origins of such groups as the Quakers and the Fifth Monarchy Men are to be traced. But it should be noted that the sectarian activity after 1648 is profoundly different in its character from that of the earlier period. The latter had been the expression of an immature political consciousness, of confused hopes and aspirations, of an inchoate protest, that was gradually translated by the impact of events into secular and political terms. The movements of 1648, on the contrary, are the product of an acute class consciousness, of a deep understanding of the social needs of the oppressed and of a firm belief in the inalienable rights of every individual; and this political maturity is unmistakably reflected for several years after 1648 in the writings of the religious radicals. But the failure of political agitation and the repressive measures that had been taken to crush progressive activity reversed the earlier process; and social aspirations, though no longer confused

---

[1] Lilburne, *The Second Part of England's New Chains Discovered or A Sad Representation of the Uncertaine and Dangerous Condition of the Commonwealth* (March 1649), E. 548 (16).
[2] *Infra,* Conclusion.

and immature, were translated into the terms of religious radicalism. The angels may enter where men may not venture to tread; and what political activity had failed to achieve, Divine intervention would surely effect. The rights of the individual which society should guarantee became the privileges of the Saints which God would assure; and a social order in which legislation was to abolish inequality and injustice became instead a world in which, as a result of the inner spiritual regeneration of mankind, men would cease to oppress their fellows. It may be noted that Winstanley's mystical and theological writings, which we shall later examine, are all a product of this period.

If the immediate practical achievements of the Levellers were insignificant, their importance in the history of political thought is considerable; for they anticipated, in very remarkable fashion, the development of radical liberalism. In them the individualism that had been inherent in the Reformation and in Puritanism is given its fullest expression. To the rising middle classes that individualism was primarily a function of privilege; and the rights that could be claimed in its name were those that furthered, or at least were compatible with, the interests of wealth. To the Levellers it was essentially an assertion that the State is built, above all else, of the individuals who compose it. Its activity must therefore be directed towards satisfying the needs of all rather than serving the interests of a few; for every individual by virtue of his existence has inalienably an equal claim with his fellows to share in the common good. That meant, as the Levellers clearly saw, that equality must replace privilege as the dominant theme of social relationships; for a State that is divided into rich and poor, or a system that excludes certain classes from privileges it confers on others, violates that equality to which every individual has a natural claim.

It meant, furthermore, that no individual or class could impose a system of law or government on their fellows against or without their consent. Every person in the State must therefore be able to share equally with his fellow-citizens, through universal suffrage in the election of their representatives, in the determination of public policy; and no government can claim validity which has not been sanctioned by the free consent of those who are to live under its rule. That consent, the Levellers urged, should take the form of the popular ratification of a written constitution that would clearly and unmistakably set forth the powers of government and that would define the boundaries of public authority by prohibiting interference with those individual rights that were considered fundamental—religious freedom, the right to private property, equality before the law, security of person against impressment and imprisonment without cause. To prevent the abuse of authority by those in power, the Levellers further insisted on the erection of such constitutional safeguards as periodical elections and the separation of powers.

They saw clearly that the criterion by which social institutions should be judged was not their formal constitution, but their operative effect; and that a social or political system had to be evaluated not by its external forms, but in terms of the freedom and security it accorded to the individual. The Civil War, they accordingly insisted, would have been a cruel and meaningless sacrifice of lives and energy if its effect were merely to be the transfer of power from the monarchy to the gentry and commercial classes; for the tyranny of the financial oligarchy or the army could be as oppressive as that of the landed aristocracy or the Church. Republicanism is therefore never really fundamental to the Leveller programme; it is a means rather than an end. If the King were beheaded and all power were to devolve on the army before the Agreement of the People had been accepted, Lilburne argued in opposing the execution of Charles in November 1648,

" our slavery for the future . . . might be greater than ever it was in the King's time ".[1]

But if liberty and equality were to become effective social realities, the State must have a positive character. It was not enough simply to guarantee to its citizens " liberty " and " freedom " in the abstract; for those concepts had to be translated into a series of specific " freedoms " and " liberties " measured in terms of the well-being of the people. The State must therefore abolish those institutions and practices that render economic oppression possible, and establish those conditions that will make for an equality of

[1] Lilburne, *The Legal Fundamental Liberties* (1649), E. 560 (14).

economic opportunity in whose context, alone, freedom and
equality can have meaning. The law that sanctions privilege
must be changed so that it binds all equally; and the legal
system that at present weights justice in favour of those who
enjoy superior wealth or education or skill must be reformed
by codification of the law in a form that can be understood
by everyone, by decentralization of the courts and by simplify-
ing and reducing the cost of an appeal to judicial processes.

The political and social programme of the Levellers was
far in advance of their time. In their demands for universal
suffrage, for reapportionment, for legal amendment, for
prison reform, for the abolition of monopolies, feudal tenures,
tithes, etc., for poor relief, for an adequate system of taxation,
they sketched a programme whose translation into legislation
was to prove the work of centuries. For the classes in whose
name they sought to secure those social improvements did
not have, in the seventeenth century, the economic strength
or the political organization to enable them to wring from
the triumphant capitalists the concessions the latter were
forced to extend to later generations.

The Levellers thus anticipated, in a remarkable manner,
two or three centuries of the development of much that was
embodied in liberal democracy. They drew compelling
attention to the most pressing social and economic needs of
the day. They were passionate and eloquent in their denunciation of injustice and oppression. They were categorical
in their protest against a system that sanctioned and perpetuated class division and social inequality. They emphasized
that the individual must remain the ultimate unit with which
political theory must deal and that the final purpose of all
social institutions must be to secure to each individual his
freedom and natural rights.

But despite their acute awareness of so many of the vital
problems which no adequate political philosophy can afford
to neglect, the Levellers failed to achieve a realistic analysis
of the phenomena they confronted. Despite their piercing
criticisms of its operation, they did not question, in fundamental
terms, the basic assumptions of the system on which the social
structure they wanted to renovate was being erected. The
conditions against which they protested, they repeatedly
assert, derive from the arbitrary exercise of political power;
and the privileges that buttress that power are the result of

an unjust legal system. Social and economic reform, they were therefore convinced, could be achieved by the establishment of constitutional mechanisms to prevent the abuse of governmental authority, through legislative activity and legal reform. Leveller writings are permeated throughout with that faith in the efficacy of political action and with a profound respect for the power and sanctity of law. The law, Lilburne affirmed, was

" . . . the surest sanctuary that a man can take and the strongest fortresse to protect the weakest of all ".[1]

But the Levellers failed to relate the developments with which they were concerned to the foundations of the economic system in which those phenomena had their roots. There is in their writings no consistent or serious attempt to analyse the social basis of the power of the ruling classes they opposed or to understand the historical evolution of their supremacy. Law, they fail to recognize, is but the reflection and crystallization of the social relationships it is intended to regulate, a result rather than a cause. The forms of political organization, they fully realized, were much less important than their operative content. But they were unable to perceive that no political system can transcend, in any ultimate sense, the economic relationships on whose foundation it is reared. A brief speech by Rainborough at Putney, occasional passages in Overton, scattered sentences from popular petitions or anonymous pamphlets, indicate some recognition of those problems. But it is at no point a recognition that is fundamental to the theoretical assumptions of the Leveller movement or to the programme it was urging.

For such an analysis would have meant to challenge the State on fundamentals; and that challenge could not be made by the small property-owners—the peasants, the petty tradesmen and merchants, the artisans—whose party the Levellers essentially were. It could come only from those whom the development of capitalism was transforming into the beginnings of the modern proletariat, from the landless labourers who had to live not by their holdings or trades or businesses, but by their labour-power alone. The Diggers played a negligible rôle in the political drama of

---

[1] Lilburne, *The Laws Funerall* (May 1648), E. 442 (13).

the period, and their fleeting appearance on the stage at Cobham was quickly forgotten. But, through Gerrard Winstanley, they questioned more profoundly than anyone else in the seventeenth century the foundations on which the new society was being built, and produced the one genuine proletarian ideology that emerged from the revolutionary ferment of the Civil War.

Chapter Three: GERRARD WINSTAN-LEY—A FORGOTTEN RADICAL

" Was the Earth made to preserve a few covetous, proud men to live at ease, and for them to bag and barn up the treasures of the Earth from others, that these may beg or starve in a fruitful land ; or was it made to preserve all her children? "—Winstanley, *The New Law of Righteousness* (1649).

IF history has denied to Gerrard Winstanley the prominence in the development of political thought that his genius should have merited for him, it has been equally unkind in surrounding his life with a veil of seemingly impenetrable obscurity. Not until his resurrection by Bernstein [1] was attention first directed to the fact that the most advanced thinker of the English Revolution had been completely neglected by its historians. And, if his political ideas have since been rescued from oblivion, the details of his personal activity still remain shrouded in mystery.

Winstanley was born in Wigan in Lancashire in 1609 ; the parish register of Wigan records his baptism on October 10 of that year.[2] The Winstanleys are a family of great antiquity in Lancashire and figure prominently in its local history. The name appears for what seems to be the last time among the county squires in 1575, when a Humfrey Winstanley was summoned to provide arms for the Queen's service.[3] Gerrard's father, Edward of Wigan, who is described in the records as a " mercer ", was probably a trader in cloths and wool. He is recorded as a burgess in the earliest surviving list, that of 1627,[4] and subsequently in the lists for 1635 and 1638. The notice of his burial at the parish church on December 27, 1639, describing him as " Mr." would seem to indicate that

[1] E. Bernstein, *Sozialismus und Demokratie in der grossen Englischen Revolution* (1895). Translated by H. J. Stenning as *Cromwell and Communism* (1930.)
[2] *The Registers of the Parish Church of Wigan in the County of Lancaster, 1580–1625*, ed. J. Arrowsmith, Wigan, 1899, p. 74.
[3] *Memorials of the Families of Cropper, Cubham and Wolsey of Bickerstaffe and of Winstanley of Winstanley.* N. Waterhouse, Liverpool, 1864.
[4] Sinclair, *History of Wigan*, Vol. I, p. 198.

he had been a person of considerable standing in the community.

Nothing is known of Winstanley's early years, of the family influences that shaped his development or of his education; and the rare autobiographical passages in his writings refer almost entirely to his spiritual experiences directly prior to his literary debut. Though his works offer no positive clues as to the type of education he received, they indicate that its formal content was quite limited. They reveal him as a man of profound originality; and his remarkable style at times reaches an eloquence that is surpassed during the period only by the incomparable Milton. But they give no evidence of extensive scholarship or learning. Winstanley was, of course, intimately acquainted with the Scriptures; but that was a trait common to all literate Englishmen of the century. Apart from the Bible, he makes no mention of or reference to any books he had read or studied. His writings are completely free of those classical quotations with which other contemporary authors delighted to exhibit their erudition; and his references to law or to statute, to history or to ancient or contemporary thinkers are extremely few. His pamphlets can leave little doubt that he was acquainted, at any rate, with More's *Utopia* and with the works of Bacon; but nowhere does he acknowledge their influence. His contempt for the book-learning of the orthodox ministers derived, no doubt, from the fact that he found the traditional concepts they preached meaningless and inadequate; it may also betray an envy and disappointment at having failed to receive some of the advantages of a formal education.

It is uncertain when Winstanley left Wigan; but at the age of twenty he was already in London. Apprenticed to Sarah Gater of Cornhill, the widow of William Gater of the Merchant Taylors Company, on April 10, 1630, he became a freeman on February 21, 1637.[1] It might be interesting to speculate as to the persons with whom he came into contact or the preachers to whose sermons he listened during those years of his apprenticeship in London; but Winstanley has left us nothing on which to build. Whether or not he returned to Lancashire after he came to London, he certainly must have maintained fairly intimate contact with his birthplace; for his first written work, published at least eighteen years after

[1] Manuscript records of the Merchant Taylors Company, London.

his arrival in London, is dedicated to his " beloved country-men of the Countie of Lancaster ", asking them not to despise him for having the temerity to venture into print.[1]

In 1640 he applied for a licence to marry Susan King at St. Martin's Outwhich.   The entry describes him as a " Merchant Taylor of the Parish of St. Olaves in the Old Jewry ", a bachelor about thirty.[2]   The records of the church at which the marriage was to have taken place were destroyed in the Great Fire.   Nowhere in his writings does Winstanley make mention of wife or family.

For several years he was a cloth merchant in London, and continued in business until 1643, when he fell victim to the economic depression of the period.   A bill of complaint that was presented by Winstanley in 1660, when he was being sued by the executors of the estate of one Richard Aldworth for the recovery of a debt of £114 he was said to have contracted during his brief period in business, reveals his commercial activities to have been rather modest.   Over a period of thirty months he claims his transactions with Aldworth, who evidently supplied him with cloth, to have amounted to £331 1s.:

". . . about the beginning of April 1641," he states, " your oratour being then a citizen of London had some trading with one Richard Aldworth late citizen and . . . of London, deceased, for fustian, dimities and lynnin cloth and such like commodities which trading continued for the part of two or three years ".[3]

Aldworth, he writes, was an important trader, for he employed several servants to keep his books.   Winstanley, with his more modest enterprise, did his own accounting.

" Your oratour further knoweth ", he continues, " that in the year of the Lord 1643 when the late unhappie wars in England were violent, your oratour left off his trading with the said Richard Aldworth and with all other persons by reason of the badness of the tymes." [3]

[1] *The Mysterie of God Concerning the whole Creation, Mankinde* (1648), B.M. 4377, a. 51 (1).
[2] Registry of the Bishop of London, Allegation Book 22, Jan. 1–Dec. 12, 1540.
[3] Chancery Records, Public Records Office.   Reynardson's Division, c. 9/412/269.

After his failure in business, Winstanley was forced to accept the hospitality of friends and to move to the country, probably to the vicinity of Cobham in Surrey.[1] There is no further record of his activities until the publication of his first tract early in 1648.

Here again we might be tempted to speculate on the nature of his experiences during his enforced idleness in the war period, on the effects the necessity of living on the charity of others and the misery and suffering with which he came into contact may have had on his sensitive conscience or on the thoughts that must have passed through the mind of an unsuccessful and ruined petty trader. But those influences must have remained purely subconscious ones; for his first several writings contain scarcely a hint of any awareness of the political and social problems of the period; and his political consciousness and maturity very definitely date from the end of 1648 or the beginning of 1649. It is therefore all the more remarkable that the development of his mind that is reflected in his writings should have covered the brief period of eight or nine months. His first two pamphlets of the early summer of 1648 are typical of the chiliastic mysticism so popular during the period. In the autumn he has shed that mysticism; and though he is still concerned exclusively with spiritual problems, his argument is that of a progressive rationalist. A few months later he emerges as the most advanced radical of the century, convinced that social and economic reorganization is society's most vital and immediate need.

Winstanley's writings fall into five definite groupings. There are his two mystical works of the summer of 1648, two subsequent theological pamphlets of the autumn of that year, the *New Law of Righteousness* of January 1649, that marks the transition in his development, the tracts and manifestos issued during and in connection with the Digger experiment in Surrey and *The Law of Freedom*, in which he develops in detail

---

[1] Berens (*The Digger Movement* (1906), p. 79) thinks that he moved to Colnbrook in Buckinghamshire. I do not know the evidence for that assumption. I am led to believe that he lived in the immediate vicinity of Cobham by the fact that St. George's Hill, where the Digger experiment was initiated, is within a few miles of Cobham; that in the bill presented in Kingston Court for the arrest of the Diggers for trespassing, Winstanley is described as being from Walton-on-Thames in the vicinity of Cobham; and in 1660 he is reported as residing in Cobham.

his plan for the organization of English society on the basis
of a system of common ownership.

Winstanley's first two theological tracts were published early
in 1648. The first, *The Mysterie of God Concerning the Whole
Creation, Mankinde*, evidently written in the spring of the year,
bears the name of no printer;[1] the second, *The Breaking of
the Day of God*, whose preface is dated on May 20, was printed
by Giles Calvert, who published Winstanley's subsequent
writings.[2] These tracts are typical products of the mystical
theology of the period; and there is little in them to indicate
the trend of Winstanley's later development. To search for
the sources of his theological conceptions would be as futile
as to attempt to identify the streams that have contributed to
the bucket of water one has drawn from the sea. The air of
the Civil War period, we have already indicated, was charged
with the currents of mystical, pantheistic and humanistic
thought; and Winstanley, like countless others, had breathed
deeply of its draughts. There are in his writings the certainty
in the imminence of redemption, the profound faith in the
potentialities of human nature, the insistence that salvation
can be achieved not through the medium of the visible Church
or its formal rites, but only through an inner spiritual experience of God, the affirmation of the presence of Christ in every
human soul, the conviction that suffering and persecution
are but a prelude to the redemption—that are common not
only to the sects of the Interregnum, but to so many of the
mediaeval popular movements in the stage of their political
immaturity. We have already indicated the social roots of
those ideas. They had been widely current, for example,
in Central Europe during the fourteenth and fifteenth centuries, in the Peasant Revolt and the Anabaptist agitation in
Germany.[3] They had found formal expression in the writings

[1] *The Mysterie of God Concerning the whole Creation, Mankinde to be made
known to every man and woman after seven dispensations and seasons of time are
passed over* (1648), B.M. 4377, a. 51 (1). A collected edition of Winstanley's first five theological writings was published early in 1650. All
page references to Winstanley's theological works in this chapter are to
this edition, a copy of which is to be found in the Goldsmiths Collection,
University of London Library.
[2] *The Breaking of the Day of God wherein four things are manifested, etc.*,
B.M. 4377, a. 51 (2).
[3] See K. Kautsky, *Communism in Central Europe at the time of the Reformation*
(1897); B. Bax, *The Rise and Fall of the Anabaptists* (1903); F. Engels,
The Peasant War in Germany (1927).

of men like Denck and Franck and Schwenckfeld; and authors like John Everard had popularized those concepts in England both through their translations of the Continental mystics and their own original works. It may be possible to detect in Winstanley the particular influence of Jacob Boehme and of the Familists and Seekers among the sects. But it is to the environment of the age rather than to any individual thinker or sect that Winstanley owes his religious doctrines. He himself constantly emphasized that the truths he set forth had not been culled from books or commentaries or formal study, but had come to him entirely as the result of a profound personal experience of God.[1]

We need be little concerned with the theological and mystical expositions which occupy the major portions of those early tracts. But there runs through them what one may term a spiritual interpretation of history which provided the theological foundation of his social philosophy.

The degeneration of mankind began, Winstanley asserts, when Adam, after the Creation, impelled by selfishness and the desire for self-aggrandisement, sought to set himself up as an equal with God. Since that day selfishness and lust have dominated mankind; and from that power of the Serpent within each human heart have come all the evil and misery the world has ever known. The history of the human race has essentially been the record of God's attempt to kill the Serpent and to exterminate the spirit of selfishness from the hearts of men by revealing Himself through Christ to every human soul. Every individual is saved when the Beast within him has been vanquished by the Spirit of Christ. But that redemption cannot be achieved through learning or ceremony or through the assistance of any external forms; it can come only through the power of Christ that is indwelling in man. But the strength of the Serpent is formidable, and man, under its influence, constantly refuses to recognize the presence of Christ within himself. He delights in the things

---

[1] Thus, for example, George Fox records that he was having very similar experiences at the time. " The Lord opened to me "; " The Lord shewed me, so that I did see clearly, that He did not dwell in these temples which men had commanded and set up but in people's hearts ", " My desires after the Lord grew stronger, and zeal in the pure knowledge of God and Christ alone, without the help of any man, book or writing. For though I read the Scriptures that spake of Christ and of God, yet I knew Him not, but by revelation." etc.—*Journal of George Fox.*

of the flesh; he is blind to his own sin and degeneracy; he is constantly thwarting his own redemption. But Christ has already begun to redeem mankind by revealing Himself to some individuals and freeing them from the tyranny of the Beast:

> " I lay under the bondage of the Serpent ", Winstanley relates, citing his own experience as an example, " and I saw not any bondage: but since God was pleased to manifest his love to me, he hath caused me to see that I lay dead in sin weltering in blood and death, was a prisoner to my lusts." [1]

Since that revelation

> " I see and feele that God hath set me free from the dominion and over-ruling power of that body of sin. . . . God hath freed me therefrom and taken me up into his own Being." [2]

That freedom is primarily a release from the overwhelming desire for material pleasures for

> ". . . when man is made spirituall and swallowed up in life or taken into the Being of God there will then be no more use or need of these outward creatures as cattell, corn, meat, drink and the like ".[3]

When man first becomes aware of the presence of Christ within his heart, he finds himself in the throes of an excruciating struggle; but it is a struggle that must inevitably end in the death of the Serpent. As the latter feels his end approaching, he intensifies the violence of his efforts. If anyone is therefore conscious of acute suffering and misery, he can derive consolation from the assurance that his salvation is imminent. But man himself can do nothing to hasten his own redemption.

> " If thou lie under sorrowes for sins, now know that it is God's dispensation to thee. Wait patiently upon him. If thou lie under the temptations of men, of losses, of povertie, of reproaches, it is God's dispensation to thee, waite with an humble quiet spirit upon him until he give deliverance." [4]

---

[1] *The Mysterie of God*, op. cit., p. 10.   [2] Ibid., p. 12.
[3] Ibid., p. 18.   [4] Ibid., p. 59.

The Saints to whom Christ has thus been revealed become a living testimony to the fact that God is working His redemption in the world. At first He will vouchsafe salvation only to the Saints. Ultimately He will save all mankind, for

"Jesus Christ . . . will dwell in the whole creation, that is, in every man and woman without exception".[1]

That revelation, Winstanley constantly affirms, will at the beginning not come primarily to scholars and divines, to those who have " all advantages and meanes outward " or to men "of study, learning and actings ", but rather to the " despised, the unlearned, the poor, the nothings of this world ", " to such as the world counts fools ".

Since recognition of God is born only of an inner spiritual experience, those who seek to testify to His power must themselves have felt and known that experience; and he who

"preaches from his book and not from the anointing and so speaking in experience what he hath seen and heard from God is no minister sent of God but a hireling that runs before he be sent, only to get a temporall living ".[2]

" God hath need of faithful witnesses to bear testimony thereof to the world ", Winstanley declares, but only of " such witnesses as can and will prove their testimony, not from the writings and words of others; but from their own experienced knowledge of what they have seen and heard and been made acquainted with from God." [3]

What is happening in the world at large is simply a reflection in macrocosm of what transpires in each human heart:

" If you desire to know the Beast, that treads you and the holy City underfoot; looke first into your owne hearts; for there she sits; and after that ye have beheld her confused workings there against Christ, then looke into the world; and you shall see the same confusion of ignorance, pride, self-love, oppression and vain conversation acted against Christ in States, in assemblies and in some churches in the world." [4]

---

[1] *The Mysterie of God,* p. 7.   [2] Ibid., p. 33.
[3] *The Breaking of the Day of God,* p. 14.   [4] Ibid., p. 52.

Just as the Serpent within man seeks to prevent the triumph of the spirit of Christ, those who are under its influence attempt to suppress true religion in the world. There is no method or means they are not prepared to employ. They secure from the civil magistrate, who is commissioned by God to preserve peace, a false ecclesiastical power that has no Divine sanction; they use that power to devise false forms of worship; they attempt by coercion and compulsory conformity to introduce an artificial and rigid uniformity of religion. They mercilessly persecute the Saints to whom Christ has been revealed and prevent them from spreading their message and testimony to the world:

"... sharp punishing laws were made to forbid fishermen, shepherds, husbandmen, and tradesmen for ever preaching of God any more but schollars bred up in humane letters only should doe that worke ".[1]

And all their wit and subtlety and learning are directed towards effecting those ends. That usurpation of ecclesiastical authority has wrought chaos in the civil sphere as well.

" Ecclesiastical power hath been a great troubler of magistracy ever since the deceived magistracy set it up." [2]

If the visible Church were abolished and the authority of Christ substituted for human direction in religious affairs " the pure reformation of Civil Magistracy would soon appear ".

The struggle within man is an indication that Christ is about to reveal Himself; and the violence of the Serpent increases with the realization of his impending doom. The persecution of the Saints throughout the land is similarly proof of the fact that God is redeeming mankind. The desperate efforts that are made to enforce conformity of religious worship, the fury that is directed against those who seek to spread true religion by relating their personal experiences of God, the calumny and ridicule and persecution to which they are subjected are but the frantic efforts of the fomentors of evil to avert their imminent destruction. Therefore:

" Rejoyce in the midst of this cloud of nationall troubles ", Winstanley declares to the Saints, " for your redemption

[1] *The Breaking*, p. 115.   [2] Ibid., p. 133.

E

drawes near. God is working out an inward and outward peace and liberty for you all." [1]

Thus, history, for Winstanley, is a vital, dynamic process. It is not simply the record of the arbitrary workings of God's will, but the story of a continuous conflict between opposing forces. The arena of that struggle is primarily the hearts and souls of men; but the conflict finds reflection and objectivication in the institutions and laws men create as instruments for its prosecution. Salvation and freedom for mankind will not come through some sudden miracle, but from the progressive revelation of Christ to every individual, through the triumph of love over selfishness and lust in every human being. Man himself, it is true, can do nothing to hasten his own redemption; but he can delay it by his stubborn refusal to listen to the voice of the Spirit, by his blind pursuit of the things of the flesh. Ultimately, God will save every human being; for everyone has within him, however dormant, the spirit of Christ that must inevitably conquer. But He first works His redemption in the Saints, so that they may serve as living witnesses of the salvation He is bringing to mankind. Those who have already been saved are the instruments through which He announces His purpose to the world. But those Saints are chosen not from the wealthy and the learned and the powerful of the world, but from the poor and the ignorant and the destitute. In the struggle that is constantly being waged, those who are enslaved by the Serpent, by the power of selfishness, utilize every means to avert their defeat. Organized religion, the visible Church, formal ecclesiastical authority, compulsory conformity, the book-learning of the orthodox, the oppression of the Saints are all the weapons of the Serpent in his battle against God; for they are the means by which he tries to prevent the emergence and recognition of the true religion. The Saints are reviled and persecuted because they are the class through whom the liberation of mankind and the victory of love and justice are made manifest to the world. Winstanley is conscious of the misery and suffering of the times; but it is a misery that man cannot and must not attempt to alleviate; for it is a dispensation from God, a prelude to His complete and final victory. And, funda-

[1] *The Breaking*, A. 5.

mental to his entire argument, there is throughout the insistence that men must accept nothing on the authority of others, but only that which they can verify in their own personal experience, that they should regard as truth not that which they have gathered from books or study, but only that which they have felt and known themselves.

That theme dominates his next two pamphlets. Within a period of a few months he moves from the mysticism of his earlier writings to give expression to a progressive rationalism. Where his earlier tracts are rendered almost unreadable by his lengthy mystical expositions, his writings of the latter half of 1648 are informed by a remarkable spirit of scientific rationalism. He is still exclusively concerned with man's spiritual adventures; but his argument is no longer the mystical one of his first tracts, but one that is in a large measure based on rational and prudential considerations. Scriptural history has become in them primarily an allegory for the illustration of his theme.

The Saint's Paradise,[1] published in the summer or early autumn of 1648, still maintains the spiritual interpretation of history and the conviction that man must patiently await God's dispensation before he can emerge from the bondage of the Serpent. It is mainly dedicated, however, to an explanation of the nature of God which Winstanley feels he understands adequately for the first time and to which he had given partial expression in his first tracts.

Religion, he complains, has become a sterile, meaningless body of doctrine because men have failed to appreciate the essence of God. He recalls that he was a prey to the same ignorance and blindness.

> " I worshipped a God but I neither knew who he was nor where he was . . . walking by imagination, I worshipped the Devill and called him God." [2]

But he now realizes that God is not a Supreme Being, majestically enthroned in the Heavens, above and beyond man, but a spirit that dwells in all mankind; and His presence in

---

[1] *The Saint's Paradise or the Fathers Teaching the only Satisfaction to waiting souls wherein many experiences are recorded for the comfort of such as are under spiritual burning* (1648), E. 2137 (1). On the date of this tract see Appendix I.

[2] *Ibid.*, Preface, A. 2.

every living creature establishes a fundamental interrelationship between all things in the universe:

> "So that you do not look for a God now as formerly you did to be a place of glory beyond the Sun, Moon and Stars nor imagine a divine beeing you know not where but see him ruling within you; and not only in you but you see and know him to be the spirit that dwells in every creature according to his orbe within the globe of the creation. . . . He that looks for a God without himself and worships God at a distance he worships he knows not what but is led away and deceived by the imaginations of his own heart . . . but he that looke for a God within himselfe and submits himselfe to the spirit of righteousnesse that shines within, this man knows whom he worships for he is made subject to and hath community with that spirit that made all flesh in every creature within the globe." [1]

God, for Winstanley, has thus become not a personal deity, but a First Principle through the recognition of which men become aware of the essential unity and harmony in the universe. That principle manifests itself in men as the spirit of love and righteousness that enables them to live in harmony with their fellows. An individual becomes conscious of the presence of God within himself when he has conquered his desire for material pleasures that nurtures selfishness and greed, when he no longer feels that he

> ". . . cannot live without money, lands, help of men and creatures ". [2]

Envy and selfishness which pit men in struggle against each other give way to love and humility which weld mankind into a unity.

The failure of the world to achieve this conception of God has been due primarily to reliance on traditional forms of instruction, to the insistence that knowledge is exclusively a function of formal study. Appreciation of truth, however, can come only from the "experimentall knowledge of Christ", from the recognition by men of the spirit of love and justice that dwells within them. The Scriptures, Winstanley therefore asserts, have always been incorrectly regarded as eternal,

---

[1] *The Saint's Paradise*, pp. 55–56, 58. [2] Ibid., pp. 21–2.

immutable law by which conduct should be regulated.   But they are, however, simply the spiritual autobiographies of the Prophets and Apostles; and their importance lies solely in the fact that they are the record of the manifestations of the spirit within the souls of particular individuals.   That record is therefore valid for any person as history rather than as law until, by enjoying a similar inner experience, he is able to understand adequately the testimony of the Apostles.

Towards the end of the pamphlet Winstanley introduces a new and radical note that thereafter becomes fundamental to his thought—the identification of God and the Spirit with Reason.

> ". . . the spirit that will purge mankind ", he asserts " is pure reason. . . . Though men esteeme this word **Reason** to be too meane a name to set forth the Father by, yet **it is** the highest name that can be given him." [1]

There is, to be sure, no single or consistent definition of the term in his pages; and it manifests itself in men and in nature in various forms.   Frequently it is interpreted as a principle of order and intelligibility, an affirmation of Winstanley's conviction that there is order and purpose in the universe.

> " For it is reason that made all things and it is Reason that governs the whole Creation." [2]

At other times it is held to be an absolute moral principle implanted in the hearts of men which impels them to walk in the path of justice and righteousness and enables men to distinguish right from wrong and good from evil.

> ". . . the spirit . . . is pure reason which governs the whole globe in righteousness and shows thee thy wickednesse and the light thereof discovers thy darkness and fills thee with shame and torment. . . ." [3]

More frequently, however, it is regarded as the basis of a system of prudential rather than absolute ethics, of a practical morality.   It is the rational element within man that, in the interests of his own self-preservation, dictates that he deal justly with his fellow-man.   That rational faculty, on the basis of which a moral structure is reared and which every human

---

[1] *The Saint's Paradise*, p. 78.   [2] Ibid., p. 78.   [3] Ibid., p. 61.

being possesses, distinguishes man from the beast; for it renders social life and a realization of the natural unity of mankind a possible adventure.

> " When the curse in flesh moves a man to oppresse or deceive his neighbours or to take away his rights and liberties, to beat or abuse him in any, kind reason moderates this wicked flesh and speak within, wouldest thou be dealt with so by thyself? Wouldest thou have another to come and take away the Goods, thy Liberties, thy Life? No saith the Flesh, that I would not. Then, saith Reason, Do as you wouldest be done unto; and thereby the envious and covetous and proud flesh is killed and the man is made very moderate. . . . For let reason rule the man and he dares not trespasse against his fellow creatures but will do as he would be done unto. For Reason tells him is thy neighbour hungry and naked today, do thou feed him and cloathe him, it may be thy case tomorrow and then he will be ready to help thee." [1]

Winstanley gives no clue whatever to this remarkable development within a few months from a mystical to a rational theology; and there are no indications of the influences that might have operated on him to produce that development. There was, of course, the rationalism of men like Overton, which was being given increasing expression in their writings; but, if Winstanley was consciously influenced by their ideas, he does not seem to have had any direct contact with Overton or members of his circle. It is possible, however, that William Everard, with whom Winstanley came into contact about this time, may have exerted a very important influence in shaping his ideas.

Everard, who at the beginning of the Digger experiment at St. George's Hill in April 1649 shared its leadership with Winstanley, had been one of the soldiers arrested in the autumn of 1647 for promoting the First Agreement of the People in the ranks of the New Model.[2] Released from im-

---

[1] *The Saint's Paradise*, p. 79.

[2] *England's Freedom, Souldiers Rights . . . Delivered to his Excellency Sir Thomas Fairfax* (Dec. 14, 1647), E. 419 (23), by W. Thompson. Attached is a petition of his fellow-prisoners in which " Will Everard " appears among the nine signatories.

I have been unable to establish any relationship between William Everard and John Everard, the mystic.

prisonment in December of that year, he had been cashiered
from the army.   The short accounts of him in the newspapers
that commented on the Digger venture indicate him to have
been an aggressive, impetuous, defiant, fanatical personality;
he is variously described as a " mad prophet ", as " seduced ",
as a " lunatic ".   By the autumn of 1648 he had already
met Winstanley; for the latter in his next tract declares that
it was written to defend both Everard and himself against
accusations of blasphemy and the denial of " God, Christ
and the Scriptures ".   Those accusations had probably been
directed against Winstanley as a result of the publication of
The Saint's Paradise.   Everard, who had evidently urged similar
views with more vigour and less discretion, had been arrested
at Kingston in Surrey and imprisoned for a week.

> " Now, I was moved to write what here followes ", de-
> clares Winstanley in the preface to *Truth Lifting Up its
> Head Above Scandals* after referring to Everard's arrest,
> " as a vindication of the man and my selfe being slandered
> as well as he (by some of the ministers) having been in his
> company that all the world may judge of his and my
> innocency in these particular scandals." [1]

By October, then, their friendship had become intimate
enough for Winstanley to take up the pen in Everard's defence.
There is no positive evidence to indicate that Everard had
been one of the Agitators; but it is likely that as an active
radical in the army he was intimately acquainted with the
writings of Overton and Walwyn.   His influence on Winstanley
through his knowledge of Leveller concepts and his familiar-
ity with the rationalism of some of the Leveller theorists may
have been decisive in the development Winstanley had already
reflected in *The Saint's Paradise.*

In *Truth Lifting, etc.,* Winstanley elaborates the interpretation of God and the Scriptures he had advanced in his
previous pamphlet and defends his use of the term " reason "
instead of God.   He still employs the concept both as an
absolute moral imperative which " guides all men's reasonings
in right order and to a right end " and as the principle of
common and mutual preservation that is the foundation of

---

[1] *Truth Lifting Up its Head Above Scandals* (Oct. 1648), B.M. 4372, a.a. 17.
" To the Gentle Reader."

a prudential social ethics. To live by reason, he explains, is essentially to live moderately in all things.

> ". . . not to be excessive in drunkenness and gluttony . . . to act righteously to all fellow creatures, till the ground according to reason, use the labour of your cattle according to reason; follow your course of trading in Righteousness as Reason requires; do to men and women as you would have them do to you ".[1]

He has become much more profoundly impressed by the interdependence of all human beings and by the fact that reason operates in society as a principle of order for their common preservation.

> " The Spirit of the Father is Pure Reason; which as he made so he knits the whole creation together into a onenesse of life and moderation; every creature sweetly in love lending their hands to preserve each other and so uphold the whole fabrique." [2]
>
> " The spirit Reason doth not preserve the creature and destroy another, as many times mens reasonings doth being blind by the imaginations of the flesh; but it hath a regard to the whole creation; and knits every creature together into a onenesse; making every creature to be an upholder of his felow; and so every one is an assistant to preserve the whole." [3]

Winstanley now sees a similar interdependence and order operating not only in human affairs, but in the processes of nature as well.

> " The cloudes send down raine, and there is great undeniable reason in it, for otherwise the earth could not bring forth grasse and fruit. The earth sends forth grasse, or else cattle could not be preserved. The sunne gives his light and heate or else the Creation could not subsist. So that the mighty power Reason hath made these to give life and preservation one to another." [4]

This profound sense of the unity of society and nature, it should be noted, sharply distinguishes Winstanley's cosmology

---

[1] *Truth Lifting, etc.*, pp. 49–50. 　　[2] Ibid., pp. 3–4.
[3] Ibid. " To the Gentle Reader." 　　[4] Ibid., pp. 4–5.

from the atomism that formed the philosophic foundation of
the Levellers' individualism.

The universe, then, is not an irrational, purposeless phenomenon directed in some mysterious fashion by the arbitrary
will of a Divine Being.   Rather, it is a rational, intelligible
order that operates in accordance with certain natural laws
whose purpose is the well-being and preservation of mankind.
A knowledge and understanding of these laws, furthermore, can be achieved through experience by every human
being.

We shall see later how Winstanley transferred his philosophical and cosmological conceptions from religion and
morals to politics and economics.

He devotes considerable space to his allegorical interpretation of the two Adams, the first of whom, by succumbing to
the temptations of the flesh, filled the earth with corruption
and the second whose revolutionary appearance

> " will change times and customs and fill the earth with a
> new law, wherein dwels righteousness and peace and
> justice and judgement shall be the upholders of his King-
> dom ". [1]

He vigorously denounces the ministers for praying when
they have felt no inspiration, for repeating stereotyped
formulæ they have learned by rote rather than waiting until
God would put words in their mouths by filling their hearts
with spirituality.   He recognizes the right of the authorities to
inflict punishment for civil offences; but he emphatically
denies them the right to a compulsive power in religious
affairs, to impose a conformity of worship, to restrict the
freedom of preaching or to demand the payment of tithes;
for religion, if it is to be true, must be a free and personal
and inner experience.

He still feels that man, by his own efforts, can do little to
improve the state of affairs until spiritual perfection is
achieved; and every individual must still " wait with a quiet
and humble spirit until the Father be pleased to teach " him.
But he advises people to begin in the meantime to " do as
you would be done unto ", to read the Scriptures and to speak
with those who have known the testimony of the Spirit within
themselves.

[1] *Truth Lifting, etc.*, p. 24.

E 2

His postscript is a eulogy, in verse, of reason.

> " If Reason, King do rule in thee
> There's truth and peace and clemencie.
>
> · · · · ·
>
> When Reason rules in whole man-kind
> Nothing but peace will all men find ;
> Their hearts he makes both meek and kind
> And troublesome thoughts he throws behind,
> For he is truth and love and peace
> Makes wars and lewdnesse for to cease.
>
> · · · · ·
>
> And why do men so clamour then
> Against this powerfull King in men? "

It was to that final question that Winstanley now addressed himself; the answer he formulated constituted the most progressive social doctrine the Civil War produced.

What seems to have been an influence of decisive importance in Winstanley's rapid development from his rational theology of the autumn of 1648 to his practical communism of the spring of 1649 was the activity of a group of advanced country Levellers in Buckinghamshire. Winstanley, living near the borders of that county, may have come into personal contact with some members of that group, but at any rate the influence of their first short tract, *Light Shining in Buckinghamshire* of December 1648, is unmistakably reflected in his remarkable work, *The New Law of Righteousness*, of the following month. For the first time he has become directly concerned with the social problems of the period; and in his recognition of the institution of private property as the source of all social conflict and his argument for a system of common ownership he has already passed far beyond all other thinkers of the period. It is an argument that is still fundamentally religious in its inspiration and emphasis; but the foundations for its transfer to the secular and political plane have already been securely laid.

Light Shining in Buckinghamshire,[1] which its authors announce

---

[1] *Light Shining in Buckinghamshire or a Discovery of the main ground ; original cause of all the slavery in the world but chiefly in England ; presented by way of a Declaration of many of the well-affected in that country to all their poor, oppressed country men of England ; and also to the consideration of the present army under the conduct of the Lord Fairfax* (1648), E. 475 (1). It is dated by Thomason on Dec. 5. A second edition was published, together with *More Light Shining in Buckinghamshire*, in March 1649.

The tract has generally been attributed to Winstanley and the Diggers. A close study of the pamphlets, however, points to the conclusion that, together with *More Light, etc.*, of March and *A Declaration of the Well-*

in the sub-title to be "A Discovery of the main ground; original cause of all the slavery in the world but chiefly in England", can scarcely be considered a Digger tract. It would seem, instead, to represent the impact of Leveller propaganda on a number of peasants whose position had been seriously affected by enclosure. Its language and argument are generally derived from Leveller literature. Its political and constitutional discussion is primarily Leveller. It is essentially a plea for equal rather than for common ownership. But in its advanced application of Leveller theory, in its historical interpretation and in its analysis of the technique of class domination, it gave remarkable expression in political and social terms to forces whose operation Winstanley had been describing in terms of the spiritual life-history of mankind.

That is not to say, of course, that *Light Shining, etc.*, is a purely secular document. It is still couched in the religious phraseology of the period; but, like most Leveller tracts, it leans but little on theological support for its validity. Its point of departure is the assertion, common to most Leveller writings, that God, in creating man, gave him permission to dominate "inferior creatures", but not to exercise arbitrary authority over his fellow-man. Where others, however, had emphasized

---

Affected in the County of Buckinghamshire of May 1649, it was the work of a group of advanced Leveller peasants whom enclosure had seriously affected and who translated Leveller concepts into terms relevant to their own situation. The language, the argument, the programme of these three tracts owe much more to the Levellers than to the Diggers. None of them represents as advanced a viewpoint as that of *The New Law of Righteousness*. Winstanley's favourite phrase, "a common treasury", appears in none of these tracts. Unlike the pamphlets Winstanley wrote both before and after the publication of *Light Shining, etc.*, they were not printed by Giles Calvert. One or two expressions, it is true, may reflect the influence of Winstanley. ". . . this light I take to be that pure spirit in men which wee call Reason . . . from which there issued out that golden rule or law which we call equity". That concept, however, was not exclusively Winstanley's; it is not unlikely, too, that some of the group may have been acquainted with his earlier tracts.

I have therefore been unable to follow Berens, James, etc., in regarding *Light Shining, etc.*, as a Digger tract that reveals the pen of Winstanley, but have considered it as the product of some extreme country Levellers that profoundly influenced Winstanley in his advance towards his communistic principles.

It is interesting that on the same day (Dec. 5) that Thomason received his copy of *Light Shining, etc.*, he secured a tract from a Northumberland regiment that pursues a line of argument remarkably similar to *Light Shining, etc.* See *The Humble Representation of the Desires of the Soldiers and Officers in the Regiment of Horse for the County of Northumberland*, E. 475 (13).

as the most important implication of that fact the natural equality of political rights or of economic opportunity that all individuals should enjoy, the authors of *Light Shining, etc.*, stress that it confers on all men a right to equal property.

"... all men being alike privileged by birth so all men were to enjoy the creatures alike without propertie one more than the other ... that is to say no man was to lord or command over his own kind; neither to enclose the creatures to his own use to the impoverishing of his neighbours ".[1]

"But man following his sensualities", they continue, "became a devourer of the creatures and an encloser, not content that another should enjoy the same privilege as himself, but encloseth all from his brothers ".[2]

Through murder and violence, some men proceeded to rob their fellows of their share of the land, to enclose those areas into estates and to set themselves up as Lords of Manors. Thus, the natural order that had known no distinction between men was corrupted by the violent introduction of social division based on the unequal ownership of land. The original community of equals was thus dissolved, and in its place there emerged the society of propertied and propertyless we know to-day. The majority of the people, deprived of their means of subsistence, were forced, in order to maintain themselves, to become the slaves of those who had stolen their land; and the latter have since lived, not, as God had commanded, by the products of their own labour but on the exploitation and oppression of those they had plundered.

To secure themselves in their enjoyment of their spoils they introduced that " heathenish innovation ", the monarchy. They gave their privileges the forms of legality through a complicated system of charters, monopolies, patents, tenures and enclosures that were issued in the name of the King and that derive their validity from his authority. In England that process began when William set up his rule by conquest. The monarchy is thus the keystone in the arch of tyranny that has been erected in the country. "... all tyranny shelters itself under the King's wings ". There arose, as a consequence, a class of lawyers who intensify the exploitation of the people by complicating the legal system and adding

---

[1] *Light Shining, etc.*, pp. 1–2. [2] Ibid., p. 2.

to its expense. A clergy was established and subsidized to preach the duty of subservience to the people. Those who were responsible for the introduction of division in society have thereby created a complex system centred in the monarchy that is designed to preserve their privileges; and the clergy, the lawyers, the judges, have all a vested interest in its maintenance, for to question the validity of the monarchy would be to undermine the source of their own power and functions.

Popular agitation occasionally forced the King to grant certain concessions to the people; but, impressive though they might have been in form, they were meaningless in fact. Parliament, for example, was rendered impotent as a popular body from the moment of its creation by limiting the choice of the majority of the members of the House of Commons to freeholders, by having the Lords appointed only by the King and by reserving for the monarch the power to veto acts of both Houses.

The Leveller programme, they urge, can strike down this " kingly Power ". The principles of freedom, they insist, must include " a just portion for each man to live so that none need to beg or steal for want but every man may live comfortably ", " a just rule for each man to go by, which rule is to be the Scriptures ", the application of the Golden Rule in social relationships and the administration of government and law, without charge and complication, by popularly elected elders. They further demand that a public stock be created for the maintenance of the poor and that all bishops, forest and Crown lands be taken over for that purpose. They warn their oppressors, the landlords, that

> " the people will no longer be enslaved by you for the knowledge of the Lord shall enlighten them " that " it is not lawful nor fit for some to work and others to play; for it is God's command that all work, let all eat and if all work alike, is it not fit for all to eat alike and enjoy alike privileges and freedome? " [1]

That *Light Shining, etc.*, should have exercised a profound influence on Winstanley is hardly surprising when we realize that he had been concerned to describe in his earlier tracts the phenomena to which its analysis was applied. He had sought to understand the chaos and violence of the Civil War

---

[1] *Light Shining, etc.*

and the oppression to which " the despised and the poor " were being subjected. He had interpreted those events as a pale reflection of the inner conflict within man of the spirit of selfishness and the spirit of Christ. That continuous and dynamic struggle, which he felt to be approaching its climax, was that of the flesh and the spirit. It was expressed externally in man's pursuit of material pleasures and in the attempt to prevent the general appreciation of the principles of righteousness by the persecution of those to whom they had been revealed. Human laws and institutions, he had seen; were the agencies by which the domination of the flesh was secured. The eventual triumph of Christ, foreshadowed by the suffering of His Saints, would restore to the world the original unity that the spirit of selfishness had destroyed. But, whereas he had hitherto described that struggle on the external and social plane in vague generalities, *Light Shining, etc.*, gave him a much more adequate understanding of its nature. The internal struggle in each individual is still fundamental for him; but he now realizes the independent and vital importance of its objectivication in the social conflict. That conflict, he now appreciates, has a law of development of its own that he proceeds to examine. It is a measure of the remarkable quality of his mind that he was able, within a very brief period, to expand the suggestions of *Light Shining, etc.*, into a comprehensive social philosophy that so completely transferred his interests from man's spiritual difficulties to his social and economic problems.

The New Law of Righteousness [1] marks the transition in Winstanley's development. It is a fascinating blend of the mystical with the practical, of his theological conceptions with the new social understanding he has achieved. He is still profoundly concerned with the struggle of the spiritual forces within man; and more than half the pages of his book are dedicated to an allegorical interpretation of Scriptural history in those terms. But he is now equally interested in

---

[1] *The New Law of Righteousness Budding forth, in restoring the whole Creation from the bondage of the Curse Or A Glimpse of the new Heaven, and a New Earth wherein dwels Righteousness Giving an Alarm to silence all that preach or speak from hear-say or imagination* (Jan. 1648).

The New Law of Righteousness is a very rare tract. It is to be found in the one volume edition of Winstanley's theological works in the Goldsmiths Collection, University of London, in Jesus College Library, Oxford, and the Manchester Free Reference Library.

the external manifestations of that struggle; and for the first time he ventures a detailed description of those phenomena. He is impelled, at least consciously, not so much by sympathy with the suffering of the people or an abstract economic argument, as by the conviction that the prevailing social system has destroyed the natural perfection of the universal scheme. For, man at the time of his creation was a perfect being; and that perfection was paralleled in the social sphere by the unity that obtained when everything was owned in common and mankind knew no division or strife. But that harmonious integration of man was destroyed when selfishness arose within him. It shattered social unity, for it translated itself into a selfish desire for the exclusive possession and enjoyment of material things; and from that desire private property was born.

> ". . . and this is the beginning of particular interest, buying and selling the earth from one particular hand to another saying this is mine, upholding this particular propriety by a law of government of his own making thereby restraining other fellow creatures from seeking nourishment from their mother earth." [1]

Thus, too, the domination of man by man was introduced. As the earth became the private property of a few, the rest of the people were forced to labour for them in order to maintain themselves. When, in this manner, some men had gained power over their fellows, they intensified their exploitation for

> " everyone that gets an authority into his hands tyrannizes over others ".[2]

Throughout the book Winstanley discusses in detail the technique by which the owners of property have maintained their domination. Having taken possession of the land by force and violence, they erected a system of law and government that secures and protects their privileges. To aid them in enslaving the people they established a visible Church that had no divine sanction; and they subjected man to the rule of the priest from the cradle through the altar to the grave. More outspokenly than anyone else in the century, Winstanley denounced the leaders of organized religion for

---

[1] *The New Law of Righteousness*, p. 6.   [2] Ibid., p. 5.

the support they had given to the oppressors. They told the common man tales of an

> " outward heaven which is a fancy your false teachers put into your heads to please you with while they pick your purses ".[1]

As a result of the private ownership of the soil there arose the buying and selling of land and commodities; and, by making trading the art of thievery, the rich have further extended their oppression of the poor. If the latter seek redress through law, the Justices of the Peace apply different standards to the rich and poor. By corrupting the universities, the ruling classes have made certain that truth will not issue from the houses of learning.

Winstanley is fully aware of all the implications and subtle results of class division. Private property, he claims, has been the cause of all the misery and strife the world has ever known:

> " self-propriety . . . is the curse and burden the creation groans under ".[2]

By impoverishing people, it inevitably drives them to crime; and hanging for theft has made death the price of poverty:

> " . . . this particular propriety of mine and thine hath brought in all miserye upon people. For, first it hath occasioned people to steal from one another. Secondly, it hath made laws to hang those that did steal. It tempts people to do an evil action and then kils them for doing of it." [3]

Their enjoyment of power has bred in the rich the conviction that their domination is part of the natural order of things.

> " The man of the flesh judges it a righteous thing that some men that are clothed with the objects of the earth and so called rich men whether it be got by right or wrong should be magistrates to rule over the poor; and that the poor should be servants, nay rather slaves to the rich." [4]

There is, Winstanley insists, but one solution to all this— the abolition of the system of private ownership. He has

---

[1] *The New Law of Righteousness*, p. 97. [2] Ibid., p. 61.
[3] Ibid., p. 62. [4] Ibid., p. 34.

no allusions that oppression can be ended so long as men own unequally and some not at all.

> " . . . so long as such are rulers as cals the Land theirs, upholding this particular propriety of mine and thine, the common people shall never have their liberty nor the land ever freed from troubles, oppressions and complainings ".[1]

Only if the earth is made a " common treasury " again, he declares, introducing the phrase that was to re-echo throughout all of his subsequent writings, can the original harmony of the social order be restored and the misery of mankind be ended.   For, if a man

> " have meat and drinke and clothes by his labor in freedome and what can he desire more in earth. Pride and envy likewise is killed thereby for everyone shall look upon each other as an equal in creation ".[2]

If everyone will be able to satisfy his needs by honest labour, there will be no incentive to crime; and the necessity for laws, prisons and punishment will ultimately disappear. If men will share in common the results of their labours, there will be no need for extensive trading, and " buying and selling " will be eliminated.   Ending the system of " mine and thine " will uproot the source of social strife; for where private ownership divides men, common ownership will unite them.

He recognizes, however, that the abolition of the existing system will not be a simple adventure; but he is convinced that there is a law of development in social institutions that renders its disappearance a certainty:

> " . . . as everything hath his growth, his raign and end so must this slavery have an end ".[3]

The instruments through which the system will be abolished are the poorest and most oppressed strata of society:

> " The Father now is rising up a people to himself out of the dust, that is out of the lowest and most despised sort of people, that are counted the dust of the earth, mankind, that are trod under-foot. In these and from these shall the Law of Righteousnesse break forth first." [4]

---

[1] *The New Law of Righteousness*, pp. 6–7.   [2] Ibid., p. 7.
[3] Ibid., p. 102.   [4] Ibid., p. 42.

But social change will be strenuously opposed by

" . . . covetous, proud, lazy, pamper'd flesh that would have the poor still to work for that devil (particular interest) to maintaine his greatnesse that he may live at ease ".[1]

But Winstanley insists that the poor must not make violence their avenue to a better social order:

" Weapons and swords shall destroy and cut the powers of the earth asunder but they shall never build up ".[2]

Writing immediately before the execution of Charles and at the time of the seizure of power by the army, he makes no direct reference to the political developments of the day. But he would seem to be addressing the Army and the Independents when he declares that

" . . . this is not to be done by the hands of a few or by unrighteous men that would pull the tyrannical government out of other men's hands and keep it in their own heart, as we feel this to be a burden of our age ".[3]

He sets himself firmly against violence as a method of social reform and death as a form of punishment:

" I do not speak ", he emphasizes, " that any particular man shall go and take their neighbours goods by violence or robbery . . . but everyone is to wait till the Lord Christ spread himself in multiplicities of bodies making them all of one heart and minde acting in righteousnesse one to another." [4]

He constantly returns to the theme that had been the burden of his earlier writings, that men can do nothing but wait with a meek and quiet spirit for the coming of Christ; but he has moved to a realization of the necessity of anticipating that revelation with positive action:

" You dust of the earth that are trod underfoot," he earnestly appeals to the oppressed, " you poor people that makes both schollars and rich men your oppressours by your labours, take notice of your priviledge." [5]

---

[1] *The New Law of Righteousness*, p. 56.   [2] Ibid., p. 37.
[3] Ibid., p. 35.   [4] Ibid., p. 38.   [5] Ibid., p. 53.

The rich, of course, will refuse to surrender their property. But the propertyless can begin to effect their own freedom by refusing to work for their masters. It is no less a crime to maintain the domination of man by man by working for another than by directly exploiting one's fellows; and in a land, Winstanley argues, where less than one-third of the total area is under cultivation there is no need for anyone to starve or to work for his oppressors. If the rich insist on saying " this land is mine ", they must work it with their own hands. No man, he asserts in anticipation of Locke, can claim more land than he can labour with his own hands " neither giving nor taking hire ". The propertyless must therefore begin to free the world by working and producing together on the common lands and sharing the results. The rich may claim as their own possessions the estates on which they dwell. But the common lands and the heaths are undeniably the common property of the poor. The latter should begin to make the earth a common treasury and to teach mankind by example by establishing that community on their own lands.

All this, Winstanley affirms, has come to him through a Divine Revelation. While he was in a trance, texts darted at him from the sky:

> " Likewise I heard these words ' Worke together, Eat bread together, declare all this abroad '. Likewise I heard these words. ' Whosoever it is that labours in the earth for any person or persons that lifts up themselves as Lords and Rulers over others and that doth not look upon themselves equal to others in the creation, The hand of the Lord shall be upon the labourer. I the Lord have spoke it and I will do it. Declare this all abroad: ' " [1]

We have already indicated the possible rôle that *Light Shining in Buckinghamshire* may have played in inducing the trance which gave Winstanley his inspiration. He is prepared, he announces, to move from theory to practice, to become priest instead of prophet as soon as God will give him his instructions:

> " I have now obeyed the command of the Spirit that bid me declare all this abroad, I have delivered it and I will

---

[1] *The New Law of Righteousness*, p. 48.

deliver it by word of mouth, I have now declared it by my pen. And when the Lord doth shew unto me the place and manner how he will have us that are called common people to manure and work upon the Common lands, I will then go forth and declare it in my actions." [1]

Fortunately, the Lord, in a very convenient revelation, was soon to indicate St. George's Hill, a few miles from Winstanley's home, as the site for the beginning of the Digger experiment.

Thus, within a period of six or seven months Winstanley had traversed a path that led from a chiliastic mysticism through a progressive rationalism to a practical communism. Only on one subsequent occasion did he again cast his ideas wholly in a theological mould; and that tract seems to have been writen during a period of profound disappointment at the failure of his practical venture.[2]

We have indicated in an earlier chapter that Winstanley began to write at a time when, as a result of the failure of political effort, there was an increasing tendency to turn from politics to a mystical theology, to reverse the process of the early years of the war by translating political aspirations into theological and spiritual terms and to invoke the assistance of the Almighty to achieve those social reforms that political agitation had failed to secure. Winstanley's earlier tracts were a manifestation of that tendency. He had already recognized the Civil War as a struggle for supremacy between opposing forces. He saw from the fact that there was a continual and determined effort to suppress and exploit the poor that the conflict was definitely one between social groups. Ecclesiastical authority, political institutions, the judiciary, law, were the weapons of the wealthy in the war they were waging. In the poor who were demanding no more than the right to live like human beings and to worship

[1] *The New Law of Righteousness*, pp. 53–54.
[2] *Fire in the Bush, The Spirit Burning, not consuming but purging mankinde* (1650), Bodleian Library, also bound together with the single volume edition in the Goldsmiths Collection and the Manchester Free Library.
I do not know on what evidence Berens has given its date as March 1649. The four copies of the tract I have seen, the Bodleian, Manchester, Seligman, and Goldsmiths copies, all bear the date 1650 on their·title-pages; and I have seen no references to any earlier editions. The fact, too, that it was not included in the one-volume edition (as is indicated by the common title-page), the preface to which Winstanley wrote in Dec. 1649, would seem to indicate that it was first published subsequent to that date.

God freely, he recognized the only people who were animated not by a selfish desire for power and privilege, but by a spirit of justice and righteousness. The fury of persecution, as a result, was being directed against them and those who sought to act as their spokesmen.

In the beginning, Winstanley interpreted those phenomena in purely theological terms. They were the reflection of a fundamental conflict of spiritual forces, the clash of good and evil within man. That interpretation is the burden of his early tracts. By January, however, Winstanley had begun to translate that version into secular terms. The struggle became not merely one between spiritual forces, but between economic classes, between the wealthy who were seeking to retain their privileges and the poor who were demanding that they be shared. That social division, with everything that it implied, was rooted in the private ownership of property; and human history was essentially the record of continual conflict between the rich and the poor. The poor were being persecuted not merely because they were the Saints of true religion, but because they were the prophets of a new social order. And not until common ownership had been established would strife and misery disappear from society. Essentially, then, in *The New Law of Righteousness* Winstanley had translated his theological concepts and his historical interpretation into political language. That he himself did not regard his social ideas as a contradiction of his religious views, but rather as their logical development, is indicated by the fact that he published a collected edition of his theological works early in 1650 while the St. George Hill adventure was still in progress and in the preface he wrote in December 1649 for that edition.

We should note at this point, however, that there had been throughout the entire decade a continuous demand for " common property ". It is, to be sure, a demand of whose existence we know largely through the fulminations of its opponents rather than through any explicit formulation by its advocates. But the volume of opposition that was expressed to any scheme of common ownership leaves no room for doubt that the suggestion achieved considerable popularity. The demand for some sort of community of goods is conspicuous in all the popular movements of the mediaeval period.[1] We

---

[1] See Kautsky, op. cit. ; Box, op. cit. ; Engels, op. cit.

have already noted that during the early years of the Civil War the sects were feared and denounced because " they would have all things common ".[1] Edwards, writing in 1646, catalogues as one of the errors of the sects their assertion

" that all the Earth is the Saints and there ought to be a community of goods and the Saints should share in the Lands and Estates of the Gentlemen and Rich Men ". [2]

The movement for some form of communism seems to have grown rapidly after 1646. The Congregational Societies of London, for example, were forced to deny in a lengthy and reasoned statement that they

" intended to throwe down those hedges that are set about men's estates and to lay both one and the other common ". [3]

The Levellers' persistent affirmation of their loyalty to the principle of private property was required as an answer both to those who repeatedly accused them of seeking to " level all estates " and to those in their own ranks who were applying the principles of natural equality to the economic as well as the political sphere.[4] The denial of men like John Cooke and Henry Parker that they favour the principle of common ownership betrays an anxiety to dissociate themselves from a current of opinion that must have become increasingly prominent.[5] There were, too, from the very beginning of the war, serious and constant riots in all parts of the country against enclosures and the frequent destruction of fences and hedges.

But in none of these manifestations did communism achieve the status of a social doctrine. With the rioting peasants, it is the spontaneous expression of their anger with those who had enclosed their lands and an attempt to regain what had been taken from them. The communism of the mediaeval movements and of most of the sects of the Interregnum is

[1] *Supra*, Chap. II, pp. 91–3.
[2] Edwards, *Gangraena* (1646), Part I, p. 34.
[3] *A Declaration of the Congregationall Societies in and about the City of London as well as of those commonly called Anabaptists as others. In way of vindication of themselves Touching : 1. Liberty. 2. Magistracy. 3. Propriety. 4. Polygamie* (Nov. 1647), E. 416 (20).
[4] *Supra*, Chap. II, pp. 150–3.
[5] John Cooke, *Unum Necessarium or the Poor Man's Case* (Jan. 1648), E. 425 (1) ; Henry Parker, *Of a Free Trade* (1648), E. 425 (18).

generally a vague and mystical affair, and, at best, a general demand for a common and equal division of the social product rather than for a system of common production. In no instance does it derive from a reasoned examination of social and historical forces.

With Winstanley, however, the demand for common ownership was rooted as early as January 1649 in a comprehensive social philosophy that became the basis of a political programme. It emerged as the result of a reasoned analysis of the rôle of private property in history and of the results of social division. Unlike the mediaeval varieties, it proposed communism not only in distribution, but in production as well.

Several aspects of Winstanley's position of January 1649 must be noted. He still retains his conviction that only God can achieve the final redemption of mankind; but, unlike his earlier insistence, he urges that man himself must begin that process through direct action by the propertyless classes. Where in the summer of 1648 he had conceived human freedom as a form of asceticism, as essentially an escape from the necessity for material things, he now regards it, on the contrary, as a function of the guarantee to every individual of an adequate minimum of material comfort. He is not concerned with the forms of political organization; for he realizes that institutions and laws are simply the expression of the economic relationships they reflect and by which they are limited. Nowhere in the writings we have thus far examined is there any extended discussion of political forms or constitutional mechanisms. In fact, his social analysis has not been at all applied to the development of English history; and the argument or illustration from the Norman Conquest has yet to appear in his pages.

But we must at the same time recognize the limitations of the position he has achieved in *The New Law of Righteousness*. The ultimate causes of social change, he still maintains, are to be found in the minds and hearts of men, though he has vaguely sensed that human nature may, after all, not be an eternal and fundamental phenomenon, but simply the way human behaviour expresses itself under particular social conditions. His communism is conceived not as the product of an inevitable historical development, but as the recognition of a basic principle of justice and morality. Common ownership is for him, as yet, not dictated by any political or economic argument; and there is no attempt to discuss the economic advantages such a system might confer. It is to him, above all else, a method of restoring the original and natural perfectibility of Creation that had been destroyed by the introduction of private property.

We shall examine in subsequent chapters the degree to which his position of January 1649 was modified and his outlook broadened by his practical experiences of the ensuing year.

Chapter Four : THE DIGGER MOVEMENT

> " My mind was not at rest because nothing was acted, and thoughts ran in me that words and writings were all nothing and must die, For action is the life of all and if thou dost not act, thou dost nothing."—
> Winstanley, *A Watchword to the City of London and the Armie* (1649).

WITH Pride's Purge, England entered on a period of military dictatorship. John Goodwin's defence of the army's action was eloquent and persuasive; but it could not mask the fact that the Government rested on the power of the sword rather than on the will of the people.[1] His argument that

> ". . . the cals of the miseries and extremities of men for reliefe are more authorizing, more urging, pressing and binding upon the consciences of men who have wherewith-all to afford reliefe unto them, then the formall requests or elections of men to places of trust or interest when the electors have no such present or pressing necessity upon them for the interposall of the elected on their behalfe. The necessities of men call more effectually than men themselves ".[2]

could be urged with equal validity against the Commonwealth as against the Presbyterian Parliament the army had purged.

During the entire year the country seethed with discontent. Economic conditions were growing steadily worse. The disastrous harvest of 1648 caused an acute scarcity of commodities, and prices rose to famine levels.[3]

" Never was there in England so many in want of relief as now ",[4] the inhabitants of London complained in March on

---

[1] The average attendance at Parliamentary divisions, for example, during the first three months after the establishment of the Commonwealth was fifty-six (Gardiner, *Commonwealth*, Vol. I, p. 9).

[2] John Goodwin, *Right and Might Well Met* (Jan. 2, 1649), E. 536 (28).

[3] Thorold Rogers, *History of Agriculture and Prices* (1887), V. 826.

[4] *The Humble Petition of Divers Inhabitants of the City of London and Places Adjacent in the behalfe of the Poore of this Nation* (March 10, 1649), E. 546 (15).

behalf of the poor of the country.   Civilian disturbance was
continuous during the year, particularly in the North, the
Midlands and the West.   The Royalists, attempting to rally
their forces, were intriguing, organizing, arming in many
parts of the country.   At home they were exploring the
possibility of an alliance with the Levellers; abroad they
were feverishly negotiating for foreign assistance and intervention.   The City, alarmed by the revolutionary purge of
Parliament, maintained an attitude of active opposition, at
best, of cold indifference, to the Commonwealth during the
first few months of its existence.   The Levellers, seriously
weakened by the months of political truce and by the firm
control Cromwell had established over the army, returned to
the fray with a series of vigorous and powerful pamphlets de-
nouncing the Commonwealth as a military dictatorship no
less arbitrary than the regime of the King or the Presbyterians
had been.   Tyranny had altered its vestments; its body remained substantially the same.   Monarchy, it was claimed a
few weeks after the execution of the King,

> " had lost its name but not its nature, its form but not its
> power, they making themselves as absolute as ever the King
> in his reign, dignity and supremacy." [1]

About the middle of February the Levellers began urging the
soldiers to demand the reappointment of the Agitators and
the re-establishment of the General Council of the Army.
The reply of the Council of State was effectively to abrogate
the soldiers' freedom of petitioning by decreeing that all petitions from the ranks had to be submitted through the officers
and to prohibit any private meetings of officers or soldiers.
Several soldiers who protested against the Council's behaviour
were cashiered from the army; in their subsequent attack on
Cromwell and Ireton they produced one of the most remarkable tracts of the entire period.[2]

> " We were before ruled by King, Lords, and Commons,
> now by a General, a Court Martial and House of Commons;

---

[1] *A Rout, A Rout or some part of the Armies Quarters Beaten Up By the Day
of the Lord stealing upon Them* (Feb. 10, 1649), E. 542 (5).
[2] *The Hunting of the Foxes from New-Market and Triploe-Heaths to Whitehall
by Five Small Beagles.* By Robt. Ward, Thos. Watson, Simon Graunt,
George Jellis, William Sawyer (March 1649), E. 548 (7).

we pray you what is the difference? . . . The old King's person and the old Lords are now removed and a new King and new Lords with the commons are in one House; and so under a more absolute Arbitrary Monarchy than before. We have not the change of a Kingdome to a Common-wealth; we are onely under the old cheat, the transmutation of names but with the addition of New tyranies to the old . . . and the last state of this Commonwealth is worse than the first." [1]

Similar charges were elaborated by Lilburne in a number of tracts. In *England's New Chaines Discovered* [2] and in *The Second Part of England's New Chaines Discovered*,[3] he does not challenge the legality of the Rump; but he insists that it is being coerced by the officers and appeals to it to free itself from that coercion. For publishing the latter tract, Lilburne, Overton, Walwyn and Prince were arrested on March 26 and confined to the Tower. Their imprisonment again aroused a tremendous agitation for their release; the petition of April 2, alone, is said to have borne over 80,000 signatures.

Among the many pamphlets that appeared during those months we should note the second publication of the authors of *Light Shining in Buckinghamshire*, whose influence on Winstanley we have already discussed. The argument of *More Light Shining in Buckinghamshire* [4] is substantially that of the earlier tract; but it repeats with greater emphasis the insistence that no one can claim anything but that which he has produced by his own labour.

"None is our bread but what we work for . . . therefore those that work not have no right to eat." [4]

It again demands freedom of speech, equality of rights and privileges, the abolition of patents, corporations and monopoly grants, the adjudication of controversies and the administration of law by popularly elected elders, the removal of enclosures and the prohibition of " buying and selling ". " Above all ", it pleads, " look to the poor ". It rejects the Agreement of the

---

[1] *The Hunting of the Foxes*, p. 14. [2] Feb. 26, 1649, E. 545 (27).
[3] March 24, 1649, E. 548 (16). [4] March 1649, E. 548 (33).

People that had been suggested by Ireton and the Officers because it is

"... too low and too shallow to free us for it doth not throw down all these arbitrary courts, Patents and powers as aforesaid; and what stock or way is provided for the poor, fatherless, widows, and impoverished people? And what advancement or encouragement for the laboring and industrious as to take off burthens is there?" [1]

Dissatisfaction and unrest were again spreading rapidly in the army. During February and March the Council of State revived the plan of an invasion of Ireland that had always obsessed so many of its members. The invasion attracted the Council not merely because it would prevent the use of Ireland by the Royalists as a base of operations against England, but because of the prospect of plunder the Commonwealth so desperately required and for the diversion it was hoped foreign adventure would provide. Cromwell, after waiting for several weeks for his instructions from the Lord—weeks during which, no doubt, he was able to evaluate the domestic situation more accurately—accepted the leadership of the Irish campaign. But the troops chosen for the venture failed to share the enthusiasm of their leaders. None of the outstanding demands of the soldiers had as yet been met; payment was still considerably in arrears. Those soldiers who indicated their refusal to serve in Ireland were dismissed from the army in April without payment. Open mutiny broke out in Colonel Whalley's regiment, as a result of which six men were sentenced to death. The lot for execution fell on Lockyer, a young, popular and able veteran of the war. His execution on April 27 aroused tremendous indignation throughout the army; and his funeral on the 29th witnessed a vast popular demonstration of sympathy with the Levellers and the soldiers.

With the execution of Lockyer, revolutionary ferment developed rapidly. Opposition to the Irish venture and grievances over pay were more outspokenly and vehemently expressed. The practice of court-martialling protesting soldiers, of dismissing them without sufficient remuneration and the denial to the soldiers of the elementary rights and liberties for which they had fought intensified their conviction that unless

[1] *More Light, etc.,* op. cit.

the military dictatorship were overthrown England would be permanently enslaved to the arbitrary will of the officers.

" Our undoubted Liberties never more encroached upon by the Military power and Law-Martial ", protested several soldiers in petitioning for a reprieve of Lockyer's sentence, " Soldiers and others of late being frequently seized, restrained and adjudged to death, and reproachful punishments without any regard to the Law of the Land or tryall by twelve sworn men of the Neighborhood; as is manifest in your present proceedings against those soldiers and others now under restraint and censure of the Council of War." [1]

In their petition they were clearly reflecting the mood of no inconsiderable section of the army.

From the Tower, Lilburne and his associates continued their agitation. In a letter to Fairfax they condemned Lockyer's execution as an act of murder; for

" . . . it is by law fully proved that it is both treason and murder for any general of the Council of War to execute any soldier in time of peace by martial law ".[2]

On May 1 they issued a new version of *The Agreement of the People*, a version, let it be noted, in which future Parliaments were again forbidden " to level men's estates, destroy propriety or make all things common ".

When Cromwell reviewed the troops in Hyde Park on May 9 most of the soldiers were sporting the sea-green emblem of the Levellers. In a conciliatory speech he promised to put the Agreement of the People into effect and to settle all grievances arising out of arrears of pay. Meanwhile serious mutiny had developed in the army. William Thompson was leading several hundreds of Colonel Whalley's regiment in mutiny at Banbury. In their manifesto, *England's Standard Advanced*,[3] Thompson demanded the implementation of the Agreement, satisfaction for the murder of Lockyer and the release of the Leveller leaders. They were joined by most of Scroope's and Ireton's regiments, who were in revolt at Salisbury; and

[1] *The Army's Martyr* (April 1649).
[2] *The Copie of a Letter Written to the General by Lt-Col. J. Lilburne and Mr. Richard Overton* (April 27, 1649), 669, f. 14 (23).
[3] May 6, 1649, E. 553 (2).

Harrison's and Skippon's regiments mutinied in Buckinghamshire. Scroope's and Ireton's men asserted in their Declaration that they were driven to revolt against the officers and the
Council of War because of

> " the sad and wofull experience of the present proceedings
> of the Officers and divers Regiments of the Army against
> the Souldiery, in depriving us of our Native Liberties, cast-
> ing lots upon our persons and thereby designing us for the
> Irish Services without our consent or knowledge, which we
> beleeve no Age can parallel and after the designation to
> force us (contrary to English Right) by unequall terms for
> the said Service, so as if we should deny, to be presently
> cashiered from the Army, with little or no pay at all in hand,
> whereby we must either be forced to beg, steal or starve. . . .
> Wherefore we are now resolved no longer to dally with our
> God but with all our endeavours to pursue what we have
> before promised in order to the settling of this poor Nation,
> and the restitution of our shaking Freedom, and redeeming
> ourselves out of the hands of Tyrants; for which cause (the
> safety of the Nation involved together with our own) hath
> forced us to deny obedience to such Tyrannical Officers
> whose unsufferable proceedings tend manifestly to the
> obstructing of our Peace, the hindrances of the Relief of
> Ireland, the re-inslaving of the consuming Nation. . . ." [1]

Writing in defence of their action some months later, a number
of the soldiers who had revolted declared that they had no
alternative to mutiny when they saw

> " . . . the whole fabrick of the Common wealth faln into
> the grossest and vilest tyranny that ever English men groaned
> under; all their Laws, Rights, Liberties and Properties
> wholly subdued (under the vizard and form of that Engage-
> ment) to the boundless wills of some deceitfull persons, hav-
> ing devolved the whole Magistracy of England into their
> Martial Domination, ruling the people with a Rod of Iron
> as most mens wofull experience can clearly witness ".[2]

Cromwell and Fairfax, aware that, in the state of distress the
country was experiencing and that because of the general

---

[1] *The Unanimous Declaration of Colonel Scroope's and Commissary Gen. Ireton's
Regiments at a Rendezvous at Old Sarum* (May 11, 1649), E. 555 (4).
[2] *The Levellers (falsely so called) Vindicated* (Aug. 21), E. 571 (11).

dissatisfaction and unrest in the army, the revolt might easily assume nation-wide proportions, marched at once to Oxford with picked men to prevent the garrison at Banbury from effecting contact with the Buckinghamshire regiments. On the 12th the Agents for Ireton and Scroope's regiments sent a letter to Fairfax declaring

> " All we require is the performance of our Engagement made at Triplo Heath, and we shall promise never to depart from your Excellencies Command in any thing which shall not be contrary to the said Engagement." [1]

In the ensuing interchange of letters the troops in revolt urged Fairfax to restore a measure of democratic discipline in the army by the re-establishment of the General Council of the Army.

> " This we beg earnestly of your Excellency to grant in respect of your duty to God, this Nation and the Army," they wrote, " that we may thereby recover our Peace and procure the happinesse of this Nation. This is the desire of our soules, if you deny this we must lay at your doore all the misery, bloodshed, and ruine which will follow." [1]

Their appeal was unanswered. On May 14 the Army Levellers, betrayed, as they later claimed, by some of their own comrades, were surprised at Burford and, after a spirited fight, they were overwhelmed and defeated. With the defeat at Burford, the army revolt collapsed.

On the day the Levellers were being crushed at Burford, the Council of State was issuing an act declaring it a treasonable offence for anyone to assert that the Government were

> ". . . tyrannical, usurped or unlawfull; or that the Commons in Parliament assembled are not the Supreme Authority of this Nation; or shall plot, contrive or endeavour to stir up or raise force against the present government or for the subversion or alteration of the same . . . or shall attempt to stir up mutiny in the army." [2]

[1] *A Full Narrative of All the Proceedings betweene His Excellency the Lord Fairfax and the Mutineers* (May 1649), E. 555 (27).
[2] Firth and Rait, Vol. II, p. 120 (May 14, 1649).

The rule of force was being sanctioned by the formality of law.

On their return from Burford, Cromwell and Fairfax were honoured with degrees at Oxford for the distinguished service they were deemed to have rendered the State by their suppression of the Leveller revolt. A few weeks later the City merchants and financiers, recognizing that Cromwell was not the dangerous revolutionary they had feared, but, like themselves, a solid and conservative man of property who would brook no threat to its security, made their peace with the new regime. The defeat of the mutiny and the new accord between the City and the Government were celebrated by a banquet in the City on June 7.[1] The following day the City, in token of its gratitude, presented Fairfax with a basin and ewer of gold and Cromwell with plate valued at £300 and 200 pieces of gold. By crushing the Leveller revolt, Cromwell had removed the most serious threat to his dictatorship; by offering such unanswerable proof of his conservatism, he regained the support of the City merchants.

If the army mutiny had failed, civilian agitation continued unabated. It had been reported at the time of the Burford encounter that 1500 Somersetshire Clubmen were marching to the support of the Levellers.[2] There were riots in many parts of the country. In the summer there was a particularly serious rising of the Derbyshire miners, dissatisfied with their conditions of labour. In September the Levellers began to urge direct economic measures against the Government. In the same month the garrison at Oxford rose in mutiny. Throughout, the Royalists continued to intrigue for an alliance with the Levellers; the latter, defeated on all fronts, began to give the suggestion serious consideration.

It is against this background of military dictatorship, of economic distress, of Royalist intrigue, of civilian revolt, of Leveller agitation and of army mutiny that we must set the beginnings of the Digger experiment in practical communism in April 1649.

After the publication of *The New Law of Righteousness*, Win-

---

[1] It is extremely interesting to note that in the Prayer specially composed for the occasion was included the Biblical injunction, " Cursed be he that removeth the mark of his neighbour's land." *A Form of Prayer to be used for both the days of Public Thanksgiving for the Seasonable and happy reducing of the Levellers* (June 6, 1649), E. 558 (22).

[2] *Mercurius Philo-Monarchicus* (May 14–21, 1649), E. 555 (34).

stanley awaited a revelation from the Lord as to the point from which to begin to make the earth " a common treasury ". Two months later he had evidently been vouchsafed that divine guidance; for on April 1, Everard, Winstanley and several of their companions appeared at St. George's Hill, in the Parish of Walton-on-Thames in Surrey, began to dig the waste-land and to plant some vegetables. The following day their number had been augmented; and for a few weeks they continued their work of digging and planting. Although they do not seem to have numbered more than thirty or forty persons during those weeks, they confidently asserted that they would shortly be joined by 5000 of their fellows. They extended a general invitation to the people of the district to join with them, promising that everyone would share equally in their venture. From the very outset, however, they encountered the violent opposition of the local populace. Writing some eight months afterwards, Winstanley relates that during the first weeks of the St. George's Hill colony, the Diggers were attacked by a mob of over 100 people, who burned a house they had erected, carried off and destroyed their tools and forcibly dragged several of the Diggers to Walton Church, where they were struck and molested before being released by a Kingston justice.

News of the little communist group must have spread rapidly; for on April 14 the Leveller leaders, in a manifesto issued to counter accusations that had been made against them, were primarily concerned to deny that " we would level all men's estates ". They make no mention of the Diggers; but the length at which they elaborated their opposition to common ownership leaves little doubt that they were already being publicly associated with the little band of Diggers in Surrey. They insist that they would never agree to any form of communism unless it had been unanimously sanctioned by the people, and that it was beyond the competence of any representative body to abolish private property. Primitive Christian communism, they assert, was purely voluntary; at best, it was a very limited and temporary affair.

" We profess, therefore," they declare, " that we never had it in our thoughts to level men's estates, it being the utmost of our aim that the Commonwealth be reduced to

F

such a pass that every man with as much security as may be enjoy his propriety." [1]

Despite the hostility of the local populace, the Diggers continued with their sowing and planting. On April 16 their persistence brought them to the attention of the Council of State. On that date the Council was informed of their activities by Henry Sanders of Walton.[2] The Council promptly forwarded the information to Fairfax, suggesting that he take immediate action for

". . . although the pretence of their being there by them avowed may seeme very ridiculous yett that conflux of people may bee a beginning whence things of a greater and more dangerous consequence may grow to a disturbance of the peace and quiett of the Commonwealth." [2]

The Justices of the Peace for Surrey were similarly instructed

". . . to send for the contrivers or promoters of those riotous meetings and to proceed against them ".[3]

Two troops of horse were despatched to Kingston to investigate what was occurring. Captain Gladman, reporting the results of his investigation to Fairfax three days later, wrote that Winstanley and Everard had agreed to come to London to explain their action in person to the General. Gladman himself planned to visit them at St. George's Hill " to persuade those people to leave off this employment ".

" Indeed," his report concluded, " the business is not worth the writing nor yet taking notiss of; I wonder the Council of State should be so abused with informations." [4]

On Friday, April 20, Everard and Winstanley appeared before Fairfax in London. Insisting that they could recognize no distinctions of rank, they refused to remove their hats in

---

[1] *A Manifestation from Lilburne, Prince, Overton and Walwyn* (April 14, 1649), E. 550 (25). In June, however, Lilburne specifically repudiated " the erronious tenets of the poor Diggers at George Hill in Surrey and laid down in their late two avowed books called *The True Levellers Standard* and *The New Law of Righteousnesse* ".—*The Legal Fundamental Liberties*, E. 560 (14).
[2] *Clarke Papers*, Vol. II, p. 210.
[3] *C.S.P., Dom., 1649–50*, April 16, 1649, p. 95.
[4] *Clarke Papers*, Vol. II, p. 212.

the presence of the General.[1] Everard, in a speech to Fairfax, declared that, since the Conquest, England had lived under a tyranny more ruthless than the Israelites had experienced under Pharaoh. But God had revealed to the poor that their deliverance was at hand and that He would soon restore to them their freedom to enjoy the fruits of the earth. In a vision, Everard had been commanded to " arise and dig and plant the earth and receive the fruits thereof ". He assured Fairfax that he and his fellows did not intend either to interfere with private property or to destroy enclosures, but that they were merely claiming the commons which were the rightful possession of the poor. They intended to cultivate the waste-lands in common and to provide sustenance for the distressed. They hoped that the poor throughout the country would follow their example; they, themselves, intended to extend their activities to Newmarket, Hounslow and Hampstead Heath. They were certain that ere long all men would voluntarily cede their property and join with them in " community ". In no circumstances, not even in self-defence, Everard declared, would the Diggers resort to the use of force.[2] At the same time they issued a manifesto to the country setting forth a reasoned statement and elaboration of their social programme.[3]

With their notice by the Council of State and the appearance of their leaders before Fairfax, the Diggers enjoyed the spotlight of national attention for a brief period. Most of the news-sheets of the last weeks of April note their activities; and it is interesting to observe the reception they were accorded by the various journals. Some, like A Perfect Diurnall, contented themselves with brief and factual accounts of the information that had reached the Council and the interview with Fairfax.[4] Others, reporting the affair, dismissed it as the work of a few

[1] In 1647 Saltmarsh had similarly retained his hat in the presence of Fairfax.—Dictionary of National Biography. Article on "Saltmarsh", by Rev. Alexander Gordon.
[2] The Declaration and Standard of the Dwellers of England, E. 551 (11). See also A Modest Narrative of Intelligence (April 14–21), E. 551 (9).
[3] The True Levellers Standard Advanced or the State of Community opened and presented to the Sons of Men, E. 552 (5). Everard's name heads the list of signatories. The preface is dated April 20. Thomason received his copy on April 26. In the Thomason Catalogue the date is incorrectly given as 1650.
[4] A Perfect Diurnall (April 16–23), E. 529 (18), notices on April 18 and 20.

madmen; Everard, particularly, is described by most papers as " a mad prophet ".

" They are a distracted crack-brained people that were the chief." [1]

The Kingdome's Faithfull and Impartiall Scout printed a cynical account:

" The new-fangled people that begin to dig on St. George's Hill in Surrey say they are like Adam, they expect a generall restauration of the Earth to its first condition, that themselves were called to seek and begin this great work which will shortly go on throughout the whole Earth; (one of them getting up a great burden of thorns and briars thrust them into the pulpit of the Church at Walton to stop out the Parson). They professe a great deal of mildness and would have the world believe they have dreamed dreams, seen visions, heard strange voices and have dictates beyond man's teaching. They professe they will not fight knowing that not to be good for them." [2]

Mercurius Pragmaticus was sarcastic and abusive in its report:

" Our sugamores this evening consulted how they might take our great prophet Everet sometime a champion unto their holy cause who for his perseverance in iniquity pretends to be rewarded with the gift of lunacy instead of Revelation. He and some 30 of his disciples intended to have converted Catland Park into a wilderness and preach liberty to the oppressed deer; they have begun to plant

---

[1] *A Perfect Summary of an Exact Diary of some Passages of Parliament* (April 16–23), E. 529 (19).
Similar accounts in *The Impartiall Intelligencer* (April 18–25), E. 529 (20). *Continued Heads of Perfect Passages in Parliament* (April 20–27), E. 529 (23).
[2] April 20–27, E. 529 (22). In its report of an incident at St. George's on April 23, the paper refers to the " party of Diggers ". This seems to be the first occasion on which the group was designated by that name. During the first few weeks they generally referred to themselves as " True Levellers ", though Winstanley subsequently adopted the term " Diggers ". The name appears during the enclosure riots of 1607 in a manifesto issued by " The Diggers of Warwickshire to all other Diggers ", protesting the tyranny of the landlords. The manifesto is printed in full in *The Marriage of Wit and Wisdom*, edited for the New Shakespeare Society by James Halliwell (1846), p. 140, sec. 15. My attention was first drawn to this fact by R. H. Tawney, *The Agrarian Problem in the Sixteenth Century* (1912).

their colony with hermits' fare, parsnips, beans, and such other castigatue nourishment; but nevertheless they intend in pure zeal to increase and multiply, if any of the sisterhood but once resolve to relinquish the pomps and vanities of this wicked world and kennel with them in their caves which (in the imitation of the seven sleepers) they have dug good store of and like meek saints intend to inherit under the earth all the privileges of darkness, that their revelations may be freelier inspired in dreams from below; they are insolent in their frenzy and threaten the countrymen's cattle, they intend to plough and have pulled down that barricade of tyrannous prerogative, the Park-pale." [1]

But the writer adds a note of warning.

" What this fanaticall insurrection may grow into cannot be conceived for Mahomet had as small and despicable a beginning whose damnable infections have spread themselves many hundreds years since over the face of half the Universe." [2]

The Moderate Intelligencer, in similar vein, lightly regards the incident as the result of the hallucinations of a few individuals

". . . wanting reason and parts to beare them up and keep them ".[3]

Generally, writers confused the Diggers with the Levellers and regarded them merely as offshoots of the latter group.[4] That identification of the Diggers with the Levellers displeased the Royalists; for the latter, regarding the Levellers as potential and valuable allies in the struggle against Cromwell, were anxious that the popular appeal of the Levellers should not be impaired by the taint of communism. Thus, the Royalist journal *Mercurius Pragmaticus* (*for Charles II*) pro-

---

[1] April 17–24, E. 551 (12).
[2] *Mercurius Pragmaticus*, op. cit.
[3] April 19–26, E. 552 (4).
[4] e.g., *A Modest Narrative of Intelligence* (April 21–28), E. 552 (7) ; (April 28–May 5), E. 553 (1).
" You see how contradictions are necessary to State Disturbers. Lately the four Fathers of the People told us they were not against propriety, etc. But their children now tell us in their Declaration etc. that particular propriety is cursed Devil " (June 2–9), E. 559 (5).

tested the attempt to bring the Levellers into disrepute. After referring to the petition to free Lilburne, it writes:

". . . and men truly understood what they are which we call Levellers; not that they aim at the Levelling of men's estates but at the new state tyranny; and therefore it is that the merciful Hoghen Mogens of Derby House having nigh starved the Kingdom and a few poor people making bold with a little waste ground in Surrey to sow a few turnips and carrots to sustain their families, they wrest this act to the disrepute of the Levellers as if they meant to make all common; and to make a large business of it, their pamphleteers proclaim it about the Kingdom and divers troops of Janisaries were sent prancing into Surrey to make a conquest over those feeble souls and empty bellies. But that you may not be scared with the Levellers hereafter I tell you they are such as stand for an equal interest in freedom against the present tyranny and are so much the more tolerable in that a little experience will teach them that a just monarch is the best guardian of public liberty; besides the passage is very quick and easy from a popular government to a well-regulated monarchy." [1]

The article drew a sharp retort from *Mercurius Brittanicus*, who took *Pragmaticus* to task for its tolerant references to the Levellers. In turn, *Brittanicus* accused the Royalists of having instigated the Digger venture in order to increase the general confusion and unrest so that the Royalists might have the opportunity of seizing power.[2]

Several days after the interview with Fairfax, the Diggers were driven off St. George's Hill by the local populace.[3] A few days later, however, they returned to the Hill, determined to resume their work.

During May, Everard seems to have severed his connection

---

[1] April 17–24, E. 551 (15).
[2] April 24–May 5, E. 552 (27).
[3] *A Perfect Summary of an Exact Diarie of Some Passages of Parliament* (April 23–30), E. 529 (34).
April 26: " The new plantation at St. George's Hill in Surrey is quite relevelled and their new creation utterly destroyed and by the country people thereabouts they are driven away—and as seekers, gone a-seeking." Similar accounts appear in *A Perfect Diurnall* (April 23–30), E. 559 (26); *The Impartiall Intelligencer* (April 25–May 2), E. 529 (28); *Continued Heads of Perfect Passages in Parliament* (April 27–May 4), E. 529 (30).

with the little band of Diggers. At the outset, he had generally been regarded as the practical leader of the group. Impetuous and aggressive, he had attracted public attention much more readily than the mild Winstanley; in the interview with Fairfax he had spoken in the name of the Diggers; his name had headed the list of signatories to the first Digger manifesto, *The True Levellers Standard Advanced*.[1] After its publication, however, he no longer figures in any Digger activities; his name is missing from the second manifesto issued in May. Some newspapers reported that he had joined the Levellers in their revolt at Burford.

"One of the chiefest ring leaders deputed by John Lilburne", wrote *Mercurius Brittanicus*, "is Evers (i.e., Everard) who was not long since sowing carrots and turnips in the waste grounds in Surrey." [2]

"Mr. Everard, the quandum digger with his company", reported another journal, "being molested in their new plantation have thrown aside the spade and taken up the sword and tis said he commands 4 or 5 hundred horse." [3]

The report of his presence at Burford, however, was probably due to his confusion with Captain Robert Everard, a leading Leveller, and the "Buff-Coat" of the Putney Debates, who actively participated in the mutiny.[4] The notoriety Everard

[1] The pamphlet, however, is unmistakably from the pen of Winstanley.
[2] May 8-15, E. 555 (15).
[3] *The Kingdomes Faithfull and Impartiall Scout* (May 4-11), E. 530 (2).
[4] In August several of those who had participated in the revolt published their version of the affair together with a vindication of their action. The presence of Captain Robert Everard among the signatories leaves no doubt that the "Captain Everard's troop" mentioned by several papers in their account of the fighting was the company Robert Everard was leading. *The Levellers (falsely so-called) Vindicated* (Aug. 21), E. 571 (11). "Captain Everard's troop" is mentioned in *The Kingdomes Weekly Intelligencer* (May 8-15), E. 555 (18); *The Declaration of the Levellers*, E. 555 (26). I have been unable to find any trace of William Everard after he left the Diggers. Baxter, however, in discussing the growth of the sects in the 1650's, mentions the Bethemists: "The chiefest of them in England are Dr. Pordage and his family who live together in community." Pordage, Baxter declares, wrote a book in defence of his views, in which he attributed the evil spirits in his house "to one Everard whom he taketh to be a conjuror who stayed so long with him as desiring to be of their communion". Baxter, however, does not know to which Everard Pordage was referring, "there being two of that name that were sectaries in Cromwell's army". Baxter, *Reliquiae Baxterianae* (1696), pp. 77-9.
There were at least four Everards in the army, two of them named William.

the Digger was enjoying at the moment was probably responsible for his confusion with the Leveller captain.

Despite the optimistic predictions of the Diggers that they would shortly be joined by several thousand of their fellow-poor, there is little evidence that the example of the St. George's Hill pioneers was emulated elsewhere during the early months of the attempt; and the immediate impact of the Diggers seems to have been negligible in its effects. During the summer and autumn of 1649, the Levellers held the centre of popular attention; and radical minds were almost exclusively concerned with the fate of the imprisoned leaders and the progress of the army mutiny. From their Leveller friends in Buckinghamshire, however, the Diggers received a message of encouragement and sympathy. In a declaration embodying many Digger and Leveller arguments, the " middle sort of men " of Buckinghamshire asserted that they had been waiting for eight years for relief from arbitrary oppression.

"We shall help to aid and assist the poor ", they declare, " to the regaining all their rights, dues, etc. that do belong unto them and are detained from them by any tyranny whatsoever. . . . And likewise will further and help said poor to manure, dig, etc. the said commons and to sell those woods growing thereon to help them to a stock etc. All wel-affected persons that join in community in God's way as those Acts 2 and desire to manure, dig and plant in the waste grounds and commons shall not be troubled or molested by any of us but rather furthered therein." [1]

The central authorities, worried by the army revolt and Leveller and Royalist agitation, seem to have taken no further notice of the Diggers for a time; for Fairfax had evidently satisfied himself that they were a group of harmless

[1] *A Declaration of the Wel-Affected in the County of Buckinghamshire, being a Representation of the Middle Sort of men within the three Chilterne Hundreds of Disbrough, Burnum, Stoke and Part of Alisbury Hundred whereby they declare their resolution and intentions with a Removall of their Grievances* (May 10), E. 555 (1). There is a brief item mentioning the Declaration in *The Kingdome's Faithfull Scout* of May 9: " Letters from Buckingham say that those called by the name of Levellers have rendezvoused near Alisbury and have agreed upon this ensuing Declaration to be published throughout the Nation, a copy whereof followeth." A summary of the Declaration follows, E. 530 (2). A similar notice appears in *England's Moderate Messenger* (May 7-15), E. 530 (5).

pacifists. He met them again on May 29, when he passed by St. George's Hill on his way to London. Finding a dozen people at work on the common, he stopped " to give them a short speech by way of admonition ". Winstanley in his reply to the General again asserted the claim of the poor to the common land and reassured Fairfax that the Diggers intended no resort to force. The incident was briefly reported by some newspapers, who dismissed it as " a businesse not worth the mentioning ". Some, however, were rather favourably impressed by the " sober answers " of Winstanley. The Diggers, commented one journal, " seemed rather to minde their work than fear an army ".[1]

But, if the Council of State was concerned with graver problems than what it conceived to be the efforts of a handful of men to cultivate a bit of barren ground, the inhabitants of Walton and Cobham recognized in the Diggers a direct challenge to their rights of private property. They met that challenge with force and ruthless violence. The grain and vegetables the Diggers attempted to plant were time and again uprooted; their tools were smashed; houses they erected were torn down. Undaunted, however, by the opposition they were encountering, the Diggers issued a second manifesto in May announcing their intention of cutting and selling the wood on the common in order to maintain themselves while they were waiting for their crops. The wood of the common, they claimed, belongs to the poor no less than the land. They warned the lords to cease carrying off the wood, and appealed to the merchants and the populace to boycott those who after stealing the wood from the common might attempt to sell it.

> " But if you will slight us in this thing, blame us not if we make stop of the carts you send and convert the woods to our own use as need requires, it being our own equal with him that calls himself the Lord of the Manor and not his peculiar right shutting us out but he shall share with us as a fellow-creature."

---

[1] *The Speeches of the Lord-General Fairfac and the officers of the armie to the Diggers at St. George's Hill in Surry and the Diggers severall answers and replies thereunto* (May 31, 1649), E. 530 (24) ; *England's Moderate Messenger* (May 28–June 4), E. 530 (27) ; *A Modest Narrative of Intelligence* (May 26–June 2), E. 557 (13) ; *A Perfect Diurnall of Some Passages in Parliament* (May 28–June 4), E. 530 (28).

F 2

"We intend ", they furthermore declare, " that not one, two or a few men of us shall sell or exchange the said woods but it shall be known publicly in print or writing to all how much every such and such parcel of wood is sold for and how it is laid out either in victualls, corn, ploughs or other materialls necessary." [1]

Winstanley, convinced that the unanswerable justice of his position would immediately be recognized by the entire nation, certainly exaggerated the interest the Diggers were arousing when he told Fairfax in a letter on June 9 that " we understand our digging on that common is the talk of the whole land ". But there were many pamphleteers, at any rate, who were quick to employ the communist venture of the Diggers to the disadvantage of the Levellers. *The Discoverer*, in a lengthy attack on the Levellers published early in June, makes no distinction between Winstanley and the Levellers. To support its accusation that the Levellers favour the abolition of private property, it quotes extensively from *The New Law of Righteousness, Light Shining in Buckinghamshire, The True Levellers Standard Advanced* and *The Declaration of the Poor Oppressed People of England*.[2] *The Discoverer* drew an immediate reply from the Levellers, in which the latter accused the author of employing unfair tactics in his attack.

---

[1] *A Declaration from the Poor Oppressed People of England directed to all that call themselves or are called Lords of Manors through this nation that have begun to cut or that through fear and covetousness do intend to cut down the Woods and Trees that grow upon the Commons and Waste Land* (June 1), E. 557 (9) (Thomason). Berens gives its date as March–April and assumes that it was published before the beginning of the St. George's Hill colony. Here again I have failed to ascertain his evidence. It is evident from the pamphlet that the Diggers had already begun to plant the land: ". . . while we labor the earth to cast in seed and to wait till the first crop comes up ". Everard's name no longer appears in the list of forty-five signatories headed by Winstanley. Thomason received his copy on June 1. There is an unmistakable reference to the manifesto in *A Modest Narrative of Intelligence* of June 9–16, E. 560 (12). The tract would therefore seem to have been written during the last weeks of May.

[2] *The Discoverer wherein is set forth (to undeceive the nation) the real plots and stratagems of Lt. Col. John Lilburne, Mr. William Walwyn, Mr. Thomas Prince, Mr. Richard Overton and that partie and their several seditious ways and wiles a long time practised by them to accomplish and effect the same* (June 2), E. 558 (2) (Thomason). An abstract of *The Discoverer* was published a few days later, in which the principles credited to the Levellers are almost all exclusively Digger arguments. *England's Discoverer or the Levellers Creed* (June 6), E. 559 (2) (Thomason) ; see also *Prince Charles ; His Message to the Parliament of Scotland* (June 11), E. 559 (9) (Thomason).

". . . to impose upon them the deviations of other men not of their party, and yet to make the world believe they are. . . . Alas how you deceive the world! They are citations out of a book none of us own, called The New Law of Righteousness. What an inference is here! A certain man to whom we have no relation has written a book wherein are many particulars, from whence you infer the deniall of a deity (and that falsely too as he will tell you) . . . the expressions cited and the books out of which they cite them are no more ours or owned by us then by them that cited them; and what dealing I pray is this to lay other men's infirmities upon our shoulders." [1]

While the Levellers were thus repudiating any association with the Diggers, the latter were continuing to suffer the fate of all social pioneers. Early in June, several infantry-men under a Captain Stravie came to St. George's Hill, attacked a man and a boy at work, seriously wounding the latter, and burned a house. Winstanley, in a letter he delivered by hand to Fairfax, protested the soldiers' action.[2] Two days later, several men attacked four Diggers on the common. The Diggers, who refused to resist, were brutally beaten; one was not expected to live. A cart in which the Diggers were carrying wood with which to rebuild their house was smashed and their horse seriously wounded.[3] Early in July, Winstanley was arrested, together with some of his fellow-Diggers, on a charge of trespassing on St. George's Hill, the property of a Mr. Drake, the Lord of the Manor and a member of Parliament, and brought to Kingston Court.[4] The Court refused to tell them

---

[1] *The Crafts-mens Craft or the Wiles of the Discoverer* (June 25), E. 561 (11).

[2] *A Letter to Lord Fairfax and his Councell of War with Divers Questions to the Lawyers and Ministers proving it an undeniable equity that the Common People ought to dig and plow and dwell upon the Commons without hiring them or paying rent to any* (June 9), E. 560 (1). The letter is reprinted in *The Harleian Miscellany*, Vol. 8, p. 586. An abridged version of Winstanley's letter, evidently a plagiarization by some Levellers, appeared a week later. Several paragraphs are copied verbatim but with all references to the Diggers omitted. Several news items follow. " The aforesaid Mr. Winstanley doth declare", it concludes, quoting the final paragraph of Winstanley's letter. *The Leveller's New Remonstrance or Declaration sent to his Excellencie The Lord General Fairfax* (June 15), E. 560 (10).

[3] *A Declaration of the bloudie and unchristian acting of William Star and John Taylor of Walton with divers men in women's apparell in opposition to those that dig upon St. George's Hill in Surrey* (June 1649), E. 561 (6).

[4] The original bill of presentment is preserved in the Public Records Office, Assizes Records, South-Eastern Circuit. Surrey, 1649, .35/90/.

the charge on which they had been arrested until they had engaged a lawyer.   Refusing to accept legal assistance, the Diggers were denied the right to plead their own case.   The Court similarly declined to read the written declaration Winstanley submitted in lieu of a plea ; and having heard only the plaintiff, the jury imposed a fine of ten pounds per person for trespassing and twenty-nine shillings and a penny each for costs.   Two days after the sentence had been passed, Bickerstaffe, one of the men arrested with Winstanley, was imprisoned for three days.   In execution of the sentence, bailiffs came to Winstanley's dwelling and drove away four cows, which strangers subsequently rescued.   Winstanley penned an eloquent appeal to the House of Commons protesting the action of the Court.[1]   But, like the plea of Fairfax, the appeal to the

---

Gerrard Winstanley, Henry Barton, Thomas Star, John Cobham, William Everard, John Palmer, Jacob Hall, William Combes, Adam Knight, Thomas Edcer, Richard Goodgreene, Henry Bickerstaffe, Richard Mudley, William Boggeral and Edward Longhurst, all described as labourers of Walton-on-Thames, are accused of having

" on April 1, 1649 by force of arms at Cobham riotously and illicitly assembled themselves and came together to the disturbance of the public peace and that the aforesaid did dig up land to the loss of the Parish of Walton and their inhabitants."

[1] *An Appeal to the House of Commons desiring their answer whether the Common People shall have the quiet enjoyment of the Commons and Waste Land ; or whether they shall be under the will of Lords of Manors still* (July 11), E. 564 (5) (Thomason).

There is an interesting item in *The Perfect Weekly Account* of July 18–25, E. 565 (28), that refers either to the presentation to the House of Winstanley's appeal or a similar petition on behalf of the Diggers :

" A petition was this day (Tues. July 24th) presented to the House by one Pelsham and divers other persons called Diggers on behalf of themselves and the rest of their friends which began the new Plantation on St. George's Hill in Surrey wherin they would be thought (though at present a despised people) instrumentall in a restoration from Adam and Noah.   In prosecution whereof they have oftentimes bin molested, their corn and roots (planted with the labour of their hands and the sweat of their brows) maliciously troden down and trampled under foot ; and last of all, three of their friends arrested at the suit of the Lord of the Soyl and bound to answer the Law, etc.   The House were upon other weighty matters when this petition was presented and therefore the Petitioners must expect to stay some time longer for an answer.

" The men seemed to bee of sober life and conversation and say their rule is to do unto others as they would be done unto.   But the grand question is whether they do not take the consequent for the matter or substance, for as man fell before the curse came so must it follow that (before the earth) man should be restored to the first estate in Adam, and propriety is butt the consequent effect of the first offence."

None of the other papers seems to have noted the incident.

House met with no response. The local people continued to destroy the Diggers' crops and to tear down their houses. In August, Winstanley was arrested a second time and fined four pounds for trespassing.

> " One of the officers of that court told a friend of mine ", he declared, " that if the Diggers cause was good he would pick out such a jurie as should overthrow him." [1]

The bailiffs again unsuccessfully attempted to drive away some cattle that a neighbour was pasturing on Winstanley's land. Five Diggers were attacked by the townspeople in the presence of the Sheriff and later carried off to prison for five weeks. Under orders from the Manor Lords, several soldiers and countrymen, on November 27 and 28, destroyed the houses the Diggers had again erected and carried off their belongings. Some of the soldiers and countrymen, Winstanley records with appreciation, performed their task with considerable reluctance; one very sympathetic soldier, in fact, left the Diggers a small sum of money. But the Diggers persisted in their efforts. Returning to St. George's Hill, they planted several acres with wheat and rye, built " little hutches like calf cribs " and declared that only starvation could deter them from their mission of making the earth " a common treasury ".

The Surrey ministers, meanwhile, were urging the people to refuse the Diggers lodging or food. The Diggers were denounced to the Council of State as Royalists, as atheists, as libertines, as polygamists. In February, Winstanley issued a brief statement denying accusations that sought to identify the Diggers with the Ranters.[2] In a postscript to the statement penned on March 4, Winstanley drew attention to the fact that several men were travelling through the country soliciting funds for the Diggers by producing a letter purporting to have been signed by himself, but which was a forged document. A Digger delegation, however, visited several counties in the spring urging the poor to emulate the example of St. George's Hill and seeking financial assistance for the little group. Their travels took them through more than thirty towns and

---

[1] *A New Yeer's Gift for the Parliament and Armie* (Jan. 1, 1650), E. 587 (6).
[2] *A Vindication of those whose endeavors is only to make the Earth a Common Treasury, Called Diggers* (Feb. 20, 1650), E. 1365 (1). The pamphlet is incorrectly dated in the Thomason Catalogue as 1649.

villages in Buckinghamshire, Surrey, Hertfordshire, Middle-
sex, Berkshire, Huntingdonshire and Northamptonshire.
Two of the original Diggers carried a letter from Winstanley
and signed by twenty-five of the Diggers declaring that,
despite all opposition, they would persist in their determination to cast off the yoke of oppression by freeing the land.
But it warned that, the summer's crop having been destroyed,
poverty and dire necessity might force the Diggers to cease
their work; and it earnestly appealed for assistance and
relief.[1]

The Digger emissaries were arrested at Wellingborough in
Northamptonshire; but in the latter town, at any rate, their
efforts met with success. In March the " poor inhabitants "
of the town announced that they had begun to dig upon the
" common and waste-ground called Bareshank ", that several
free-holders had agreed to surrender their claim to the commons and that some farmers had already offered them seed.
But the Wellingborough Diggers met with no better fate than
their Surrey comrades; for the Council of State wrote Mr.
Pentlow, the Justice of Peace for Northampton, some weeks
later commending him on the prompt measures he had taken
against the " Levellers in those parts ", and advising him to put
into immediate execution the laws " against those that intrude
upon other men's properties ".[2] Another group began similar
activity at Coxhall in Kent. In June there were serious riots
in Slimbridge and Frampton in Gloucestershire, where " rude
multitudes " were " levelling enclosures ".[3]

The parent colony at Cobham, however, was struggling
desperately for its existence. On February 23, the Council of
State wrote Fairfax of complaints that had been received from
Surrey, evidently from Cobham, that the woods were being
despoiled and ordered him to apprehend the offenders; for
such action

[1] *A Perfect Diurnall of Some Passages and Proceedings* (April 1–8, 1650),
E. 534 (25), which prints a copy of the letter and an account of the arrest
in Wellingborough.
[2] *C.S.P., Dom., 1650,* April 15, 1650, p. 106. For the Declaration of the
Wellingborough Diggers see *A Declaration of the Grounds and Reasons why we
the poor inhabitants of the town of Wellingborrow in the County of Northampton
have begun and give consent to dig up, manure and sow corn upon the Common and
Waste ground called Bareshanke belonging to the inhabitants of Wellinborrow by
those that have subscribed and hundreds more that give consent* (March 12, 1650),
669, f. 15 (21).
[3] *C.S.P., Dom., 1650,* June 27, p. 218.

". . . besides the loss, encourages the looser and disordered sort of people to the greater boldness in other designs by their impunity in this in which they have so far proceeded that they cannot be brought to justice by the ordinary course ".[1]

By the end of March the Diggers had been driven off St. George's Hill, but continued their work on a little heath near by. In a manifesto they issued, they congratulated their comrades at Wellingborough and Coxhall:

" Likewise ", they declared, " we write it as a letter of congratulation and encouragement to our dear fellow Englishmen that have begun to dig upon the commons thereby taking possession of their freedom in Wellinborrow in Northamptonshire and at Coxhall in Kent." [2]

Shortly afterwards, however, the little communist venture came to an end. A week before Easter, Parson Platt, one of the Diggers' most persistent persecutors, together with a Mr. Sutton, pulled down a house and struck a man and a woman working on the heath. Despite Platt's promise that if the Diggers cut no wood from the heath he would no longer molest them, he returned a week later with several men, set fire to the Diggers' houses, burned their furniture and scattered their belongings. The Diggers were threatened with death if they attempted to resume their activities. To prevent their return, Platt and Sutton hired several men to maintain a twenty-four hour vigil on the heath. With that, Winstanley's practical attempt to introduce communism into England seems to have come to an end. In April he addressed " An Humble Request to the Ministers of both Universities and to all Lawyers in every Inns-a-Court " detailing Platt's behaviour and publishing the written statement he had submitted to him.[3] But no further effort seems to have been made to resume the work of planting the commons.

With the collapse of his effort to introduce communism by practical example, Winstanley seems to have dedicated him-

---

[1] C.S.P., Dom., 1649–50, Feb. 9, p. 510; C.S.P. Dom., 1650, Feb. 23, p. 10.
[2] An Appeale to all Englishmen to judge between Bondage and Freedome sent from those that began to digge upon George Hill in Surrey ; but now are carrying on that publick work upon the little Heath in the Parish of Cobham (March 26, 1650), 669, f. 15 (23).
[3] April 1650. Forster Collection, Victoria and Albert Museum, South Kensington, London.

self exclusively to the task of peaceful and reasoned persuasion ; for there is no further record of his activities until the publication of *The Law of Freedom* early in 1652.[1]

---

[1] I am inclined to believe that *Fire in the Bush*, whose date has already been discussed (Chap. III, p. 148, n. 2), belongs to the months immediately after the end of the St. George's Hill venture. There is no reference whatever in the pamphlet to the Digger experiment ; but the tract would seem to be the expression of a profoundly religious man who, disappointed in the failure of practical effort, has found consolation in the realization that his experience is but the reflection of the eternal conflict between God and the Serpent, the struggle between good and evil, in which good will inevitably conquer.

Chapter Five : THE POLITICAL AND SOCIAL PHILOSOPHY OF THE DIGGER MOVEMENT

> "True Freedom lies where a man receives his nourishment and pre-servation and that is in the use of the earth."—Winstanley, *The Law of Freedom* (1652).
> "True Religion and undefiled is this, To make restitution of the Earth which hath been taken and held from the common people by the power of Conquests formerly and so set the oppressed free."—Winstanley, *A New Yeers Gift for the Parliament and the Armie* (1650).

IF the Diggers were a factor of negligible importance in the political developments of their period, they bequeathed a legacy of enduring value to political thought. For Winstanley was writing at a time when the edifice of English life was being re-shaped in a form it has largely maintained to our day. If a few contemporary thinkers quarrelled with some details of its structure, none questioned as profoundly as Winstanley the foundations on which it was being erected. The challenge he issued has lost none of its pertinence for our time; if anything, as the problems with which Winstanley, in a period of social transition, was concerned have once again become the paramount issues of the day, its significance has greatly increased during the intervening centuries.

The political philosophy of the Digger Movement found its expression in the several manifestos and declarations and the few lengthier tracts—mainly the work of Winstanley—that were issued during the course of the St. George's Hill venture and in Winstanley's last work, *The Law of Freedom*. From those writings there emerges a body of doctrine that served as a guide to action and that was in its turn modified and expanded by the practical experience its exponents encountered. It was essentially, it must be emphasized, less an integrated, doctrinal system than a series of brilliant perceptions and profound insights. But it was none the less a comprehensive social philosophy embodying an interpreta-tion of history and social development, a theory of government and law, an analysis of economic processes and a programme of social reconstruction based on that analysis.

Winstanley retained to the end his profound spirituality; and he was constantly tending to express in spiritual terms the social and material forces he was seeking to describe. The mystic and the political theorist remain, if not in actual conflict, at least in uneasy partnership with each other. The ideas of the one are constantly being clothed in the language of the other; and the profundity of his social insights is frequently obscured by the theological symbols that he employed in their description. But it must be emphasized that there was no fundamental dichotomy in Winstanley between his religious convictions and his social concepts; for both were simply different aspects of his reaction to the events and problems of his time. It is of vital importance, however, to stress that in Winstanley both the tendency of the mystic to await the intervention of the Lord and the natural detachment of the philosopher were conquered by the realism of the practical reformer.

> "My mind was not at rest", he wrote, recalling the weeks that followed the publication of *The New Law of Righteousness*, "because nothing was acted, and thoughts ran in me that words and writings were all nothing and must die, For action is the Life of all and if thou dost not act, thou dost nothing." [1]

Winstanley's attempt to translate his ideals into reality is fundamental to an understanding of his thought.

But the theological framework within which his social ideas had originally been contained gradually lost its significance and function. Ultimately, the validity of his argument rested on a foundation that was wholly secular in its nature, if primarily spiritual in its original inspiration. In his last work, his position was an almost purely materialistic one. Nature emerges as the final and ultimate reality; and social and environmental influences were seen as the paramount factors conditioning human behaviour. Both natural and social phenomena are to be explained not by external forces, but in terms of their interrelationships and by laws inherent in those processes themselves. Religion finally became for Winstanley a concept to which supernatural

[1] *A Watchword to the City of London and the Armie* (Sept. 1649), E. 573 (1).

considerations were wholly alien; it was essentially a broad radical humanitarianism concerned exclusively with human relationships rather than with any mystical communion with the supernatural. In fact, it may be said that Winstanley tended to use religion as a concept synonymous with the. class consciousness of the oppressed, with their recognition of their social rights:

> "True religion and undefiled is this, To make restitution of the Earth which hath been taken and held from the common people by the power of Conquests formerly and so set the oppressed free." [1]

God, as he had already affirmed in his earlier writings, was not a personal deity over and beyond man or a principle independent of nature and matter. The conception of a personal God or devil, of an actual heaven and hell were the psychological result of the inability to understand the nature of the physical world, the refuge of those who felt impelled to substitute fancy and imagination for the knowledge they were unable to achieve:

> " . . . it is a doctrine of a sickly and weak spirit who hath lost his understanding in the knowledge of the Creation and of the temper of his own Heart and Nature and so runs into fancies ". [2]

The idea of God to Winstanley was the expression of certain laws operating in the natural order and in human society— the principle of motion and interdependence in nature and of love, reason and justice in human affairs. Essentially, it was a description of those principles through which natural phenomena could be explained and made meaningful and on which alone an adequate social order could be erected:

> "To know the secrets of nature, is to know the works of God; And to know the works of God within the creation, is to know God himself, for God dwells in every visible work or body. And indeed if you would know spiritual things, it is to know how the Spirit or Power of Wisdom and Life, causing motion or growth, dwels within

[1] *A New Yeers Gift for the Parliament and the Armie* (Jan. 1, 1650), E. 587 (6), p. 24.
[2] *The Law of Freedom in a Platform or True Magistracy Restored* (1652), E. 655 (8), p. 60.

and governs both the several bodies of the stars and planets in the heavens above and the several bodies of the earth below as grass, plants, fishes, beasts, birds and mankinde." [1]

Knowledge of God was therefore knowledge of nature and its laws; and that knowledge could be achieved only through scientific observation.

In common with all progressive thinkers of the period, Winstanley based his political philosophy on a theory of natural law. But where others, like the Levellers, had conceived natural law as endowing every individual with a series of inalienable rights, not least among which were the right to property and the claim to political equality, Winstanley interpreted natural law as conferring on the entire community the right of free and collective access to the means of subsistence. Natural law gave to every individual the one fundamental right of sharing in common with all his fellows the ownership of the land:

" The earth with all her fruits of Corn, Cattle and such like was made to be a common Store-House of Livelihood, to all mankinde, friend and foe, without exception." [2]

It should be pointed out, however, that there was no consistent interpretation of natural law in Winstanley. In the physical world he constantly identified it with the principle of motion and growth, with that interrelationship of phenomena that operated as the principle of preservation in the natural order. In the sphere of human affairs, however, Winstanley tended to impart several meanings to the concept. We have already indicated that difficulty in our discussion of his early works. Frequently he regarded natural law as an absolute moral principle implanted by God in every human being, which enabled him to recognize right and wrong, good and evil; and much of his writing seems to testify to his belief in the existence of an absolute morality. In his later writings, however, he generally adopted the position that some of his earlier tracts had suggested—that natural law was simply a system of ethics based on social experience. The end or purpose of natural law, whether conceived as an absolute system or as the

---

[1] *Law of Freedom*, p. 58.
[2] *A Declaration from the Poor Oppressed People of England*, loc. cit.

product of experience, is, above all else, the preservation of man. For preservation is the fundamental impulse both in nature and in man. Winstanley may not have finally repudiated a belief in an absolute moral order that existed independently of man and that required no reference to human experience for its validity. It is likely, however, that those passages in his later works that suggest that belief were a residue of his earlier, mystical period. For Winstanley did not believe that man was necessarily and innately a moral creature. He rejected the view that contemporaries generally associated with the name of Hobbes:

" Now, this same power in man that causes divisions and war is called by some men the state of nature which every man brings into the world with him. . . . But this law of darknesse is not the State of Nature." [1]

Nor was man created exclusively with the attributes of an angel. The human being is largely a product of his environment; and his behaviour is primarily conditioned by the circumstances in which he lives. Natural law Winstanley defined simply as

" . . . the power of Life (called the Law of Nature within the creatures) which does move both man and beast in their actions; or that causes grass, trees, corn and all plants to grow in their several seasons; and whatsoever any body does, he does it as he is moved by this inward Law. And this Law of Nature moves twofold viz. un-rationally or rationally." [2]

But there is no innate moral sense in man that determines the operation of that law except the desire for preservation and security. Moral categories, therefore, have no validity or meaning except in reference to the preservation of man and nature. Man acts rationally if his behaviour tends to secure his preservation; he behaves irrationally if his actions frustrate that end. But men do have the ability to learn from their experiences; and it is on the basis of those experiences that morality is developed. Men may frequently consider that their preservation can be achieved only in competition with their fellows; and well-being is oft-times regarded as a function of excessive material satisfaction.

[1] *Fire in the Bush* (1650), p. 72.   [2] *Law of Freedom*, p. 78.

Men learn by bitter experience, however, that a system of social ethics based on those assumptions is a wholly inadequate one; for competition breeds strife and violence, and over-indulgence destroys physical health. " Experimentall observation ", Winstanley was convinced, would teach men that individuals can guarantee their own security and well-being only through common co-operation for the welfare of the community; and it is only on the basis of that realization that a satisfactory code of social morality can be developed. Men act rationally and in accordance with natural law—whose end is the preservation of all things— when they recognize that preservation of self is dependent on the welfare of the whole. That, I believe, was the essential meaning of the doctrine of the " inner light " that figures so prominently in Winstanley's writings. That " inner light " is kindled in man not by any supernatural revelation, but when he recognizes as a result of experience that his own preservation demands common co-operation with his fellowmen. It is potentially present within every man; for its recognition is born of a deduction from practical experience that every human being can achieve. The inner light represents the maturation of political consciousness.

Natural law, Winstanley therefore asserted, gives to every individual an equal claim to preservation—or, in other words, a common claim to the soil as the source of human sustenance. The natural state of mankind—that is, the state in which all men were aware of their fundamental interests—was a co-operative society united, like the order of nature, by the principle of common preservation. It was a society in which everything was owned in common and in which everyone was able to provide himself with the necessities of life by his own labour on the soil. Because there was no concept of ownership, there were no distinctions of rich and poor; and because everyone had free access to the means of subsistence, no one was subjected to or enslaved by his fellowman. On the whole, Winstanley regarded this view of natural society as historically authentic; and the conference of the communal right to the land was implicit in the fact of Creation. It is possible that when he had repudiated the idea of a personal creation, the state of nature became for him a purely analytical concept rather than an historical fact. Essentially, it was an assertion that every individual had a claim on nature to preservation; and that claim vested in the community of which he was a member the collective ownership of the land as the most effective method of guaranteeing that preservation to every person.

That the original state of society had been one in which common ownership had prevailed was a concept that had been widely held by philosophers since the Middle Ages. But the general deduction had been that, although common ownership might represent an ideal form of social organization, there was something innate in human nature—at any rate since the Fall—that made private property the only basis on which any form of organized social life could be established. In none of those thinkers, therefore, was there any effort to consider the methods by which that natural order could be restored. Instead, accepting man, as they knew him, as final and human nature as an unchanging and unchangeable phenomenon, they sought to construct the most adequate social system those human limitations would permit. In Winstanley, alone, do we find the profound conviction that the restoration of the natural order by the abolition of private property is a possible adventure; for human nature is primarily a product of the social conditions under which men have been living and constitutes no insuperable barrier to fundamental change:

> ". . . I am assured that if it be rightly searched into the inward bondage of the minds as covetousnesse, pride, hypocrisie, envy, sorrow, fears, desperation, and madness are all occasioned by the outward bondage that one sort of people lay upon another." [1]

Common ownership of the land was for Winstanley the basis of individual freedom and social equality. Freedom, he insisted, could not be defined in terms of specific rights or privileges, as exemption from certain restrictions or in its application to particular groups and classes; for that would be to place too narrow and limited a definition on the concept. For Winstanley, its essence lay, above all else, in the establishment of those social conditions that would permit the free and adequate development of every individual. Freedom became a function not of particular political institutions or rights, but of the fundamental nature of the social order. And its basis

[1] *Law of Freedom*, p. 18.

was the guarantee to every individual of an adequate minimum of material satisfaction. Man, Winstanley realized, did not live by bread alone; but without bread there could be no life:

> ". . . better not to have a body than not to have food and rayment for it ". [1]

Freedom could therefore have meaning only in a social order that enabled everyone freely to enjoy the necessities of life:

> " True freedom lies where a man receives his nourishment and preservation, and that is in the use of the Earth." [2]

For it is under those conditions alone that spiritual and cultural development becomes possible:

> ". . . when men are sure of food and raiment, their reason will be ripe, and ready to dive into the secrets of the Creation that they may learn to see and know God ".[3]

For Winstanley, writing at a time when land was still able to provide the essential items of an adequate standard of living, access to the soil became the essential condition of freedom and liberty.

But freedom, he saw, could have no meaning unless it was set in the context of equality. To grant that freedom to some and to deny it to others was to admit inequality to the heart of the State, by positing the inadmissible assumption that some men had a superior claim to preservation. To grant access to the soil unequally meant, furthermore, to open the door to the ultimate denial of freedom and the possibility of preservation to vast masses of the people. For unequal privilege would mean an unequal interest in its maintenance. Personal interest in the maintenance of that inequality would take precedence over a general concern for the common welfare. It would place in the hands of the privileged the temptation and the power to exclude others from the land, and thus to force them into slavery and bondage. Freedom, based on the provision to every individual of the necessities of life, could be adequately secured only in a social system where that freedom was equally enjoyed. For Winstanley, that fact implied a

---

[1] *New Yeers Gift*, p. 21.   [2] *Law of Freedom*, p. 17.   [3] Ibid, p. 71.

common and equal claim of every individual to till the soil and to wrest from nature his material sustenance—in other words, a system in which the land, as the basic means of subsistence, was commonly owned. To declare, therefore, as with one recent writer,[1] that the Diggers belong to the history of equality rather than to that of liberty is to overlook one of Winstanley's most profound perceptions; for, to him, both ideals were vitally interdependent. More than any other thinker of the period, he saw that liberty could be made an effective reality only if it were firmly rooted in equality, and that the common condition of their realization was the establishment of an adequate material basis in which they could thrive.

The original state of common ownership was ended by the introduction of private property in land. Generally, Winstanley ascribed the origin of private property to force. Some men, impelled by greed and covetousness, convinced that their security demanded that they take advantage of their fellows, began to convert what had hitherto been common into their personal possession by enclosing the land:

> ". . . the power of inclosing Land and owning Propriety was brought into the Creation by your ancestors by the Sword which first did murther their fellow-creatures men and after plunder or steal away their land ".[2]

Men came to own unequally, and some not at all; and from that fact emerged the phenomenon of social division. As increasing numbers were excluded from the soil, they learned that they could maintain their existence only by working for wages for those who were now in exclusive possession of the land, particularly for those who had enclosed a larger area than they were themselves able to cultivate. A fundamental distinction was thus created between those who lived by virtue of their ownership of land and those who were able to subsist only by the sale of their labour-power; and the latter became completely dependent on the former. Men lost the liberty they had enjoyed by virtue of their ability freely to provide themselves with the necessities of life. They similarly lost the equality that had derived as a result of the possession of that liberty by the entire community. Social equality based on

[1] Woodhouse, op. cit., Introduction, p. 99.
[2] *A Declaration from the Poor Oppressed People, etc.*

common ownership was superseded by social division rooted in the private possession of the soil.

With the divorce of masses of people from the land and their conversion into landless wage-labourers, exploitation became the motif of social relationships. The propertyless were forced by dire necessity to work for a mere pittance; and the landlords, by appropriating the surplus the labourers produced over and above the wages they received, increased both their wealth and their power:

> " They have by their subtle imagination and covetous wit got the plain-hearted poor or younger brethren to work for them for small wages and by their work have got a great increase." [1]

Winstanley thus clearly perceived that the separation of the people from the land was the basis of modern economic development. He failed to give that perception the sophisticated expression it was to receive from later economists; but it was a perception that was none the less central to his entire doctrine. Enclosure, as he saw, created on the one hand a mass of landless labourers who, because they could exist only by selling their labour-power, were enslaved to the owners of property. It produced, on the other, greater wealth for the landlords, who were able to live solely by their exploitation of others. With their wealth they were able to engage in the sale and purchase of land; and by their superior skill in the art of trickery, they were able to enlarge their estates at the expense of less unscrupulous owners. Winstanley failed to appreciate the significance of the new commercial and industrial development. He recognized, it is true, that the increase of wealth enabled the new commercial and industrial classes to acquire landed estates:

> " By large pay, much Free-Quarter and other Booties which they call their own they get much Monies and with this they buy Land." [2]

But he saw the new commercial development as an unnecessary excrescence on the agricultural economy of the country. His denunciation of the practice of " buying and selling " and

---

[1] *The True Levellers Standard Advanced*, E. 552 (5).
[2] *True Levellers Standard*.

his insistence on its prohibition partly reflect his own unhappy business experience. It suggests as well that in the communal order he envisaged need would be the sole criterion governing the distribution of products. But it indicates his failure to recognize that the expanding commercialism was establishing a set of social relationships no less important than those that were based on the land, that industrialism was creating an economy whose relationship to the soil was far less fundamental than he was prepared to admit and that both commercial and industrial developments were creating new forms of economic power that were entirely divorced from the ownership of land. That he did not appreciate the importance of those facts, however, in no way lessened the significance of his perception that the basis of those developments was the expulsion of the peasantry from their lands.

Essentially, then, Winstanley was affirming that the rich could justify their claim neither to their land nor their wealth. Their land had originally been acquired by force and murder. In selling or exchanging it, they were transacting business with that of which they had no right to dispose; for the land is collectively the property of the entire community. Nor is their title to their wealth more valid; for their fortunes were created only by virtue of their unlawful possession of the soil. Furthermore, Winstanley declared, a man can claim as his own only that which he has produced with his own labour and effort. But the wealth of the rich is created wholly by the efforts of their labourers; and to that surplus product the landlords have no legitimate title:

> "No man can be rich, but he must be rich, either by his own labors, or the labors of other men helping him: If a man have no help from his neighbor, he shall never gather an Estate of hundreds and thousands a year: If other men help him to work, then are those Riches his Neighbors, as well as his own; For they be the fruit of other mens labors as well as his own. But all rich men live at ease, feeding and clothing themselves by the labor of other men and not by their own; which is their shame and not their Nobility: for it is a more blessed thing to give than to receive. But rich men receive all they have from the laborers hand, and what they give, they give away other mens labors not their own." [1]

[1] *Law of Freedom*, p. 12.

Thus, at a time when the middle classes, through Puritanism, were attempting to rationalize their accumulation of capital by insisting that not the possession of riches but the methods in which they were gained and the manner in which they were spent were the moral criteria by which economic activity was to be judged, Winstanley was arguing that the very possession of wealth was in itself inevitably illegitimate. And that affirmation derived not from any ascetic renunciation of material goods, but from the realization that the whole process of the acquisition of wealth was based on robbing the labourers of that which their work had produced.

The private ownership of the means of subsistence is, for Winstanley, the fundamental fact of social life. It is the key to the understanding of history; and on the foundation of the social relationships that the system of private ownership creates is reared the superstructure of government and law, of religion and education. For private ownership created private interests; and the security of those individual interests became men's prime concern. Luxury enjoyed without labour bred the desire for its own perpetuation and expansion; and the satisfying experience of power over one's fellows impelled men to seek its extension. Because the maintenance of property, of wealth and of power required the continued exploitation and impoverishment of the propertyless, the positions that had been won by the sword had to be maintained by the sword. Economic power was the avenue to political domination; and those who by their ownership of the land controlled the fate of their fellow-men soon achieved the ability to shape political and social institutions to their own ends and purposes:

"... if once landlords, then they rise to be Justices, Rulers and State Governours as experience shewes ".[1]

Social organization in the communal society of the natural order was dedicated, declared Winstanley, to the welfare of all; government in a system of private ownership is simply an agency for the protection of property. Government, he asserted, was not a neutral agency, impartially arbitrating between conflicting claims. It was essentially a set of institutions that was designed by the men of property to safeguard their interests and whose operation was determined

[1] *True Levellers Standard.*

and limited by their purposes. Because the government of
the wealthy rested on the exclusion of the common people
from their rightful access to the soil, it could exact no moral
claim to obedience; and its security and authority were wholly
a function of the force it could command. Government and
State power were thus, in Winstanley's view, that exercise
of force by which the owners of property maintained their
privileged position. It was, if we may borrow a modern
phrase, simply supreme coercive power:

> ". . . the power of the murdering and theeving sword
> formerly as well as now of late years hath set up a govern-
> ment and maintains that government; for what are prisons
> and putting others to death, but the power of the Sword
> to enforce people to that Government which was got by
> Conquest and sword and cannot stand of itself but by the
> same murdering power ".[1]

It was on that foundation, as well, that Winstanley rested
his definition of law. Law in a society divided into rich and
poor, he claimed, was something more than a series of formal
rules regulating social relationships. It was a body of regulations that sought to fulfil the purpose of government; and its
substance was predominantly determined by the nature of
those purposes. The ends it would seek to realize would
always be largely those of the people who exercised effectively
the power to declare the law. In a society based on the
private ownership of land and the unequal enjoyment of
privilege, the function of law became the preservation of the
existing property relationships and the protection of privilege:

> ". . . the Kingly power sets up a Law and Rule of Govern-
> ment to walk by; and here Justice is pretended but the
> full strength of the Law is to uphold the conquering Sword
> and to preserve his son Propriety. . . . For though they
> say the Law doth punish yet indeed the Law is but the
> strength, life and marrow of the Kingly power upholding
> the Conquest still, hedging some into the Earth, hedging
> out others; giving the Earth to some and denying the Earth
> to others which is contrary to the Law of Righteousnesse
> who made the Earth at first as free for one as for another.
> . . . Truly most Laws are but to enslave the Poor to the

[1] *Declaration from the Poor Oppressed, etc.*

Rich and so they uphold the Conquest and are Laws of the great Red Dragons." [1]

But government could not continue to rest solely on naked coercion. Stable and secure rule demanded that at some point the processes of coercion be translated into passive acquiescence. To a considerable degree that process was fostered and accelerated by the social system itself. The mere fact of their slavery induced in the people a sense of their own inferiority. At the same time, it bred in those who ruled a conviction of innate superiority. Gradually, men came to accept their inherited status in the social order as natural and preordained. The ruling classes had been destined by God to command; the common people equally had been fated to serve. Social division thus

> ". . . forces one part of the Creation man to be a slave to another, and thereby the spirit is killed in both. The one looks upon himself as a teacher and ruler and so is lifted up in pride over his fellow-creatures. The other looks upon himself as imperfect and so is dejected in his spirit and looks upon his fellow creature of his own image as a Lord above him." [2]

To encourage that submission by lending to the social system the sanction of ecclesiastical approval had been the prime and traditional function of organized religion. The clergy was established to teach the people the virtue of unquestioning acceptance of their lot, of resignation to one's status in life as the inscrutable will of the Almighty. Those who cast doubt on the moral validity of the existing order were confused and misled by the priests:

> " If any poor enslaved man that dares not steal, begins to mourn under that bondage and saith, We that work most have least comfort in the earth and they that work not at all enjoy all contrary to the Scripture which saith the poor and the meek shall inherit the earth. Presently the tithing priest stops his mouth with a slam and tels him that is meant of the inward satisfaction of mind which the poor shall have, though they enjoy nothing at all." [3]

---

[1] *New Yeers Gift*, pp. 39–40.   [2] *True Levellers Standard.*
[3] *New Yeers Gift*, pp. 40–1.

The poor were consoled by the assurance that they would find compensation for their suffering and misery in the dazzling heaven they were certain to occupy; and the fear and insecurity that were the inevitable accompaniment of their poverty predisposed the people to an acceptance of those teachings. The Church thus shifted the emphasis of religion from a consideration of man's status on earth and converted it into a fantastic other-worldly doctrine remote from the realities of daily life. The minds of men were diverted from a consideration of a sordid reality against which they might have been moved to revolt to a contemplation of a chimerical paradise which they were counselled to await with patience and resignation:

> ". . . this divining spiritual Doctrine is a cheat; for while men are gazing up to Heaven imagining after a happiness, or fearing a Hell after they are dead, their eyes are put out; That they see not what is their birthrights, and what is to be done by them here on Earth, while they are living ".[1]

Religion, Winstanley protested, had thus served as one of the most important bulwarks of the existing order. His intense and bitter anti-clericalism is a theme he introduces into every one of his pamphlets; and it was certainly not moderated by the violent antagonism the Digger experiment in Surrey provoked from the clergy. The clergy, he constantly repeated, were repudiating by their actions all the fundamental precepts of a Christianity in which they professed to believe. They had become a distinct social group with a vested interest in the maintenance of the prevailing social system. They were rewarded for the not inconsiderable services they had rendered the owners of property by the grant of tithes; and they had been so corrupted by their function that they are now prepared to serve any master who bids for their services:

> " And do we not yet see ", Winstanley asks, " that if the Clergie can get Tithes or Money they will turn as the Ruling power turns, any way . . . to Papacy, to Protestantisme; for a King, against a King; for monarchy, for State Government; they cry who bids most wages, they will be on the strongest side for an earthly maintenance." [2]

---

[1] *Law of Freedom*, p. 62. [2] *New Yeers Gift*, p. 6.

Because they are dependent for their income on the ruling classes, they must always be subservient to those in power:

". . . there is a confederacie between the Clergy and the great red Dragon. The sheep of Christ shall never fare well so long as the wolf or red Dragon payes the Shepherd their wages." [1]

No less important than the influence of the property system on religion had been its effect on education and knowledge. A system that rested on a denial to men of their social rights must, because of its very essence, discourage independent thought and study lest people become aware of the claims they can legitimately make on society. Scientific research in such circumstances could not be a disinterested quest for truth, for its frontiers were fixed by the interests of property:

". . . this Kingly Bondage is the cause of the spreading of ignorance in the Earth ". [2]

The poverty and insecurity that were of the essence of the social order, had more than anything else retarded the progress of scientific study and experiment:

". . . for fear of want and care to pay Rent to Taskmasters hath hindered many rare Inventions ". [3]

The clergy, whose power derived largely from their monopoly of education, attempted to prevent the spread of popular instruction lest their own ignorance and hypocrisy be revealed. And by their insistence that knowledge was identical with tradition and that experiment and observation were no avenues to understanding, they had erected a most formidable barrier against scientific progress:

" ' I ', but saith the Elder Brother, ' You must not trust to your own Reason and Understanding, but you must beleeve what is written and what is told you. . . .' " [4]

As a result

". . . the secrets of creation have been locked up under the traditional parrot like speaking from the Universities and Colleges for Scholars ". [5]

---

[1] *New Yeers Gift*, p. 39. [2] *Law of Freedom*, p. 57.
[3] Ibid., p. 71. [4] Ibid., p. 61.
[5] *Declaration from the Poor Oppressed People, etc.*

The institution of private property and the social groups that derive from its existence were, for Winstanley, the major clues to the explanation of history.   The story of the human race is largely a sordid record of violence and social strife; and those conflicts are born of the struggle for the mastery of the land and the power it confers.   More then a century before Madison was to write that property is the only durable source of faction, Winstanley had declared that

> " particular propriety . . . is the cause of all wars, bloodshed, theft and enslaving laws that hold the people under miserie ".[1]

> " Wherefore is it ", he asked, " that there is such wars and rumours of wars in the nations of the Earth? and wherefore are men so mad as destroy one another?   But only to uphold Civil Propriety of Honor, Dominion, and Riches one over another which is the curse the Creation groans under waiting for deliverance." [2]

For private property dissolves a general concern in the corporate well-being by creating a series of unequal and private interests; and from the existence of those separate interests faction and conflict inevitably emerge:

> " Propriety and single interest divides the people of a land and the whole world into parties and is the cause of all wars and bloodshed and contention everywhere." [2]

Wealth habituates men to the enjoyment of luxury.   It creates a craving for its extension.   It breeds a restless jealousy of those who enjoy similar or greater privileges.   Because property confers on its owners the power to dominate their fellow-men, it inevitably fosters the struggle among those who wield that power for exclusive and supreme mastery. It sets up a fundamental distinction between those who own and those who are excluded from ownership.   The propertyless cannot fail to observe that comfort and well-being are directly a function of the possession of land; and they are impelled by sheer desperation to challenge for its ownership:

> " Indeed the Government of Kings is a breeder of Wars ", declared Winstanley, " because men being put into the

---

[1] *Declaration from the Poor Oppressed People, etc.*
[2] *True Levellers Standard.*

G

straits of poverty are moved to fight for Liberty, and to take one anothers Estates from them, and to obtain mastery." [1]

Social strife is therefore a result of the division between rich and poor that is rooted in the private ownership of the means of subsistence; and wars are always in the final analysis contests for that economic superiority that is the key to power and luxury. No war, Winstanley asserts, has ever brought freedom to the common people. For all wars are fought by particular interests for their own advantage. Wars have achieved changes of masters; they have never succeeded in abolishing slavery. That, he insists, is clearly the testimony of history:

> " Look into all Armies ", he urges, " and see what they do more but make some poor, some rich; put some into freedom, and others into bondage; and is not this a plague among Mankinde? " [1]
> " This is the fruit of War from the beginning, for it removes Propriety out of a weaker into a stronger hand but still upholds the curse of Bondage." [2]

It was on the basis of that analysis of social development that Winstanley interpreted the general course of English history. He made no attempt, it should be emphasized, at a detailed examination of its content; but its major outlines, he asserted, had been traced by the development of private property.

Private property was introduced into England by the Conquest when William parcelled out the land to his followers who set themselves up as Manor Lords. Government was established to maintain the rule of the monarchy and the landlords. A legal system was created to crystallize the social relationships that had been established and to confirm the lords in the possession of their estates. To confuse and enslave the common people, the laws were rendered complicated and involved. They were written in a foreign language so that their administration could remain the monopoly of those who were privileged to enjoy special training. There thus came into existence a class of lawyers

---

[1] *Law of Freedom*, p. 14.　　　[2] *New Yeers Gift*, p. 4.

whose function was the maintenance of the *status quo* and whose prosperity increased with the complexity of the legal system and the delays they introduced into the administration of justice. The clergy was set up to lull the people into an acceptance of the new order by preaching its sanctity. Through the institution of tithes, the priests were given a vested interest in the maintenance of the system; and by exacting payment from the poor, they themselves became directly oppressors of the people.

All subsequent English history was the record of the enslavement of the people inaugurated by the Conquest. Divorced from the land, most of the people became the bondsmen of the landlords. The kings who succeeded William were the heirs of the Conquest; and their claim to obedience rested solely on the use of force. The original title of the lords to their land was unlawful because the soil was rightfully the possession of the entire people. Nor can they now argue their right of possession by virtue of the charters they hold; for those documents were issued in the name of kings who exercised a usurped and illegal authority.

The common people were therefore oppressed by a political system that vested power in the person of the King, by a legal fabric administered by unscrupulous lawyers and by a corrupt clergy. That structure of oppression was founded on the private ownership of the land and the exclusion of the masses of the people from access to the soil.

Frequently there were contests for power between various sections of the ruling classes themselves. In every instance the brunt of those wars had been borne by the common people who were impoverished by the conflict and who were rewarded for their sacrifice by a change in the person of the tyrant. That was for Winstanley the essential meaning of the Civil War. More than any of his contemporaries, he was able to pierce through to the central significance of the developments of his period and to perceive, with remarkable clarity, that the Civil War had been above all else a struggle for economic and political supremacy between the monarchy and the rising gentry whose development the monarchy had retarded. To aid them in the prosecution of the war, the gentry had enlisted the assistance of the common people by promising them their freedom from oppression. The victory of the gentry had been rendered possible largely through the sacrifice of life and money by the people. With the overthrow of the monarchy and their accession to power, the gentry had achieved their victory. But the common people remained in bondage; for the essence of tyranny, the private ownership of land, remained unimpaired:

> "While this Kingly power reigned in one man called Charls", Winstanley declared, "all sorts of people complained of oppression, both Gentrie and Common People, because their lands, Inclosures and Copieholds were intangled and because their Trades were destroyed by Monopolizing Patentees and your troubles were that you could not live free from oppression in the earth. Thereupon you that w   rie when you were assembled in Parliament, y   on the poor Common People to come and he   cast out oppression and you that complained   nd freed and that top bow is lopped off the tr   ie, and Kingly power in that one particular is   ut alas oppression is a great tree still, and kee   un of freedome from the poore commons still, he hath many branches and great roots which must be grub'd up before everyone can sing Sions songs in peace." [1]

If the abolition of the monarchy were to be the only result of the Civil War, then the people had shed their blood in vain. For their slavery was to be attributed to no particular individual or political institution; it was of the very essence of the social system under which they lived. The mere removal of Charles was therefore in itself of minimal significance:

> "for the King's power lies in his law, not in his person".[2]

Whatever freedom it might be argued the common people had gained by the War was superficial and illusory; for the poor could not be free until they had the opportunity to till the soil. The freedom they had been promised by Parliament and for which they had fought could be achieved only by fundamental social change that would witness the abolition of private property and the restoration of the common ownership of the land:

[1] *New Yeers Gift*, pp. 5–6.   [2] *Law of Freedom.*

" We know that England cannot be a free commonwealth unless all the poor commoners have a free use and benefit of the land; for if this freedom be not granted we that are the poore commoners are in a worse case than we were in the King's days, for then we had some estate about us though we were under oppression but now we are under oppression still of Lords of Mannors tyranny." [1]

That recognition that the Civil War would have meaning only if it were to result in a reshaping of the economic foundations of the country was spreading among the common people, Winstanley told both Parliament and Fairfax. The desperate poverty of the people was impressing on them the fact that their slavery was directly the result of the economic order and that the luxury of the rich was built on the destitution of the poor:

" Now saith the whisperings of the people, The inferior Tenants and Laborers bears all the burdens in laboring the Earth, in paying taxes and freequarter beyond their strength and in furnishing the Armies with Souldiers, who bear the greatest burden of the War, and yet the Gentry who oppress them and that live idle upon their Labors carry away all the comfortable livelyhood of the Earth . . . and is not this slavery, say the People. That though there be Land enough in England to maintain ten times as many people as are in it, yet some must beg of their brethren or work in hard drudgery for day wages for them, or starve or steal, and so be hanged out of the way as men not fit to live in the earth . . .? " [2]

That complaint, he warned them, would become even more serious if Parliament persisted in its refusal to free the people by freeing the land:

". . . for then it will appear to the view of all men that you cut off the King's head that you might establish your-selves in his chair of government and that your aym was not to throw down tyranny but the tyrant ". [3]

What more than anything else, I believe, distinguishes Winstanley among the forerunners of modern socialism is his

[1] Letter from Winstanley to Fairfax, Dec. 1649, *Clarke Papers*, Vol. II, p. 217.
[2] *Law of Freedom*, pp. 8–9.   [3] *An Appeal to the House of Commons*.

profound concern with the methods by which the communist order is to be achieved. The vision of a collectivist society as the only adequate solution to the social problem is shared throughout history by many thinkers. But until the nineteenth century, certainly until Babeuf, few of those thinkers appreciated the problems its establishment involved or boldly confronted the practical tasks its achievement implied. Where they were aware of those difficulties, they despaired of their solution; and their communist societies were utopias set in another and distant world. Only God, by effecting a change in the hearts of men, could bring down those utopias from the realms of fancy to the actuality of daily life. In Winstanley there is at once a keen perception of the problems that fundamental social change involves, a consideration of the methods by which it can be instituted and the optimistic conviction that the task is not beyond the limits of human possibility. The methods, he urged, it is of course true, were conceived in terms too simple to permit of effective application in a society of even the degree of complexity that seventeenth-century England had attained. Certainly, he overestimated the strength of the objective forces making for the type of society he envisaged. In the mere fact of his application to the problems of method, however, he had reached a position considerably more advanced than that which other socialist pioneers were to achieve in the following 150 years.

One cannot claim for Winstanley a completely consistent or detailed conception of those methods. His writings reveal the profound dilemma in which he was caught by his own ideas. Logically, he had already concluded, even before his practical experience at St. George's, that men will seldom voluntarily relinquish the privileges they enjoy.[1] But he shrank from pushing that perception to its logical, practical conclusion. A profound pacificism dominates his later, no less than his earlier [1] writings. That pacificism, I should remark in passing, is not an absolute doctrine; for in *The Law of Freedom* he reversed an earlier position he had expressed in *The New Law of Righteousness*, indeed as late as March 1650 in his *Appeal to all Englishmen*, by recommending capital punishment for certain offences. It is not unlikely that the numerical weakness of the Diggers played some part in shaping his views on the use of

[1] *Supra*, Chap. III.

force; but I do not believe it to have been a decisive factor. Throughout, Winstanley condemned violence as a method of effecting social change:

> " We abhor fighting for freedom ", he declared, " it is acting of the curse and lifting him up higher. . . . Freedom gotten by the Sword is an established bondage to some part or other of the Creation. . . . Victory that is gotten by the Sword is a victory that slaves get one over another." [1]

In every one of his writings he constantly expressed the hope that the spirit of love would ultimately triumph in all men by virtue of its own power and strength. Together with many of his contemporaries, he shared an increasing faith in the efficacy of rational persuasion. His manifestos and tracts were primarily reasoned appeals to Parliament, to the Army, to Cromwell, to the lawyers, to the clergy, to the general populace, seeking to convince them by argument of the justice of his claims:

> " The cause of this our Presentment to you ", his *Appeal to the House of Commons* began, " is an Appeal to you desiring you to demonstrate to us and the whole Land the equity or not equity of our cause." [2]

But it is nevertheless true to say, I believe, that the essence of his doctrine was his realization that social change had to be initiated neither by the spirit of love nor by the force of reason, but only through the direct action of politically-conscious individuals. If that recognition is not explicit in his utterances, it is certainly implicit in his practical activities. The claim of the poor to the common lands that is the burden of his political manifestos derives directly from his realization that the ideal communal society would be established through no sudden miracle, but only through several preliminary stages. Common ownership was for Winstanley the ultimate end of social effort; the co-operative cultivation of the commons by the poor was the first stage in its achievement.

Thus, while Winstanley was convinced that common ownership would benefit all classes in society, he felt that the initiative for changing the existing order had to come primarily from those propertyless classes whose position had forced on them

---

[1] *New Yeers Gift*, p. 29.   [2] *An Appeal to the House of Commons.*

the realization that their freedom demanded the abolition of private property; and it was in those classes that Winstanley saw the first awareness of the necessity for that fundamental change:

> " I see ", he declared, " that the poore must first be picked out and honoured in this work, for they begin to receive the word of righteousnesse but the rich generally are enemies to true freedome." [1]

In urging that the progress of mankind towards a better social order could come, in the first instance, only through the action of the propertyless classes in effecting their own emancipation, Winstanley was definitely the spokesman of a class rather than of all of humanity. Undoubtedly, the failure of the Leveller Movement impressed on Winstanley the futility of relying solely on argument to bring about social reform. But the necessity for direct action by the propertyless classes was a conclusion that flowed logically from the premises on which his social philosophy was based. That perception becomes all the more remarkable when we realize that Winstanley was writing at a time when an industrial proletariat in the modern sense of the term hardly existed and when even the problem of the landless peasantry had not assumed the proportions it was to reach in the following century.

These two themes, then, run through Winstanley's writings —the argument for common ownership as the only adequate form of social organization and the development of the waste and common lands by the poor as the means by which it was to be achieved. Some of Winstanley's writings—*An Appeal to the House of Commons*, for example—are exclusively concerned with the claim to the commons. Others, like *The Law of Freedom*, are dedicated to a discussion of the communal organization of society. In others little attempt is made to distinguish the ultimate ideal from the means by which it is to be effected. On the whole, however, Winstanley rested his case for common ownership on an appeal to natural law and a theoretical analysis of its superiority as a system of social organization in terms of the benefits it would confer; the claim to the commons was urged on more immediate and practical considerations.

By the cultivation of the commons, Winstanley constantly

---

[1] *Watchword to the City of London.*

emphasized, he intended no direct attack on the existing system of property rights. It was, the Diggers admitted frankly enough, their first stage in the abolition of private property. They dug on the commons, they declared, so

> ". . . that we may work in Righteousness and lay the foundation of making the Earth a Common Treasury for all, both rich and poor ". [1]

But it was a stage that could be accomplished within the framework of the existing order and with no prejudice to the landlords. By demanding recognition of the right of the poor to the commons, they were simply asking that

> ". . . the freeholders have their freedom to work quietly in their inclosures and let the common people have their commons and waste lands quiet to themselves ".[2]

Moreover, as Winstanley was to argue, even the landlords would benefit immeasurably from the scheme:

> " We digg upon the Common to make the Earth a Common Treasury because our necessity for food and raiment require it." [3]

Natural law, the Scriptures, the law of righteousness, they repeatedly insist, give to every person a claim to share in the fruits of the earth in order to preserve his own life.

> " The Earth was made by Almighty God to be a Common Treasury of Livelihood to the whole of mankind in all its branches, without respect of persons." [4]

But their title to the commons could be justified entirely on the assumptions of the existing system. For, just as the landlords claimed the enclosures as their private possessions, the commons were undeniably the collective possession of the poor. It was as illegal under the law of the land to exclude the poor from access to the commons as to deny the landlords their title to their estates:

---

[1] *True Levellers Standard.*
[2] *Appeal to the House of Commons.*
[3] " To His Excellency Lord Fairfax and the Counsell of Warre, the Brotherly Request of those that are called Diggers " (Dec. 1649), *Clarke Papers*, Vol. II, p. 215.
[4] *Watchword.*

G 2

"This Common Land now is as freely the common peoples as you can say the Inclosures are your propriety." [1]

That claim had been immeasurably strengthened by the events of the war and the victory over the King. For the victory that had been achieved had been won jointly by Parliament and the people. If anything, the contribution of the common people to the triumph over Charles had been the more important of the two:

"All sorts have assisted you in person and purse and the common people especially seeing their estates were weakest and their misery in the wars the greatest." [1]

The partnership in victory must therefore imply an equal sharing of its results:

"All sorts of people have lent assistance of purse and person to cast out the kingly order as being a burden that England groaned under. Therefore, those from whom money and blood were received, ought to obtain freedom in the Land to themselves and posterity, by the Law of Contract between Parliament and People. But all sorts, poor as well as rich, Tenant as well as the Land Lord, have paid taxes, free-quarter, excise, or adventured their lives to cast out the kingly office. Therefore all sorts of people ought to have freedom in this the Land of Nativity without respecting persons, now that kingly power is cast out by their joynt assistance." [2]

If Parliament continues to refuse that freedom to the common people, it will be repudiating every solemn pledge it made to the people and on the strength of which alone the latter undertook to support the war:

"You called upon us to assist you with plate, taxes, free-quarter and our persons and you promised us in the name of the Almighty, to make us a free people. Thereupon you and we took the National Covenant with joynt consent to endeavour the freedom, peace and safety of the people of England." [1]

[1] *An Appeal to the House of Commons.*
[2] *Watchword.*

Furthermore, Winstanley argued, Parliament was obligated by its own acts to free the land for common use. For it had passed legislation abolishing the monarchy and declaring England a commonwealth. The abolition of the monarchy meant that all charters and grants that had been held in the name of the King and by which the landlords and the priests justified their power were rendered null and void. The land, therefore, automatically reverted to its former owners, the common people. For the abolition of kingly power did not mean solely the removal of the person of the monarch; it must effectively mean the end of all the laws and institutions that the Conquest had introduced. The death of Charles had to undo all the work of William. Similarly, the act declaring England a free commonwealth bound Parliament— if the Act were to have any meaning at all—to establish those conditions under which alone freedom could be effectively guaranteed; and that, Winstanley asserted, meant freedom of access to the land for every individual.

The cultivation of the commons, Winstanley was convinced, would confer vast social and economic benefits on the country. It would inaugurate a period of unparalleled prosperity in which every section of the populace would share. Valuable unused economic resources would be rescued from neglect and deterioration.

> " The common lands hath laid unmanured all the date of his Kingly and Lordly power over you, by reason whereof both you and your fathers (many of you) have been burthened with poverty. And that land which would have been fruitful with corn, hath brought forth nothing but heath, moss, turfeys, and the curse. . . ." [1]

Poverty and unemployment would be eliminated, for there was ample waste and common land in England on which every poor and unemployed person could work to provide himself with the necessities of life.

> " By this means, within a short time, there will be no beggar or idle person in England." [1]

The increase in production would effect a reduction of the

[1] *An Appeal to all Englishmen to judge between bondage and Freedome* (March 1650), 669, f. 15 (23).

excessive prices which had so seriously oppressed the people
since the beginning of the war:

> " The waste and common land being improved will bring
> in plenty of all commodities, and prevent famine, and pull
> down the price of corn to 12d. a bushel or less." [1]

Robert Coster, one of the Digger pamphleteers, expressed
the opinion that the increase in the area under cultivation
would help to reduce the price of land and thereby the price
of agricultural commodities.

> " If poor men which want employment and others which
> work for little wages would go to dress and improve the
> commons and Waste Lands, whether it would not bring
> down the price of Land which doth principally cause all
> things to be dear? " [2]

No less important than the economic advantages that would
result from the development of the commons were the social
benefits the country would enjoy. Crime, largely the product
of economic distress, would be materially reduced.

> " This freedom in planting the common land will prevent
> robbing, and stealing and murdering and prisons will not
> so mightily be filled with prisoners." [1]

The occupation of the commons would not threaten the
stability of the existing social order; on the contrary, it would
enable landlords to enjoy their estates in greater security. For
general prosperity and the provision of an adequate standard
of living to the poor would reduce social tension and considerably lessen the antagonism that now exists between the
rich and poor:

> " Now sir," Winstanley told Fairfax, " if you and the
> Council will quietly grant us this freedom, which is our
> own right, and set us free from the kingly power of the
> Lords of the Manors, that violently now as in the King's
> days hold the commons from us (as if we had obtained no
> conquest at all over the Kingly power) then the poor that
> lie under the great burden of poverty, and are always

[1] *An Appeal to all Englishmen.*
[2] Robert Coster, *A Mite Cast into the Common Treasury* (Dec. 18, 1649),
E. 585 (4).

complaining for want, and their miseries increase because they see no means of relief found out, and therefore cry out continually to you and the Parliament for relief, and to make good your promises, will be quieted. . . . If this freedom were granted to improve the commons lands, then there would be a supply to answer everyone's inquire, and the murmurings of the people against you and the Parliament would cease. . . ." [1]

National unity would be immeasurably strengthened and the security of the nation effectively assured; for if everyone were to have an equal interest in the results of the operation of the State, there would similarly be an equal interest in its defence:

" This Commonwealth Freedom will unite the hearts of Englishmen together in love; so that if a foreign enemy endeavour to come in, we shall all with joint consent rise up together to defend our inheritance, and shall be true one to another. Whereas now the poor see if they fight and should conquer the enemy, yet either they or their children are like to be slaves still, for the gentry will have all. And this is the cause why many run away and fail our Armies in time of need. And so through the Gentry's hardness of heart against the Poor the Land may be left to a foreign enemy for want of the Poor's love in sticking to them. For, say they, we can as well live under a foreign enemy, working for day wages as under our own brethren, with whome we ought to have equal freedom by the Law of Righteousness." [2]

Finally, declared Winstanley, England would enjoy the honour of being the first country in the world to establish an enlightened social order and to translate the principles of Christ into an effective and living reality in terms of a progressive and just society. And its example would inspire all the nations of the world to similar action.

But the cultivation of the commons was simply the first stage in the advance of society towards a general system of common ownership. For, despite the vast advantages the country would reap from that policy, complete freedom and

[1] " Letter to Fairfax " (Dec. 9), *Clarke Papers*, Vol. II, p. 217.
[2] *Appeal to all Englishmen.*

social harmony could be achieved only when, with the abolition of private property, all social distinctions had disappeared:

> " So long as the earth is intangled and appropriated into particular hands and kept there by the power of the sword . . . so long the creation lies under bondage." [1]

Winstanley's argument for common ownership rested largely, as we have already discussed earlier in this chapter, on the appeal from Creation, the Law of Righteousness, reason, the Scriptures, religion:

> " The plaine truth is the law of propriety is the shamefull nakedness of mankinde and as farre from the Law of Christ as light from darkness." [1]

Natural law, which recognized no inequality or distinctions of class and person, vested the collective ownership of the land and its products in the entire community. That claim, I have sought to argue, was unlike that of *The New Law of Righteousness* not primarily a moral argument. Despite the theological garb in which Winstanley's ideas were so frequently clothed, moral and ethical concepts, for him, did not derive from any absolute or supernatural principle of justice; they had reference simply to the problems of preservation and human welfare. The insistence, therefore, that communal ownership was dictated by natural law derived, let me repeat, from his conviction that common ownership was the most effective method of assuring preservation to every individual:

> " In the beginning of time, the great Creator, Reason, made the earth to be a Common Treasury, to preserve beasts, birds, fishes and man." [2]

The belief that common ownership alone could secure the well-being of all members of society was largely the result of his analysis of the rôle and effect of private property throughout history. That analysis, as we have already seen, led Winstanley to the realization that the private ownership of land was the basis of social division. Ownership of land conferred absolute power over one's fellows. It substituted

---

[1] *Fire in the Bush.*   [2] *True Levellers Standard.*

slavery for equality in human relationships.   Poverty was an inevitable result of exclusion from the soil.   Destitution and want bred fear, crime, a sense of inferiority and degradation; power and wealth fostered greed, arrogance and pride.   The conflict of private interests led to war and social strife; and the maintenance of the distinction between the rich and the poor required the constant and ruthless use of force and suppression.   The character and substance of government and law, of religion and education, Winstanley had seen, were primarily determined by the fact that power was the monopoly of the owners of property; and their interests and privileges imparted to all social institutions their essential nature.

The evils from which society was suffering, Winstanley therefore affirmed, could be finally ended only with the abolition of private ownership.   In the first place, as he had reasoned in developing the claim of the poor to the commons, common ownership would eliminate the haunting spectre of poverty by providing everyone with the necessities of life; for poverty was purely an artificial product of the property system:

> " This is the bondage the poor complain of, that they are kept poor in a Land where there is so much plenty for everyone." [1]

> " If any say, This will bring poverty, surely they mistake," he declared in reply to objections urged against his scheme, " for there will be plenty of all Earthly Commodities, with less labor and trouble than now it is under Monarchy. There will be no want; for every man may keep as plentiful a house as he will and never run into debt; for common stock pays for all." [2]

Nor, he was convinced, was the vision of a society producing in abundance for all its members a utopian fantasy;   on the contrary, it could be immediately achieved in England for

> " there be land enough in England to maintain ten times as many people as are in it ".[3]

Furthermore, the encouragement of invention and research, both through a deliberate programme of aid and assistance

---

[1] *Law of Freedom.*   [2] Ibid., pp. 13–14.
                    [3] Ibid., p. 9.

and through the stimulus of the new social environment, would considerably increase production. Under private ownership, the productive capacity of the country is not dedicated to the welfare of the entire community but simply enables

> " . . . the Gentry to have abundance, and to lock up Treasures of the Earth from the poor; so that rich men may have chests full of gold and silver, and houses full of corn and good to look upon, while the Poor who work to get it can hardly live; and if they cannot work like slaves, then they must starve ".[1]

In the communal order the social product will be freely distributed in accordance with need:

> " As everyone works to advance the Common Stock, so everyone shall have a free use of any commodity in the Storehouse, for his pleasure and comfortable livelihood, without buying and selling, or restraint from any." [2]

By allowing everyone free access to the soil and to raw materials, unemployment would be eliminated. An end would similarly be put to the luxurious idleness of the rich; for no one would be permitted to share in the common stock unless he had contributed by his own labour to the common welfare:

> " If you say, some will live idle," declared Winstanley, replying to the age-old argument against socialism, " I answer, No. It will make idle persons to become workers, as is declared in the Platform; There shall be neither Beggar nor Idle Person." [3]

If men were thus able to satisfy their needs by productive labour and to assure themselves of an adequate livelihood, the fear and insecurity that are the deposit of poverty would disappear. The wealthy, by being forced to work for their living and by being reduced to a standard of equality with their fellows, would be cured of the jealousy and pride that their luxury and idleness had bred. Men would live more normal, healthier lives; and more wholesome human relationships would be established in society.

---

[1] *New Yeers Gift.*   [2] *Law of Freedom*, p. 74.   [3] Ibid., p. 14.

The abolition of private property would end social division by destroying its foundation. The oppression of man by man would cease to exist; for no one would have to become his fellow's bondman in order to maintain his own existence. The basis of personal power would be uprooted. By dissolving all private interests and privileges, common ownership would render war and social strife impossible by eliminating their major cause. If the general standard of living were raised, education and culture would flourish; and there would be no longer any barriers to the development of scientific knowledge and research.

In a society divided into groups on the basis of wealth, Winstanley had asserted, government had functioned purely as an agency of the owners of property for the preservation of their privileges. In a social order in which the basis of personal power had been destroyed by the establishment of a system of common ownership, men would live on terms of complete equality. A common interest in the general welfare would supersede a personal concern in the maintenance of privilege. As a result, the nature of government would be completely transformed. In such circumstances

" Government is a wise and free ordering of the Earth and the Manners of Mankind by observation of particular Laws or Rules, so that all the Inhabitants may live peaceably in plenty and freedom in the Land where they are born and bred ".[1]

The burden of law, similarly, would no longer be the protection of private interests; it would represent, instead, the collective will and interest of the entire community:

" Law is a Rule, whereby men and other creatures are governed in their actions, for the preservation of the Common Peace." [2]

We shall discuss in the next chapter the institutions and methods by which Winstanley planned to organize his communal order.

[1] *Law of Freedom*, p. 25.   [2] Ibid., p. 78.

Chapter Six: WINSTANLEY'S UTOPIA

" I never came to quiet rest and to know God in my spirit, till I came
to the knowledge of the things in this Book."—Winstanley, *The Law of
Freedom* (1652).

In none of the tracts Winstanley wrote during 1649–50 did
he attempt to describe in detail the constitution and institutional organization of the new social order he was advocating.
It was to be, clearly enough, an economic system in which
private property in the means of production had been abolished
and in which the earth and its products were to be the common
possession of the entire populace. Commerce was to be
rigidly proscribed; and money, as a result, would have no
function in the new order for the social product was to be
freely distributed:

> " We must neither buy nor sell ", the Diggers announced.
> " Money must not any longer (after our work of the Earths
> Community is advanced) be the great god that hedges in
> some and hedges out others, for money is but part of the
> Earth; for after our work of the Earthly Community is
> advanced, we must make use of gold and silver as we do of
> other metals but not to buy or sell." [1]

There is no record of the manner in which the affairs of the
St. George's Hill group were administered; but the Diggers
clearly intended their crops and woods to serve as a common
stock for their sustenance. Everyone, evidently, worked on
terms of complete equality with his fellows. But, beyond that
general outline, there was no discussion of the institutional
framework of the communal society the Diggers were seeking
to establish. That detailed elaboration was the burden of
Winstanley's last and most important work, *The Law of
Freedom*.

After the collapse of the Digger colony at St. George's Hill
early in 1650, there was no further record of Winstanley's

---

[1] *Declaration from the Poor Oppressed People, etc.*

activity until the publication of *The Law of Freedom* early in
1652. In the Epistle Dedicatory to the book, written in
November 1651, Winstanley told Cromwell that he had
intended to submit the work for his consideration two years
earlier but that events had forced him to lay it aside.

> " But this word was like fire in my bones, ever and anon,
> ' Thou shalt not bury thy talent in the earth '. Thereupon
> I was stirred up to give a resurrection and to pick together
> as many of my scattered papers as I could finde and to
> compile them into this method, which I do here present to
> you, and do quiet my own spirit." [1]

The book itself was obviously composed at various intervals.
It is unevenly written; it is poorly arranged; it follows no
logical sequence. It embodies a recital of the grievances
by which the common people are still oppressed, a discourse
on the nature of government and law, a detailed programme
for the organization of the economic, political and administrative machinery of the communal order, a number of interesting cosmological observations and a code of laws for the new
society. As in Winstanley's earlier writings, his theoretical
and general observations are distinguished more by their
profundity of insight than by their completeness as an integrated doctrinal system. His constructive, detailed proposals,
certainly, are more interesting for the depth of perception
into some of the problems of social organization that his
suggestions reveal than for the adequacy or practicability
of the complete structure.

The Law of Freedom strikingly reveals the remarkable quality
of Winstanley's mind that had been apparent in his earlier
tracts; but it equally emphasizes the serious limitations that
both his period and his own background and experience
imposed on him. His cosmological views and his general
observations on government and social processes have been
discussed in earlier chapters. His theoretical position in
The Law of Freedom was, on the whole, considerably more
advanced than that of his other writings. I have already
remarked that his interpretation of both natural and social
phenomena became an almost wholly materialistic one.
Largely as a result of that fact, due partly, as well, to the

[1] *Law of Freedom*, p. 11.

essentially practical nature of the problems with which the book is concerned, it betrays little tendency to revert to the mystical language or the theological conceptions that had marked so much of his earlier utterances. In one important respect, however, the book reflects the impact of Winstanley's failure in his practical effort to make the earth " a common treasury ". There is little of that confident, at times buoyant, optimism that had permeated his other writings. Unlike his other tracts, *The Law of Freedom* is less a political manifesto than an intellectual and academic exercise. More important, there is no longer any stirring call to the poor and the dispossessed to rise and to assert their rights. It is a memorandum for Cromwell's consideration rather than a call to action.

That is not to say, let me hasten to emphasize, that Winstanley lost his faith in the inevitability of the social order he envisaged :

" The Spirit of the whole Creation (who is God) ", he declared, " is about the Reformation of the World, and he will go forward in his work." [1]

Nor does *The Law of Freedom* represent in any way an attempt by Winstanley to moderate his views and to render them more palatable to his generation. He has lost none of his conviction that only common ownership can solve the problems of society; and he will be satisfied with nothing less than the complete abolition of the existing order. But the temper of the book is the sober realization that the propertyless themselves do not have the power to force through those changes without the support of those in power. It is a retreat from his earlier optimistic conviction that the poor of his day, by their own unaided efforts, could remake the world.

The very fact of its dedication to Cromwell is an indication of that mood. The dedication itself is largely an humble appeal to the dictator's vanity, conceived in terms of the personal honour or disgrace his policy will bring him. By establishing effective freedom, Cromwell can achieve enduring fame; by maintaining slavery, he will eternally brand himself as a tyrant and a despot. Peaceful change will assure

---

[1] *Law of Freedom*, p. 4.

him a secure and honourable regime; refusal to reform will constitute an invitation to revolution and his own overthrow.

> ". . . You must do one of these two things ", Winstanley told him. " First, either set the Land free to the oppressed Commoners, who assisted you and pay'd the army their wages . . . and so take possession of your deserved honor. Or secondly, you must onely remove the Conquerors power out of the Kings hand into other mens, maintaining the old Laws still; and then your Wisdom and Honor is blasted forever; and you will either lose yourself or lay the foundation of greater slavery to posterity than you ever knew." [1]
> " Lose not your Crown ", he urged Cromwell. " Take it up and wear it."

Cromwell alone, Winstanley frankly confessed, had the power to effect the social changes that could free the people.

> " I have set the candle at your door; for you have power in your hand to act for Common Freedom, if you will; I have no power." [2]

The book, as I have already observed, is marked by many flashes of profound insight into natural and social processes. But considerable sections, particularly those that concern the detailed and constructive programme, are conceived in far too simple and, frequently, naïve terms. There is a remarkable recognition of the rôle of the productive processes in shaping human affairs, but an equally remarkable inability to comprehend the changing nature of those processes themselves. There is a deep appreciation of the scientific temper of the century and, at the same time, a complete failure to grasp the essential and increasing complexity of social relationships. It is a combination of profound understanding and simple conception, of penetrating insight and unsophisticated suggestion. In his theoretical analyses and observations Winstanley is a social philosopher far in advance of his epoch. In his detailed proposals he remains a *petit bourgeois* tradesman seemingly unaware of the complex nature of social organization. That is not to say, let me again repeat, that

---

[1] *Law of Freedom*, pp. 3–4. [2] Ibid., p. 11.

Winstanley was an unrealistic Utopist spinning fanciful visions of an ideal world. His social analysis embodied a more adequate appreciation of the realities of social life than any of his contemporaries was able to achieve. For more than a year he struggled to give practical expression to his theoretical convictions. But his detailed programme was inadequate. It failed to take cognizance of the commercial and industrial development of the period. It was conceived on a scale too simple for practical application to a social organization of increasing complexity.

The basis of the new social order, Winstanley of course insisted, was to be the common ownership of the land and of all the natural resources. Certainly, he did not intend to compensate the manor lords for the confiscation of their estates or the priests for the loss of their tithes; for common ownership would but restore to the community that which had originally been taken from it by force:

> "When Tythes were first enacted and Lordly power drawn over the backs of the oppressed, the Kings and Conquerors made no scruple of Conscience to take it, though the people lived in sore bondage of poverty for want of it; and can there be scruple of conscience to make restitution of this which hath been so long stoln goods?" [1]

Every person was to enjoy complete freedom to till and plant the soil. A network of storehouses would be established throughout the country in which the products of the land would be collected for distribution to the people. All raw materials were to be kept in "general storehouses" from which artisans would be supplied with materials for their crafts. They would bring their finished products to the "particular storehouses". Every person in the community could draw freely from any of the storehouses. Despite the increasing importance of manufacture, Winstanley was still thinking almost exclusively in terms of simple household production. An agricultural economy, he evidently felt, supplemented by simple craft work, could supply all the goods and commodities that any society required for its welfare:

> "The Earth is to be planted and the fruits reaped and carried into the Barns and Storehouses by the assistance of

[1] *Law of Freedom*, p. 11.

every family. If a man or family want corn or other provisions, they may go to the Storehouses and fetch without money ".[1]

" The general Storehouses are such houses as receive in all commodities in the gross . . . and these general storehouses shall be filled and preserved by the common labor and assistance of every Family. . . . And from these public Houses which are the general stock of the Land, all particular tradesmen may fetch materials for their particular work as they need, or to furnish their particular dwellings with any commodities. . . .

" There are particular Storehouses or Shops, to which the Tradesmen shall bring their particular works; as all instruments of iron to the Iron-shops, hats to the shops appointed for them and so on. . . . They shall receive in, as into a Storehouse and deliver out again freely, as out of a Common Storehouse, when particular persons or families come for everything they need, as now they do by buying and selling under Kingly Government." [2]

The establishment of that chain of storehouses, Winstanley suggested, could be a very simple affair; for stores and shops that now function as retail agencies could continue to serve as the distributing centres for every community:

" Even as now we have particular trade in Cities and Towns called Shopkeepers, which shall remaine still as they be, only altered in their receiving in, and delivering out; for whereas by the Law of Kings or Conquerors, they do receive in and deliver out by buying and selling, Now they shall (by the Laws of the Commonwealth) receive into their shops and deliver out againe freely, without buying and selling." [2]

Every able-bodied person would be required by law to engage in some useful and productive occupation; no one would be permitted to employ the services of his fellow-man to labour for him. The social order was therefore to be a co-operative society based on creative, productive labour. Everyone would earn the right to a continuous share in the

[1] *Law of Freedom*, p. 72.   [2] Ibid., p. 75.

social product by virtue of his contribution through labour to the common welfare:

> " As everyone works to advance the Common Stock so everyone shall have a free use of any commodity in the Storehouse for his pleasure and comfortable livelihood, without buying or selling or restraint from any." [1]

Winstanley easily refuted the general and common objection that such a system would foster idleness and laziness:

> " Some hearing of this Common Freedom ", he remarked, " think there must be a Community of all the fruits of the Earth whether they work or no, therefore strive to live idle upon other men's labours." [2]

Penalties, however, would be provided by the law for those who refused to work. The basis of social division, the distinction between those who live by the exploitation of their fellow-men and those who subsist by the sale of their labour, would be finally eliminated; and the economic structure of the social order would render the emergence of an idle, parasitic class utterly impossible.

Winstanley was particularly emphatic in his insistence that commerce should be absolutely forbidden in the new society. From experience, he knew it to be one of the most effective media through which the crafty and unscrupulous were oppressing the poor. Trade, he saw, fostered the development of a class of merchants and business men whose wealth gave them both political power and, through the purchase of land, the opportunity to drive the peasants off the soil. " Buying and selling ", if it were to be permitted in the new order, could thus become the thin edge of the wedge for the overthrow of the new system. Anyone engaging in commerce, except in foreign trade, was therefore to be regarded as a traitor working for the reintroduction of the old oppressive order. The sale and purchase of land or commodities was therefore to be regarded as a treasonable offence, punishable by death:

> " If any do buy or sell the Earth, or the fruits thereof, unless it be to, or with strangers of another Nation, accord-

---

[1] *Law of Freedom*, p. 74. [2] Ibid., p. 23.

ing to the Law of Navigation, they shall be both put to death
as Traytors to the Peace of the Commonwealth; because it
brings in Kingly Bondage again, and is the occasion of all
quarrels and oppressions." [1]

With the proscription of commerce, there would be no
further use for money, except possibly for a limited quantity
for purposes of foreign trade. Precious metals could be
converted, instead, into useful goods and ornaments.

The common ownership of property, it should be noted,
was to extend only to the productive resources of the country.
Personal effects and goods taken from the storehouses for use
or consumption would be considered the private possession of
every family:

"Though the Earth and Storehouses be common to
every Family yet every Family shall live apart as they do;
and every mans wife, children, and furniture for ornament
of his house, or anything he hath fetched in from the Storehouses, or provided for the necessary use of his Family, is all
a propriety unto that Family for the peace thereof; And
if any man offer to take away a mans wife, children, or
furniture of his house, without his consent, or disturb the
peace of his dwelling, he shall suffer punishment as an
Enemy to the Commonwealths Government." [2]

Winstanley briefly considered the problem of incentives in
his social order, and felt that the conferring of "Titles of
Honor" on those who held public office or who, through
scientific research or exceptional ability, had rendered distinguished service to the community would be an adequate
and sufficient stimulus to effort.

"As a man goes through Offices, he rises to Titles of
Honor, till he comes to the highest Nobility, to be a faithful
Commonwealths man in a Parliament House. Likewise
he who finds out any secret in Nature shall have a Title of
Honor given him, though he be a young man. But no man
shall have any Title of Honor till he win it by industry, or
come to it by age or Office-bearing." [2]

[1] *Law of Freedom*, p. 84.   [2] Ibid., p. 13.

Those titles, merited by public service or important scientific contribution, were the only distinctions of person the new social order would recognize.

Winstanley's scheme for the administration of the co-operative society is probably the least satisfactory part of his work. In his suggestions he displayed neither the profundity nor the originality that distinguish his social theory. It is obvious that Winstanley had given little consideration to the administrative problems of a social system; and the limitations of his experience are apparent in the simplicity with which he conceived the political structure of the commonwealth.

The administration of affairs was to be in the hands of a series of officials elected annually by a system of universal manhood suffrage. Fathers were to retain their authority as heads of their families and were to be responsible for the early education of their children. Every town, city and parish was to have its peace-makers to sit in council for the administration of the general affairs of the community and to undertake the reconciliation of quarrels, overseers to supervise and direct the storehouses, production and distribution, labour and the instruction of the youth, task-masters for those who had been sentenced to a loss of their freedom for infractions of the law and executioners to carry out capital penalties. County courts consisting of a Judge, the Peacemakers and the Overseers of every town and soldiers or county marshals were to sit in every county at least four times a year and more often if need be.

Winstanley retained Parliament as the supreme governing body of the land; but he insisted that it must be elected annually. He failed to delineate its functions very clearly, but he obviously thought that its activities would be primarily judicial and administrative rather than legislative. In broad outline:

> " A Parliament is the highest Court of Equity in a Land; and it is to be chosen every year. . . . This Court is to oversee all other Courts, Officers, Persons, and actions and to have a full power being the Representatives of the whole Land, to remove all grievances and to ease the people that are oppressed." [1]

Seldom, however, in the past had Parliaments ever fulfilled

[1] *Law of Freedom*, p. 80.

their major duties of abolishing tyranny and relieving oppression:

> " For hath not Parliament sat and rose again, and made
> Laws to strengthen the Tyrant in his Throne, and to
> strengthen the rich and the strong by those Laws, and left
> Oppression upon the backs of the Oppressed still? " [1]

A Commonwealth Parliament, he suggested, that would

> " not only dandle us upon the knee with good words and
> promises till particular mens turn be served, but will feed
> our bellies and clothe our backs with good actions of
> Freedom, and give to the oppressed childrens children their
> birthright portion ".[2]

would have a four-point programme to fulfil.

Its first and immediate act should be make all common,
waste, abbey, bishops' and Crown lands available to the poor
for cultivation; it must affirm that the land

> " is their own Creation-Rights faithfully and courageously
> recovered by their diligence, purses and blood from under
> the Kingly Tyrants and Oppressors Power ".[2]

It must, in the second place, embark on a programme of legal
reform. The old legal code must be scrapped and, in its stead,
a system of laws based on reason and equity and designed to
achieve the common welfare rather than to protect privilege
and private interests would have to be adopted. No Act,
however, is to have the power of law until it has received
popular sanction. All proposed legislation must be publicly
announced throughout the country. If, within a month of
publication, no objections have been forthcoming from the
people, the Act will be deemed to have received public approval and will pass into law:

> ". . . They are to make a publike Declaration thereof
> to the people of the Land who choose them for their approbation. And if no objection come in from the people within
> one month, they may then take the peoples silence as a

---

[1] *Law of Freedom*, p. 51.   [2] Ibid., p. 52.

consent thereto . . . the enacting of new Laws must be by the peoples consent and knowledge." [1]

Parliament would be charged with the removal of all grievances and oppressions—the restoration of the common lands, the prohibition of commerce, the abolition of tithes. It would, finally, be responsible for the conduct of foreign affairs and the maintenance of an Army:

" A Parliament ", Winstanley concludes, " is the Head of Power in a Commonwealth. It is their work to manage publique affairs in times of War and in times of Peace; not to promote the interests of particular men, but for the Peace and Freedom of the whole body of the Land, viz. of every particular man, that none be deprived of his Creation rights, unless he hath lost his Freedom by Transgression." [2]

In the section on the selection and duties of public officials Winstanley makes a number of shrewd and penetrating observations. All public servants in the Commonwealth were to be elected through a system of universal manhood suffrage. " All true Officers are chosen ones." Generally, all men over forty, with the exception of those who professed sympathy with monarchical government or with the old economic order, were eligible for public office. Exception might be made, however, as far as the age qualification was concerned, in the case of younger men of outstanding ability. Elections must be free and unprejudiced; electioneering would serve as an automatic disqualification for office. No public official is to be either permitted to designate his successor or eligible for immediate re-election when his annual term of office expires.

Winstanley was particularly aware of the influence of power and authority on those who wield them; and he was anxious to prevent the emergence of a group of professional public servants by prohibiting lengthy tenure of office:

" When publique Officers remain long in places of Judicature, they will degenerate from the bounds of humility, honesty, and tender care of brethren, in regard the heart of man is so subject to be overspread with the clouds of covetousness, pride and vain-glory; for though at the first entrance into places of Rule they be of publique spirits,

---

[1] *Law of Freedom*, pp. 52–3.   [2] Ibid., p. 55.

seeking the Freedom of others as their own; yet continuing
long in such a place, where honours and greatness come in,
they become selfish, seeking themselves, and not Common
Freedom; as experience proves it true in these days according to this common proverb—' Great offices in a Land and
Army have changed the disposition of many sweet spirited
men.' " [1]

Constant rotation and short terms of office would, he hoped,
keep officials mindful of the fact that they were the servants
rather than the masters of the community.   Such measures
would prevent the development of bureaucratic indifference
and aloofness and render public servants responsive to the
needs and wills of the people :

> " When officers grow proud and full, they will maintain
> their greatness, though it be in the poverty, ruin and
> hardship of their Brethren. . . . And have we not experience
> in these days that some Officers of the Commonwealth have
> grown so mossy for want of removing, that they will hardly
> speak to an old acquaintance if he be an inferior man,
> though they were very familiar before these wars began?
> And what hath occasioned this distance among friends and
> brethren, but long continuance in places of honour, great-
> ness and riches? " [2]

Officials will be unable to entrench themselves in the citadels
of power.   Large numbers of people will share at one time or
another the responsibilities of civic administration; and this
will develop a well-informed, politically conscious citizenry.

If the sections of *The Law of Freedom* that concern the political
structure of the Commonwealth are disappointing those on
education fully reveal the progressive nature of Winstanley's
mind.   There is in them a keen perception and appreciation
of the scientific temper of the century.   There is the realization that popular instruction and knowledge are vital to any
healthy society.   There is the recognition that unequal
educational opportunity opens the door to the introduction of
social division.

We have already commented in earlier chapters on Winstanley's conviction that the improvement in the general

---

[1] *Law of Freedom*, p. 36.   [2] Ibid., pp. 36–7.

standard of living and the eradication from society of the haunting fear of insecurity and want would result in intensified cultural and intellectual activity. Ending the monopoly of education by the clergy would remove all restrictions on the popular spread of knowledge; and when research would have ceased to be the servant of a propertied class but would be dedicated to the service of the community, scientific development would be immeasurably encouraged.

Education in the new social order was to be free, general and compulsory. Children were to be instructed in the arts, sciences and languages. But Winstanley was anxious to make certain that no leisured class of intellectuals " trained up only to book-learning and to no other employment " would be allowed to develop as parasites on society. Everyone, he therefore insisted, must be taught a trade or some practical occupation. Such practical and technical training would, on the one hand, safeguard the individual from the vices of idleness and, on the other, enrich the Commonwealth by increasing production.

> " To prevent idleness and the danger of Machivilian cheats, it is profitable for the Commonwealth, that children be trained up in Trades and some bodily imployment, as well as in learning Languages or the Histories of former ages. . . . If this course were taken, there would be no Idle person nor Beggars in the Land and much work would be done by that now lazy generation for the enlarging of the Common Treasuries." [1]

The State was to be particularly active in encouraging scientific research and in providing people with every facility for scientific investigation:

> " In the managing of any Trade, let no young wit be crushed in his invention, for if any man desire to make a new tryall of his skil in any Trade or Science, the Overseers shall not hinder him therein but incourage him therein that so the Spirit of Knowledge may have his full growth in man, to find out the secret in every Art." [1]

Society was therefore to afford everyone free and ample opportunity for the full development of his potentialities.

[1] *Law of Freedom*, p. 71.

The only titles of honour that would be granted, apart from the distinction public office would confer, would be those gained for distinguished contributions to learning and science.

Winstanley reveals his profound appreciation of the importance of the scientific method that was being developed during the century in his insistence that the spirit pervading the educational system was to be, above all else, scientific and rational; for experience, he asserted, was the only valid source of knowledge. If mankind has suffered in the past through lack of knowledge, that ignorance, he claimed, has derived from the insistence of the clergy that only tradition must be recognized as truth:

> ". . . a studying imagination comes into man, which is the devil for it is the cause of all evil, and sorrows in the world; that is he who puts out the eyes of mans Knowledge and tells him he must beleeve what others have writ or spoke, and must not trust to his own experience ".[1]

In the new social order, however, men will be permitted to teach only that which has been verified or demonstrated by scientific observation and experiment:

> " Everyone who speaks of any Herb, Plant, Art, or Nature of Mankind, is required to speak nothing by imagination, but what he hath found out by his own industry and observation in tryal." [2]

Winstanley's emphasis on knowledge and information as vital to any adequate social order is reflected in his suggestion for the appointment of postmasters in every part of the country and in his stress on the necessity for improved means of communication. County and parish postmasters were to record all events of importance and to deliver periodical reports to the central postmaster in the capital. News from all parts of the country would then be compiled and issued in book form every week to all communities in the land. Fresh bonds of unity would thus be forged between all parts of the country. People would constantly be informed of developments and events of importance and interest. The results of scientific research would be more quickly dis-

---

[1] *Law of Freedom*, pp. 58-9.   [2] Ibid., p. 57.

seminated and popularized and applied for the welfare of the people.

Winstanley, similarly, planned to convert the pulpit into a medium of popular instruction. Institutionalized religion was to play no rôle in his ideal commonwealth; for the essence of religion lay in the spirit that informed human and social relationships rather than in a mechanical uniformity of practice and worship. It is significant that there is no discussion whatever in *The Law of Freedom* of the relationship of ecclesiastical organizations to the State. There was to be complete freedom of religious belief; and no one could be punished for opinion. Anyone, however, who attempted to masquerade under the cloak of religion in order to acquire land or wealth would be put to death:

> " He who professes the service of a righteous God by preaching and prayer, and makes a Trade to get the possessions of the Earth, shall be put to death for a Witch and a Cheater." [1]

The weekly day of rest was to be dedicated to social intercourse and to public instruction. Sermons were to concern themselves not with the niceties of theological dogma, but with the problems of daily life. Lectures were to be delivered from the pulpit on history and contemporary affairs, on all the arts and sciences—languages, physics, astronomy, husbandry, etc.—and on the nature of man. Throughout, the blessings and benefits of freedom were to be contrasted with the curse of slavery and " kingly government ". Such use of the pulpit for secular instruction, Winstanley was of course aware, would be denounced by the ignorant clergy as mundane and materialistic:

> " ' I ', but saith the zealous but ignorant Professor, ' this is a low and carnal ministry indeed; this leads men to know nothing but the knowledge of the earth, and the secrets of nature; but we are to look after spiritual and heavenly things.'
> " I answer," declared Winstanley, " To know the secrets of nature is to know the works of God; And to know the works of God within the Creation is to know God himself; for God dwels in every visible work or body." [2]

[1] *Law of Freedom*, p. 86.   [2] Ibid., p. 58.

Law reform was an integral and essential element of Winstanley's programme. It was to be, as we have already noted, one of the major responsibilities of Parliament. For, despite his conviction that a progressive social order would greatly reduce the incidence of crime, Winstanley was fully aware that all social organization had to be regulated by law:

> "Others think", he observed, "there will be no Law but that everything will run into confusion for want of Government." [1]

But,

> ". . . because that transgression doth and may arise from ignorant and rude fancy in man, is the Law added ". [1]

But if law would still be necessary—and law in a society in which the distinction between rich and poor had been eliminated, Winstanley constantly emphasized, would be dedicated to securing the common welfare—it could be purged of all the abuses that under "kingly government" had rendered the legal system so oppressive to the common people. Winstanley made no specific or detailed recommendation for reform of the existing legal code but advanced a number of general suggestions that should be followed in drafting the laws and in judicial procedure.

In the first place, the laws should be written simply and clearly in a language all people could understand. "Short and pithy Laws are best to govern a Commonwealth." They should be read frequently in popular assembly so that people would be intimately acquainted with their content. Popular knowledge of the laws combined with their simplicity would enable people to dispense with the services of lawyers; one of the main roots of oppression would thus wither away. In the second place, the legal code should be so formulated as to enable judges completely to dispense with the interpretive application of law. For government, Winstanley affirmed, had to be by laws and not by men. That meant, in his view, that law should be so framed that it could be applied to every situation without requiring personal interpretation from the judges. Much of the oppression from which the

---

[1] *Law of Freedom*, p. 23.

H

people had suffered, Winstanley asserted, had derived from the fact that judges enjoyed wide latitude in their application of the law. That made possible the introduction of personal prejudice into the administration of justice. Law had therefore readily been made to serve the furtherance of personal interests:

> "From hence hath arisen much misery in the Nations under Kingly Government in that the man called the Judge hath been suffered to interpret the Law . . . the Law which was a certain Rule was varied according to the will of a covetous, envious or proud Judge." [1]

It was therefore necessary, in order to safeguard freedom and equality, so to formulate the legal code that the judge would have to do no more than pronounce the bare letter of the law without elaboration or personal interpretation:

> "The Law itself is the Judge of all men's actions . . . for no single man ought to judge or interpret the Law." [2]

There would thus be no necessity whatever in the new society for the services of professional lawyers

> ". . . for there is to be no buying or selling; neither any need to expound Laws, for the bare letter of the Law shall be both Judge and Lawyer, trying every man's actions. And seeing we shall have successive Parliaments every year, there will be Rules made for every action a man can do." [2]

Any person accepting money or reward for the administration of justice would be put to death as a traitor. A judge rendering a personal decision in the absence of a law or disregarding the expressed intention of the legal code would be permanently disqualified from holding public office.

Winstanley thus held the naïve belief—a belief that derived from the essential simplicity which he conceived would mark human relationships in the new social order—that a simple legal code could be devised that would cover any situation in which dispute or difference might arise. He himself drew up a rigidly artificial code of sixty-two laws on trade, elections, production, marriage, etc. It is doubtful whether he

---

[1] *Law of Freedom,* p. 48.   [2] Ibid., p. 13.

actually intended them to serve as a legal code for a social system; more likely they were meant as suggestions as to the lines along which legislation should be drafted. It is hardly necessary to discuss those laws in any detail. They translate into legislation the suggestions for the organization of society on the basis of common ownership that we have been discussing in this chapter. They provide for the common ownership of the land and the free distribution of its products. They prescribe capital punishment for a number of offences, to several of which we have already referred. Officials who prove negligent in their duties are to be dismissed from office and disqualified for re-election. Such offences as idleness, waste of resources, slander, etc., are to be punished by public admonition or by the loss of freedom for a period of twelve months, during which the offenders will be required to perform menial tasks at the direction of the task-masters or to serve their terms as slaves to the freemen. It is particularly interesting to note that the code makes provision for free medical service.

If the institutions Winstanley devised were inadequate, because of their simplicity, for the purposes he intended them to fulfil, his suggestions nevertheless enshrined perceptions no less important than those his social analysis had embodied. They affirmed, first of all, that the goods of the earth should be dedicated to the welfare of all human beings rather than to the satisfaction of the needs of a few. Neither wealth nor birth nor ability constituted a superior claim to the opportunity to live a full and creative life. There was the recognition that the free development of personality and creative, cultural and spiritual activity were possible adventures only in a society in which poverty and insecurity had been abolished by the effective guarantee of an adequate standard of living to every person. That meant, as Winstanley saw, that society must itself own and control the things by which men live. It meant, furthermore, that the distribution of those goods should be limited solely by the capacity to produce and that need and reasonable demand were the only valid criteria by which that distribution should be effected.

If political institutions, as Winstanley had argued, are always the reflection of the economic relationships on which they are built, freedom and liberty could be made meaningful and enduring only if they were rooted in an economic equality

—which implied nothing less than the common ownership of the means of production and the canonization of productive labour as the basic principle of the social order.

But proper economic organization would not of itself automatically assure political stability and administrative efficiency. Safeguards had to be erected against the abuse of public authority and the temptations that political office so subtly holds forth to its occupants. A progressive social order required an informed, educated citizenry; the dissemination of news and information, Winstanley therefore insisted, was fundamental to intelligent government and social progress. Unlike his more famous contemporary, Harrington, Winstanley was consistently a democrat. The ability to govern, he was convinced, was the monopoly of no single class; everyone could be educated to take his share in the responsibilities of public administration. And, throughout, there was, in Winstanley, the implicit assumption that a static society is a decaying society. The social order must therefore be infused with a dynamic temper. It must deliberately foster experiment; it must encourage scientific research; it must be willing to innovate; it must set a premium on imagination and initiative.

Winstanley failed, it must be admitted, to give adequate institutional expression to those perceptions. But his insight into the fundamental problems which any realistic political science must confront and the direction he indicated for their solution remain no less valid for our day than they were for his. For the essential problem with which Winstanley was concerned was the relationship of economic power to political organization. And that is the problem to which our age, as a period of social transition, is being increasingly forced to address itself.

CONCLUSION

"... so long as such are rulers as cals the Land theirs, upholding this particular propriety of mine and thine, the common people shall never have their liberty nor the land ever freed from troubles, oppressions and complainings."—Winstanley, *The New Law of Righteousness* (1649).

THE impact of the Diggers on the political thought of their period does not seem to have been much more significant than their influence on the course of events. Winstanley himself, though he complained in *The Law of Freedom* that " my health and estate is decayed and I grow in age, I must either beg or work for day wages ", evidently retired to a quiet life at Cobham; and he does not seem to have written anything after the publication of *The Law of Freedom*.[1] The fact that he was sued in 1660 for the recovery of a debt of £114 he was said to have contracted during his business career suggests that, after his retirement from political activity, he enjoyed a period of comparative prosperity. That this conjecture is not wholly without substance is indicated by the evidence of Lawrence Clarkson, self-avowedly with Muggleton one of the Last Two Witnesses. Clarkson, in his spiritual autobiography published in 1660, relates that in his search for an adequate spiritual doctrine he came into contact with the Diggers at St. George's Hill. But human nature, he was convinced, was so selfish that he was unable to regard the Digger venture as inspired by anything more lofty than the desire for public recognition :

"I made it appear to Gerrard Winstanley there was a self-love and vain-glory nursed in his heart by which his name might have become great among the poor commonalty of the Nation." [2]

That interpretation of Winstanley's motives, Clarkson claimed, was subsequently confirmed by events :

[1] On the generally accepted belief that Winstanley joined the Quakers, see Appendix I.
[2] Lawrence Clarkson, *The Lost Sheep Found* (1660), p. 27.

" Afterwards in him appeared a most shameful retreat from George's Hill with a spirit of pretended universality, to become a real Tithe-gatherer of propriety." [1]

There can be little doubt that Clarkson was unfair to Winstanley in his estimate of his character; but it is not improbable that the erstwhile Digger did become, in his later years, a fairly prosperous farmer.

Nor do there seem to have been any particularly significant echoes of the movement itself after 1650. Few references can be found to the Diggers in the years following the failure of their practical activities. Thomas Burton records in his diary that Colonel Shapcot, urging the removal of Naylor, the eccentric Quaker, to Yorkshire at his trial in 1656–57, declared:

" Those that come out of the North are the greatest pests of the Nation. The Diggers came thence." [2]

But if Winstanley's Lancashire origin impressed itself on the Colonel's memory, few persons seem to have remembered the Digger agitation. Certainly, the people of Kent, who petitioned in 1653 for the abolition of " that image of monarchy in Lords of Mannors, in their receiving of Lords rents or homagepenny of the people which monarchy imposed on the people ", who urged that lawyers, " impropriators ", rich men and manor lords who " receive rents or homagepenny for that which is not theirs, manifesting thereby that the people are still under the Conquest of the Norman Tyrant, he being of the Normans creating and upholding the arbitrary power of Princes or Kings although that monarchy is now conquered " be disqualified from holding office, revealed an intimate acquaintance with Digger literature.[3] But the tenants of Thomas Dyke of Wartbole in Cumberland who told the Council in 1654 that they had been freed by the overthrow of " ye late monarchy of Norman race " were probably borrowing a phrase current in the popular agitation of the time rather than reflecting any direct Digger influence.[4] The activity of

---

[1] Lawrence Clarkson, *The Lost Sheep Found* (1660), p. 27.

[2] *Diary of Thomas Burton*, Vol. I, pp. 153 ff.

[3] *No Age Like Unto This Age or Times Unparallel'd, Oppression, Oppression, Oppression being the cries in Kent against the great Oppression of Tythes, Unjust Justices and Corrupt Magistrates* (June 1653), E. 702 (13).

[4] *S.P.D.*, LXXIV, pp. 78 seq. Quoted in James, op. cit., p. 101.

the Diggers may have helped to direct attention to the enclosure problem; and it is not unlikely that they were one of several factors that stimulated the enclosure controversy that flared up for a short time in the 1650's.[1] But even Moore, who so earnestly pleaded the cause of the dispossessed against the current of economic development, was motivated largely by a charitable impulse—however profound—to ease the distress of the poor rather than by any fundamental desire to reform the social order. Here again, however, one can find little trace of the direct influence of the Diggers; for none of the writers in the controversy makes any reference to them.

Some of Winstanley's theological writings seem to have enjoyed fairly wide circulation; and there is evidence that they were not entirely unknown to contemporaries. His first five theological tracts went through at least two editions. William London, in his *Catalogue of the Most Vendible Books in England*, of 1658, a bibliography recommended to the gentry and the ministers, lists *The Mystery of God*, *The Breaking of the Day of God*, *The Saint's Paradise* and *The New Law of Righteousness*; and London's list, it should be added, was a select rather than an exhaustive one.[2] Some seventeenth-century writers occasionally cite Winstanley's religious works, mainly for the purpose of proving him to have been the founder of Quakerism. Thus, Thomas Coomber, for example, writing in 1678, quoted extensively from Winstanley's early tracts in an effort to support his contention that

". . . the very draughts and even body of Quakerism are to be found in the several works of Gerrard Winstanley, a zealous Leveller ".[3]

Thomas Bennet, similarly, in 1711 referred to the time when " Winstanley published the principles of Quakerism and enthusiasm broke out ", and has a single reference to *The Saint's Paradise*.[4] The Quaker, Benjamin Furley, for example, had

---

[1] e.g. Halhead, *Inclosure Thrown Open or Depopulation Depopulated* (1650), E. 619 (2). John Moore, *The Crying Sin of England in not caring for the poor* (1653), E. 713 (7) ; *A Scripture word Against Inclosure* (1656) ; Pseudonimus, *Considerations Concerning Common Fields and Inclosures* (1653), E. 719 (9) ; *A Vindication of the Considerations* (1656).
[2] Wm. London, *A Catalogue of the Most Vendible Books in England* (1658), E. 955 (1).
[3] Thomas Coomber, *Christianity No Enthusiasm* (1678).
[4] Thomas Bennet, *An Answer to the Dissenters' Pleas for Separation* (1711).

in his library, among other works of Winstanley, the one-volume edition of his theological tracts and *The True Levellers Standard Advanced*.[1]

Winstanley's most important work, *The Law of Freedom*, however, attracted little contemporary attention.[2] Considerable sections of the book were reprinted, together with other material, in at least four pamphlets by George Horton, a London publisher; evidently they had been copied from Calvert's edition.[3] Some sections, too, appear curiously hidden among news dispatches in three issues of *The French Intelligencer*, a London newspaper that was published for about six months in 1651–52.[4] Several paragraphs of Lilburne's *Apologeticall Narration* of April 1652 seem to have been written in direct reply to Winstanley.[5] Little other notice, however, was evidently taken of the book.

It is less easy to assess the influence of the Diggers on the political thought of the 1650–60 period. I have been able to find only one other tract that presents a clear-cut, reasoned appeal for communism—*Tyranipocrit*, one of the most remarkable pamphlets of the entire period. *Tyranipocrit* is more than an eloquent and impassioned denunciation of class division and social inequality, of injustice and hypocrisy. It reveals

---

[1] *Bibliotheca Furliana.* Amsterdam, 1714.

[2] Berens, op. cit., p. 232, mentions two editions of *The Law of Freedom*. The four copies I have consulted—those at the British Museum, the Guildhall, the Bodleian Library and the Seligman Collection, New York City—all evidently belong to one edition: that of 1652.

[3] *The Levellers Remonstrance* (Feb. 1, 1652), E. 652 (12) ; *A Declaration of the Commoners of England* *(Feb. 13, 1652), E. 654 (10) ; *Articles of High Treason* (Feb. 21, 1652), E. 655 (10) ; *Bloody News from the Barbadoes* (Feb. 12), E. 655 (16).

[4] *The French Intelligencer* (Feb. 4–11), No. 12, E. 654 (7) ; (Feb. 11–18), No. 13, E. 655 (2) ; (Feb. 17–24), No. 14, E. 655 (12).

[5] " . . . in my opinion and judgment", writes Lilburne, " this silly conceit of Levelling of propriety and magistracie is so ridiculous and foolish an opinion, as no man of braines reason or ingenuitie can be imagined such a sot as to maintaine such a principle, because it would, if practised, destroy not only all industry in the world and raze the very foundation of generation and subsistence or being of one man by another. For as for industry and valour by which the societies of mankind are maintained and preserved, who will take paines for that which when he hath gotten it is not his owne but must equally be shared in by every lazy, simple, dronish sot? or who will fight for that wherin he hath no other interest but such as must be subject to the will and pleasure of another, yea of every coward and base low spirited fellow, that in his sitting still must share in common with a valiant man in all his brave and noble achievements."—Lilburne's *Apologeticall Narration* (April 1652), E. 659 (30), pp. 68–9.

a profound appreciation of the manner in which Puritanism was adapting religious principle to the needs and service of the new economic order. It insists that everyone should maintain himself by his own labour. It urges that all titles and social distinctions be ended. It earnestly appeals for the abolition of private property or, at least, for equal if not common ownership:

> "For if you should make and maintaine an equallity of goods and lands as God and nature would have, as justice and reason doth crave, then the gall of murmuration would bee broken and then mankinde might live in love and concord as brethren should doe. . . ." [1]

> "An equallity of meanes to spend is the foundation of justice and till that bee laid no justice can be administered in the Commonwealth." [2]

> "Take away the name and power of thine and mine or make and maintaine an equallity of all such of God's creatures as God hath given for the use and benefit of mankind." [3]

But if *Tyranipocrit* was inspired by any of the early Digger writings—the tract was published in August 1649—it represents, apart from the Digger pamphlets, a wholly isolated phenomenon.

Nor do the Commonwealth Utopias reveal any tendencies that can be attributed to Digger influence rather than to the general environment of the period. Certainly, they indicate a widespread feeling that the social chaos of the era demanded no minor reforms but drastic and novel experiment; but there is nothing in them that we can with certainty trace to Winstanley. Cornelius, who planned to organize his society on the lines of a joint-stock company, considered the possibility of communism but rejected the plan of establishing it by force:

> "Those that come into our society shall not be bound to make their goodes common (for according to the Tenth Commandment) none ought to covet another man's goodes." [4]

---

[1] *Tyranipocrit Discovered with his Wiles wherewith he vanquisheth* (Aug. 1649), E. 569 (5), p. 33.

[2] Ibid., p. 50.   [3] Ibid., pp. 52–3.

[4] Peter Cornelius, *A Way Propounded to Make the Poore in These and Other Nations Happy* (1659), E. 984 (7), p. 5.

H 2

And Cornelius, as the very title of his tract suggests, was more interested in alleviating the distress of the poor than, as Winstanley, in making a frontal attack on the social system. The other Utopias of the period, that of Covel,[1] for example, are similarly more noteworthy for that spirit of humanitarianism than for any practical or profound social analysis.

Harrington, of course, was, with the single exception of Hobbes, the most sophisticated and systematic thinker of the period. It is impossible to state whether he was acquainted with Winstanley's writings; though it is not unlikely that the Digger tracts did come to the attention of one of such erudition and extensive reading as Harrington's works reveal him to have been. Harrington, certainly, fully realized the fact that political domination was directly and inevitably a function of economic power; and *Oceana* was built on a distribution of land that would ensure a stable and harmonious balance of classes.

> " Equality of estates causes equality of power and equality of power is the liberty not only of the Commonwealth but of every man."[2]

But he was far less aware than Winstanley of the more indirect and subtle fashion in which the system of class relationships the economic order establishes shapes all forms and expressions of social life. And Harrington, above all else, was fundamentally an aristocrat who had little faith in the capacity of the common man to develop into a responsible citizen and to whom the gentry were the residue of all social intelligence:

> " A nobility or gentry in a popular government, not over-balancing it, is the very life and soul of it."[3]

If we are therefore to look for Digger influence, we must search for the evidence in the prolific literature of religious enthusiasm that the 1650–60 decade produced. I have already referred briefly to the fact that there was little direct left-wing political activity after 1650. The events of 1649 had effectively shattered the Leveller organization and dulled the

---

[1] Wm. Covel, *The Method of a Commonwealth* (1659), Goldsmith's Library.
[2] Harrington, *Oceana* (Renaissance Edition, New York, 1901), p. 193.
[3] Harrington, op. cit., p. 189.

revolutionary ardour of the rank and file of the Army. After 1650 the Levellers became a mere adjunct of Royalist plots. Lilburne devoted himself largely to his private affairs; and he came into public prominence only when his personal interests brought him into conflict with the Government. The feeble effort of the Diggers, we have already seen, was quickly suppressed in 1650; and they made no further attempt to convert the earth into a " common treasury ".

But if Cromwell could crush the political efforts of the common people, it was less easy for him to destroy their newly aroused class consciousness. Army agitation, Leveller propaganda, Digger activity, the impact of events had imparted to the people an acute awareness of their class interests. After 1649 and 1650 that social consciousness could no longer be given direct political expression. Instead, it found its voice in the tremendous revival of mystical enthusiasm and millenary fervour that dates from those years. If the price of political agitation was persecution and imprisonment, it was much more convenient to shift the initiative for social change to the Lord who could risk with impunity the wrath of dictators. And if the practical efforts of mortals had failed to achieve the desired results, surely God, in His time, would bring the eagerly awaited millennium.

Radical activity, then, was channelized into religious fervour; and the growth of the Quakers, the Fifth Monarchists, the Ranters and hundreds of other varieties that defy classification testifies to its intensity. But there is a remarkable difference, as I have indicated briefly in an earlier chapter, between the pre-1649 mystical religion and the post-1649 sects. The former had been, true enough, the expression of the oppressed. But it was the manifestation of an immature political understanding, of vague and undefined aspirations. Events and the work of progressive writers crystallized that sentiment into an active political and class consciousness of which the revolutionary movements of 1647–9 were the practical result. The mystical enthusiasm of the 1650's, however, was the product of an acute class consciousness the political expression of which was inhibited by the repressive policy of the Government. The Levellers and the Diggers had given to the common people the vision of a better world; and that vision had been sketched in full and attractive detail. They had sought to persuade their fellows that it was a world that was not set in a distant heaven, but that could be achieved immediately on earth. They had imparted to the people the recognition that the privileges of the wealthy were fashioned of the blood and sweat of the poor. And they had constantly emphasized that the people could expect no relief through the charity or humanitarianism of their oppressors and that the delay of the social reforms that had been promised was the result not so much of the political incapacity of their rulers as of their deliberate and conscious purpose. A profound understanding of those perceptions is present, in one form or another, in all the mystical sects in the several years after 1650. As the sects moved farther from their origins, those social perceptions were modified and finally distorted beyond recognition by the extreme religious fanaticism and abstract spiritual symbolism in which they were expressed. That this class consciousness, however, was a dominant factor in shaping the early development of those mystical movements is, I believe, indisputable.

The forms in which that consciousness was expressed, let me repeat, were infinitely varied and fantastic. To the Fifth Monarchists, the millennium, which they interpreted with a rigid faithfulness to the Scriptural description, would be ushered in by the Saints, most likely by force, when God would indicate the propitious moment. The Quakers believed that the new era in human history would be inaugurated only when all men recognized the Inner Light within them, when the power of love had triumphed in mankind. The Ranters, the wildest and most eccentric of all sects, were so convinced of the omnipresence and imminent revelation of God that they felt that every impulse, every urge, every sign of activity or motion, was a manifestation of His Being. Two things, however, are of vital significance in all of this seeming confusion—the nature of the millennium all sects envisaged and the dogmatic affirmation that only the poor, the down-trodden, the despised, could be chosen as the Saints, as the first Children of the Light, as those in whom God would first manifest himself—in other words, that the poor would be the instruments through which the millennium would be established on earth. It is probable that Digger influence was not altogether unimportant in imparting to the poor the conviction that they were to be the agents through whom the new world would be built and, more particularly, in shaping the picture of that world that the sects were continually drawing.

The origin of that religious ecstasy in acute economic distress and the formulation of its dominant characteristics by an acute class consciousness are clearly and eloquently written into the tracts of the 1650's.[1] There is vehement denunciation of the rich for their exploitation of the poor; there is fiery condemnation of class oppression. And that protest is inspired, let me emphasize, in the early years at any rate, not merely by moral or ethical considerations, but by the recognition that the luxury of the rich is the product of the exploitation and destitution of the poor. Oppression is condemned not simply because it bars the pathway to heaven for those who practice it, but primarily because of its consequences on the poor. A strong note of asceticism, it is true, begins to enter into much of this literature towards the end of the decade; during the early years, however, it is but a weak undertone in that powerful chorus of social protest.

One could quote endlessly from the tracts of the period in example of the intensity of that social protest. Naylor and Fox, Hubberthorn and Ben Nicholson among the Quakers, Aspinwall and Spittlehouse, Rogers and Mary Cary of the Fifth Monarchists. Abiezer Coppe and Salmon, Coppin and Bauthumley among the Ranters and innumerable others who reported the visions they saw and the voices they heard are all inspired by the same acute social consciousness.

"Are not your purses filled and your Estates raised in the ruines of the people?" asked Naylor, "and are not those Laws which ought to be used to preserve People from oppression by abusing made the undoing of whole Families, impoverishing Towns and Countries?"[2]

"From the Lord we are sent to declare against ail deceipt and unrighteousnesse of men", declared Hubberthorn, announcing the social purpose of his mission, "and against all who live in pride and idlenesse and fulnesse of

---

[1] For a good account of and excellent references to the literature of social protest of the 1650's see Tindall, op. cit., Chap. V *passim*, and notes.

[2] Naylor, "A Few Works . . . together with a Call to Magistrates, Ministers, Lawyers and People to Repentance" (1653), in *Works : A Collection of Sundry Books, Epistles and Papers Written by James Naylor* (1716), p. 137.

bread by whom the creation is devoured and many made poor by your meanes and you live upon the labours of the poor and lay heavie burthens upon them, grievous to be born. . . ." [1]

And there is little doubt in their minds that the poor were to be the forerunners of the millennium and that God would first reveal Himself in the hearts of the oppressed:

" The Lord shall guide the hearts of the simple and dwell with them of low degree," affirmed Anne Gargill, " . . . The exceeding wisdom of God will dwel with the poor and the rich shall be sent empty away; he that is abased shall be exalted, he dwels in the hearts of the lowly and the lofty to him is not known." [2]

" He will bring down the mighty from their seats that he may exalt those of low degree," declared Naylor. [3]

The conception of the social order the millennium was expected to establish was directly fashioned by that perception of social division; and it is here that Digger influence may have been of some importance. Certainly, men would live in peace and plenty; the poor would find ample compensation for their suffering. But terrifying pictures were drawn of the fate that awaited the rich. They were to be stripped of all their wealth and possessions; they were to suffer all the damnations of the hell the poor knew so well through their own living experiences:

" Go ye workers of iniquity into everlasting punishment ", Fox warned the rich. " Howl and weep, misery is coming upon you, enemies of God, adversaries of righteousness." [4]

" For I come and will make you howl, howl ye rich men for the rust of your silver and gold will now rise up in judgment against you," George Foster reported was the message of God to him, " for I come to destroy all things besides myself and will suddenly take from man his gods and pictures of gold and silver and will make them for

[1] Hubberthorn, *The Immediate Call* (1654), E. 812 (13), pp. 4–5.
[2] Anne Gargill, *A Warning to All the World* (1656), E. 865 (2).
[3] Naylor, loc. cit., p. 136.
[4] Fox, *Newes Coming Out of the North Sounding Towards the South Or A Blast out of the North Up into the South* (1656).

fear of me give them away, for I come to take vengeance on those that have afflicted the poor." [1]

The millennium, writers continually affirmed, would bring to the poor an abundance of material goods and comfort. The Spirit of God will teach men, declared James Parnell,

" . . . so that there be no want in the creation nor cry of oppression but the hungry will be fed and the naked cloathed and the oppressed set free and here is the blessing restored to the Creation ",[2]

Men would live on terms of complete equality with their fellows and all distinctions of person and class would be abolished; for the Lord, as everyone emphasized, was no respecter of persons.

More important, however, is the fact that a considerable number of those mystical enthusiasts conceived the social order God would establish as one in which private property had been abolished and all goods owned and shared in common; and it is not unlikely that the Diggers were an important source of that conception that for a few years shaped the social ideals of many religious extremists. The Ranters, for example, made the common ownership of all goods one of their cardinal tenets:

" They taught ", one of their former members asserted, " that it was quite contrary to the end of the Creation to appropriate anything to any man or woman but that there ought to be a community of all things." [3]

Foster, one of those who so frequently saw divine visions, declared that:

" God gave to the creature man an equall priviledge to all alike and not made man to be Lord over some part of

---

[1] George Foster, *The Pouring Forth of the Seventh and Last Vial Upon all Flesh and Fleshliness which will be a Terror to the Men that have Great Possessions* (1650), E. 616 (4).

[2] James Parnell, *The Trumpet of the Lord Blowne or a Blast Against Pride and Oppression and the Defiled Liberty which stands in the Flesh* (1655), E. 830 (5).

[3] *The Ranters Last Sermon*, by J. M. (a deluded brother lately escaped out of their snare) (1654), E. 808 (1).

the Creation and the other part of the creation to be in subjection to some other man." [1]

" Be contented, O you rich men," Foster reported was the Lord's message to mankind, " lest I smite you with a curse for behold I come and will make my saints break bread from house to house as formerly they did and will make them for to have communion and all things common so that they shall not say this is mine or that is mine." [1]

Similar expressions of that vision of a communal society can be found in many Quakers no less than in many other sects of the period.

But that powerful and bitter note of protest soon lost itself in religious ecstasy. Whatever social experience or understanding may have been its original inspiration were confused and obscured by the extreme religious manifestations in which they were expressed. Towards the end of the decade the social dissent of the sects amounted to little more than the reflection of a deep moral indignation. To a very considerable degree, too, a decided asceticism comes to dominate the social thinking of many religious enthusiasts.

But at no time, however, did the social protest of the sects have any practical significance; for it embodied no positive suggestions or proposals. There was no appeal to the common people to act for their relief from oppression. For, under the impact of events, the sects had assigned to God the responsibility for social change. Only the Lord by His own appearance or by filling the hearts of men with love and mercy could liberate the enslaved and ease the lot of the suffering.

With the Restoration even that note of moral protest largely disappears from English political thought for more than a century. The Restoration was essentially a compromise between the aristocracy and the middle classes for the exploitation of the economic opportunities an expanding society presented. The Civil War had made it certain that neither an absolute king nor an absolute Church would ever again impede economic progress. The Commonwealth had been a search for an adequate political basis for that new structure. The threat of the poor, the dissatisfaction of the dispossessed, the divisions among the victors, fostered a political

[1] Foster, op. cit.

instability to which the Restoration proved to be the effective answer.   The Bloodless Revolution of 1688 simply completed the work that the Civil War had begun.

With the results of their revolution effectively guaranteed, the propertied classes could now confront with confidence and security the period of economic expansion on which England now entered.   Locke, with his superb common sense, summed up the achievements of the Revolution and presented the middle classes with a theoretical rationalization of the claims they had already in fact established; and English political theory until Hume was little more than a commentary on his doc-trines.   The inviolable rights of private property, the estab-lishment of the claim of the individual to pursue his own inter-ests without interference by the State—a claim, rationalized, of course, by the conviction that the natural harmony of individual interests was of itself productive of the social good—these were the central problems with which thinkers were concerned.   As a result, one can search the literature of the century almost in vain for a significant note of dissent, for some consideration of the plight of the peasant or the landless labourer or the town worker.   An occasional voice, like Bellers, may be raised to plead the cause of the poor; some charitable spirit may utter a mild protest.   But, nowhere, certainly not until the last quarter of the eighteenth century, can we find in English thought any challenge to the basic assumptions of the social order, let alone the suggestion that men should act for its radical transformation.

If, then, we are to look for the expression of a social doctrine like that of Winstanley, it is in eighteenth century France rather than in England that we must seek.   For France in the eighteenth century, like England in the seventeenth, was a society that had become acutely conscious of the chains by which it was bound.   It is a society in vigorous reaction against absolute rule—against an absolute monarchy and, even more, perhaps, against an absolute Church.   It is a society with a newly aroused social conscience; it is profoundly sensitive to injustice and inequality, to suffering and oppression.

From that reaction against absolutism and that social sensi-tivity there emerges a continuous and, in many respects, a remarkable volume of social protest.[1]   There is fierce denuncia-

[1] On this literature of social protest cf. A. Lichtenberger, *Le Socialisme Français au XVIIIème Siècle* (1895).

tion of privilege in all its forms. There is eloquent and passionate condemnation of inequality. There is a bitter attack
on wealth and luxury. Above all, there is an open and
powerful challenge to the sanctity of private property. The
natural state of man, it is constantly asserted, was one in which
the concept of ownership was wholly unknown. Private
property originated in force, in theft, in avarice. It is a right
rooted not in natural law, but created solely by civil society.
With its introduction arose the division between the rich and
the poor, flagrant inequality, social strife. It bred greed,
luxury and extravagance on the one hand and indescribable
misery and slavery on the other. The luxury of the wealthy
is built on the suffering of the poor. In such a society, conflict
is inevitable and continuous. And all this, I should add, is
not the lone cry of a single soul: it is the continous protest of
a host of writers throughout the century.

But most of that protest, it should be emphasized, is little
more than the expression of a deep moral sentiment, of a
profound humanitarian impulse. Seldom does it emerge
from a reasoned analysis of social and economic processes.
Rarely is it intended as a rallying-cry for the poor. There is,
in fact, as with Voltaire and Diderot, with Holbach and
Helvetius, a deep-seated fear of the poor, a genuine alarm
at the possible consequences for property and the established
order of the emancipation and enlightenment of the common people. Much of the protest of the century is little
more than literary exercise unintended to have any practical
significance. The practical proposals that follow on that
protest are generally as moderate as the denunciation is violent.
Rousseau, more eloquently than anyone else in the century,
can describe the unhappiness and slavery of mankind in terms
of the consequences of private property; the resemblance of
the *Discourse on Inequality* to much in Winstanley is remarkable.
But with Rousseau, as with so many others, there is little more
than deep moral indignation. The state of nature may have
been so supremely happy because it knew no property; but
civil society cannot exist without private possession. The
State must therefore respect no right more zealously than that
of private property. Rousseau can see no hope for improvement; and the positive suggestions he ventures are timidly
and moderately conceived. Raynal, D'Argenson, Brissot,
Diderot—to mention but a few—all share Rousseau's passion-

ate hatred of inequality and his deep sympathy with suffering. Many of them reveal a remarkable understanding of the rôle private property has played in history. But they conclude either, as with Raynal, that property is " droit sacré et impre-scriptible ", or, as with Boissel, that educational or moral reform must precede any fundamental social change. Oc-casionally we find something more than a moral protest. Linguet, for example, sees that property originates in force and violence; he recognizes the rôle of the class struggle as the moving force in history; he knows that the full force of law has always been directed to the protection of property: " L'esprit des lois, c'est la propriété." His doctrine, too, unlike that of so many of his contemporaries, is based on a scientific analysis of economic phenomena and an examination of the condition of the peasants and the working classes. He even anticipates in remarkable fashion the theory of surplus value. But he sees from his analysis that the price of improve-ment is nothing less than revolution; and that prospect is one from which Linguet, together with almost all his contem-poraries, fearfully shrinks, " La philosophie qui l'exhorte à la patience (le paysan) estelle bien plus raisonnable que celle qui l'encourage à la révolte." [1]

Seldom, therefore, do we encounter a doctrine such as that of Winstanley—based on an analysis of social and economic forces, pushed to its logical conclusion by insisting on the complete abolition of private property and expressed practi-cally in a call to the propertyless to act for the realization of that new social order. There are, it is true, several writers during the century who are aware that the inequality they condemn and the privileges against which they protest can be finally ended only by the establishment of a system of common ownership. But where writers recognize the logical necessity of some form of communism, they either construct Utopias of whose achievement they are profoundly pessimistic, or insist that a change in the hearts of men is the first condition of drastic social reform, or conceive systems in terms that are too simple and primitive to have any practical significance. Thus, Morelly, for example, constructs a communist utopia, but urges that its establishment must depend on a change in the moral code of mankind. Mably, too, sees clearly that covet-ousness and greed are the results and not the cause of private

[1] Quoted in Lichtenberger, op. cit., p. 303.

property.   Only a system of common ownership, he insists,
can destroy those private interests that are the source of all
social conflict.   Like Winstanley, he is strenuously opposed to
the development of commerce because it unduly complicates
the natural simplicity of the social order.   He even recognizes
that nothing short of revolution can free mankind.   " Choisis-
sez entre une révolution et l'esclavage, il n'y a point de milieu."[1]
But he is profoundly pessimistic as to the possibility of introducing common ownership into society;   and as practical
proposals he can do no more than suggest certain measures of
gradual reform.   Rétif de la Bretonne, writing some years
before the Revolution, bases his utopia for mankind on a rigid
communism;   on the eve of the Revolution, he feels that only
limited reforms are within the realm of practicability and that
private property must be retained.   Gosselin resembles the
Diggers in many ways.   He is interested, above all else, in the
agrarian problem.   He agrees that only complete socialization
can eliminate injustice and inequality.   But common ownership, he feels, is an impossible adventure in modern society.
At best, it may be possible through the methods he suggests
to obtain a greater degree of equality in the ownership of
land.   But Gosselin's ideas, at any rate, were too simple to
have any practical importance.

On the whole, therefore, I think it can be said that only in
two thinkers of the century can we find a social doctrine like
that of Winstanley—in Abbé Meslier at the beginning of the
century and in Babeuf at its end.

Meslier, indeed, is probably the most remarkable socialist
thinker of the century.   In him there is, as in Winstanley, a
superb insight into all the evils of the old order.   Private
property is the source of all human misery and suffering.
The poor are enslaved to the rich because they are dependent
on them for their subsistence.   The wealthy are simply idle
parasites who live on their exploitation of the poor.   The whole
system of inequality and private property is maintained by
force by the kings and the nobility;   Meslier is particularly
violent in his attack on the monarchy.   Like Winstanley, he
is passionate in his denunciation of organized religion.   The
Church has supported and encouraged tyranny and oppression.   The belief in a personal deity is a fraud perpetrated by
the rich on the poor;   when Meslier's self-imposed starvation

[1] Quoted in Lichtenberger, op. cit., p. 235.

has brought him near to death, he asks God's pardon for having been a Christian and thus an instrument in the perpetuation of injustice. The earth can produce enough to enable everyone to live in peace and plenty. There can, then, be but one solution to the misery of mankind—the complete reorganization of the social order on a communist basis. But only the poor and the propertyless can change the social system; revolution must be their only method. The poor have the power, given the will, to rise and overthrow their kings and their priests. " Votre salut est entre vos mains, votre délivrance ne dependrait que de vous, si vous saviez vous entendre tous." [1]

Meslier's practical proposals, like those of Winstanley, frequently lack precision and clarity. They form, too, a series of profound insights rather than an integrated system. But, alone in the century until Babeuf, Meslier carried his ideas to the logical conclusion to which his analysis drove him. Without having experienced, either like Winstanley or Babeuf, the disillusionment that was the aftermath of revolution, he shared their conviction that only action by the propertyless to destroy the social order and to substitute in its stead a system of common ownership could bring freedom to society.

But Meslier was a wholly isolated phenomenon in his century; and his writings on politics were completely unknown, because inaccessible, to his generation. Not until Babeuf do we find an expression of his revolutionary spirit.

With Babeuf we are on the threshold of modern socialism. It is not too fanciful to say, I believe, that Babeuf is Winstanley plus a century of historical development. With him, as with Winstanley, there is much more than simply the conception of the communist ideal. There is a profound concern with the methods by which it is to be achieved; and there is a practical effort to realize that ideal through positive action. I need hardly emphasize the tremendous difference between the methods of the Diggers and those of the Babouvistes. The latter were revolutionary conspirators; the former a little band of well-meaning pacifists whose sole weapon was the spade. But Babeuf, we must remember, lived a century and a half after Winstanley. As a result, he could have an insight into the potential revolutionary rôle of the proletariat that the Digger could never have achieved.

[1] Quoted in Lichtenberger, op. cit., p. 82.

Both Winstanley and Babeuf were the products of a remarkably similar historical experience. Babeuf, tutored by his position as a feudal agent and his personal experience of the privileges of feudalism, had recognized the necessity of communism from the very outset of the Revolution. Like Winstanley, he regarded the Revolution in which he participated as the beginning of the liberation of the suffering masses. The measures he conceived as necessary to effect that liberation bear a striking resemblance to those of the English Digger. Men could be free only if they lived in a society organized on a basis of complete equality. That demanded, as he saw, the common ownership of all land and industry; for anything less than that would always mean the exploitation of the poor by the rich. Individual well-being was wholly a function of the common welfare. Education had to be common and equal; and everyone could thereby learn to play his rôle in the administration of affairs. Distribution had to be free and equal; money and wages had to be completely abolished. Everyone had to engage in productive labour; idleness would entail a forfeiture of political rights. As immediate measures, he suggested, as with Winstanley, the confiscation of all national lands and the cultivation of all unused areas. But, throughout, there is the insistence that nothing short of complete equality could establish effective freedom in society.

Like Winstanley, he regarded the establishment of that equality as the essential purpose of the Revolution. Increasingly, he was forced to realize that that end was none of the purpose of those the Revolution had brought to power; the latter were seeking merely the creation of a middle-class state that would give expression to their own interests. The poor who had aided in the victory were to be excluded from a share of its benefits. With the fall of Robespierre and the reign of Thermidor, that disillusionment becomes complete and final; and Babeuf is driven to conspiracy and insurrection.

It is in his conception of the organization of insurrection that Babeuf can be considered the first modern socialist. His methods and strategy flow directly from his social analysis; and they were given precision by the lessons of 1789, of 1793, of Thermidor. For, his strategy was based on his recognition of the fact that conflict between the rich and the poor was inevitable in any society divided by wealth. The rich would cede their privileges only to superior force. That meant, as Babeuf saw, that if equality based on common ownership were to be established in society, the propertyless would have to organize for the violent seizure of political power. It meant, furthermore, that, having attained power, they would have to introduce a rigorous suppression of those classes who were the enemies of freedom. Dictatorship was a necessary prelude to democracy.

I do not intend to discuss either Babeuf's organization of insurrection or the programme he envisaged to follow upon the seizure of power. Education and propaganda, the penetration of the police and the army, the occupation of the arsenals and the seat of government—all figured in his strategy. His immediate programme was based on his recognition of the necessity for a preliminary dictatorship and the need for complete social revolution. And both strategy and programme were derived from a recognition, that could never have been vouchsafed to Winstanley, of the proletariat as the sole revolutionary force in society.

With Babeuf there opens a new chapter in the history of socialism; for the basis is laid for fitting the socialist perceptions that had emerged from an agrarian society to the realities of an industrial order. The realization that social freedom must be rooted in collective ownership and that its achievement must be wholly the task of those who are excluded from ownership is transformed from a theoretical insight into a practical policy with the growth of an industrial proletariat for whom those lessons are implicit in its practical experience. It leads directly from Babeuf through Saint-Simon and Fourier to the events of 1848 and everything they implied. In the nineteenth century, the *cri de cœur* of Winstanley in the seventeenth century and of Meslier in the eighteenth is organized into a living, practical movement

APPENDIX I

THE DATE OF *THE SAINT'S PARADISE*

Nᴏɴᴇ of the editions of *The Saint's Paradise* bears a date of publication; and Thomason, in his copy, has recorded merely the month—July—and not the year in which it came into his possession. In the Thomason Collection the tract is bound together with pamphlets of the year 1658; and Fortescue in his catalogue of the tracts ascribes it to that year. Both Bernstein, in his *Sozialismus und Demokratie in der grossen Englischen Revolution* of 1895, and Dr. G. P. Gooch, in his *English Democratic Ideas in the Seventeenth Century* of 1896, evidently misled by its position in the Thomason Collection, assumed 1658 as the date of its publication. Impressed by the similarity of many of its concepts to Quaker principles, they asserted that, sometime after the publication of *The Law of Freedom* in 1652, Winstanley, like Lilburne, joined the Quaker Movement. Most historians of the period, following Bernstein and Gooch, have accepted that assumption as fact, and generally state that Winstanley ended his life as a Quaker.

Internal evidence, already discussed in the text, renders it certain, however, that *The Saint's Paradise* was published after *The Breaking of the Day of God* of May 1648 and before *Truth Lifting Up its Head Above Scandals* of October. The one-volume edition of Winstanley's theological works, published early in 1650, includes *The Saint's Paradise*, though the title-page of the latter tract again carries no date of publication. Its position in the volume, however, confirms the opinion that it was written in the summer or early autumn of 1648.

Its inclusion among the tracts of 1658 in the Thomason Collection is probably the result of an error at the time the tracts were bound in their present form. It is possible, however, that Thomason, who had none of Winstanley's other theological tracts, came into possession of *The Saint's Paradise* at a date much later than that of its original publication.

The similarity of the argument of the tract to Quaker concepts, as we have already indicated in the text, must be considered rather the result of the general environment of the period than of any direct contact between Winstanley and George Fox and his followers—for which there is no evidence whatever.

APPENDIX II

A LIST OF THE DIGGER WRITINGS

B.M. = British Museum. S. = Seligman Collection.

THERE is no complete collection of Winstanley's works and the Digger manifestos in any single library. The fullest collection is at the British Museum, which, however, lacks two or three important tracts. The Seligman Collection at Columbia University possesses a large number of the Digger writings, including *The New Law of Righteousness* and *Fire in the Bush,* both very rare tracts.

The list of Digger tracts which follows is substantially the same as that given by Berens in *The Digger Movement.* I have added one fresh item— the one-volume edition of Winstanley's first five theological works published early in 1650, the preface to which Winstanley wrote in December 1649. In some instances, however, the dates I have given differ from those in Berens' list.

On one point I have been unable to satisfy myself completely—on the order of Winstanley's first two tracts. *The Breaking of the Day, etc.,* was published in May 1648; *The Mysterie of God, etc.,* carries only the year, and not the month of publication. In the one-volume edition *The Breaking of the Day* is printed as the first tract. The contents of both tracts and the dedication of *The Mysterie of God, etc.,* to his fellow-countrymen of Lancashire has led me to accept the latter pamphlet as Winstanley's first written work. In any event, both tracts were obviously written within a very short time of each other :

The Mysterie of God Concerning the whole Creation, Mankinde. Winstanley. (April–May 1648.) (B.M.) (S.)

The Breaking of the Day of God. Winstanley. (May 1648.) (B.M.) (S.)

The Saint's Paradise or the Fathers Teaching the only Satisfaction to Waiting Souls. Winstanley. (June–September 1648.) (B.M.) (S.)

Truth Lifting Up Its Head Above Scandals. Winstanley. (October 1648.) (B.M.) (S.)

The New Law of Righteousness. Winstanley. (January 1649.) (S.) (Jesus College, Oxford.)

The True Levellers Standard Advanced or the State of Community opened and presented to the Sons of Men. Everard, Winstanley, etc. (April 1649.) (B.M.) (S.) (Guildhall.)

A Declaration from the Poor Oppressed People of England. Winstanley, etc. (May 1649.) (B.M.) (S.) (Guildhall.)

A Letter to the Lord Fairfax and his Councell of War with Divers Questions to the Lawyers and Ministers. Winstanley. (June 1649.) (B.M.) (S.) Reprinted in the *Harleian Miscellany,* Vol. 8. (1809.)

A Declaration of the Bloudie and unchristian Acting of William Star and John Taylor of Walton. (June 1649.) (B.M.) (S.)

An Appeal to the House of Commons. Winstanley. (July 1649.) (B.M.) (S.) (Goldsmith's Collection.) (Guildhall.)

A Watchword to the City of London and The Armie. Winstanley. (September 1649.) (B.M.) (S.) (Guildhall.)

" To his Excellency The Lord Fairfax and the Councell of Warre, The Brotherly Request of Those that are called Diggers." (December 1649.) (*Clarke Papers,* Vol. II.)

" To my Lord Generall and his Councell of Warr." Winstanley. (December 1649.) (*Clarke Papers,* Vol. II.)

" The Diggers' Song." (1649.) (*Clarke Papers,* Vol. II.)

A Mite Cast into the Common Treasury. Robt. Coster. (December 1649.) (B.M.)

Several Pieces Gathered into Volume set forth in fine Books (i.e., The first five Theological tracts). Winstanley. (1650.) Preface, December 1649. (Manchester Free Reference Library.) (Goldsmith's Collection.)

A New Yeers Gift for the Parliament and Armie. Winstanley. (January 1650.) (B.M.) (Goldsmith's Collection.)

A Vindication of Those whose Endeavors is only to make the Earth a Common Treasury called Diggers. Winstanley. (March 1650.) (B.M.)

A Declaration of the Grounds and Reasons why the poor Inhabitants of Wellinborrow. . . . (March 1650.) (B.M.)

An Appeale to All Englishmen to Judge between Bondage and Freedome. Winstanley, etc. (March 1650.) (B.M.)

The Diggers Mirth or Certain Verses Composed and Fitted to Tunes. (April 1650.) (B.M.)

A Perfect Diurnall. (April 1-8, 1650.) (B.M.)

An Humble Request to All the Ministers of both Universities and to all Lawyers of every Inns-a-Court. Winstanley. (April 1650.) (Victoria and Albert Museum.) (S.)

Fire in the Bush. Winstanley. (1650.) (S.) (Manchester Free Reference Library.) (Goldsmith's.) (Bodleian.)

The Law of Freedom in a Platform. Winstanley. (February 1652.) (B.M.) (S.) (Guildhall.) (Bodleian.)

BIBLIOGRAPHY

This study has been based primarily on the pamphlet literature of the 1640–60 period and mainly on the Thomason Collection at the British Museum, the collections at Friends' House and the Guildhall Library, London, the McAlpin Collection of British History and Theology, Union Theological Seminary, New York City, the Seligman Collection in Columbia University Library and the tracts in the New York City Public Library. The best biographical guides to this vast literature are the *Catalogue of the Pamphlets, Books, Newspapers, etc., Collected by George Thomason*, by G. K. Fortescue (1908), and the *Catalogue of the McAlpin Collection of British History and Theology*, by C. R. Gillett (5 vols., 1927–30). The Thomason Collection is much the richest in the popular political and social literature of the period; but Fortescue's Catalogue must be used with caution, for there are frequent errors both in date and ascription and the titles of many tracts are incorrectly given.

It is impossible to give within the limits of this bibliography a list of the large number of tracts and pamphlets that have been read or consulted during the course of this study. The most important have been cited or referred to in the text and notes. In most instances, references have been given to tracts in the Thomason Collection. Where rare tracts not at the British Museum have been cited, the libraries in which they are to be found have been indicated.

Secondary literature dealing with the development of radical political thought during the 1640–60 period is extremely limited. The bibliography, therefore, comprises almost exclusively those sources, both contemporary and secondary, that have been found most helpful in studying the general background of the Civil War period, the agrarian problem and the political, economic and religious aspects of the Civil War and the Commonwealth periods.

Abbott, W. C., *The Writings and Speeches of Oliver Cromwell*, Vol. I. (1933.)
Acts and Ordinances of the Interregnum, ed. C. H. Firth and R. S. Rait. (1911.)
Allen, J., *English Political Thought, 1604–1644.* (1938.)
Ashley, M. P., *Oliver Cromwell, The Conservative Dictator.* (1937.)

Bax, B., *The Rise and Fall of the Anabaptists.* (1903.)
Baxter, R., *Reliquiae Baxterianae.* (1696.)
Beer, M., *A History of British Socialism.* 2nd ed. (1929.)
Belasco, P., *Authority in Church and State.* (1928.)
Berens, L. H., *The Digger Movement.* (1906.)
Bernstein, E., *Cromwell and Communism.* (1930.)

Bradley, H., *The Enclosures in England*. (1918.)

Braithwaite, W. C., *The Beginnings of Quakerism*. (1912.)

Brinton, C., *The Anatomy of Revolution*. (1939.)

Brown, Louise, *The Political Activities of the Baptists and Fifth Monarchy Men in England during the Interregnum*. (1912.)

Burrage, C., *The Early English Dissenters*. (1912.)

Calendar of State Papers, Domestic, 1620–1660.

Calendar of State Papers, Venetian, 1621–1661.

Carlyle, T., *Letters and Speeches of O. Cromwell*, ed. C. S. Lomas. (1904.)

Clarendon, *History of the Great Rebellion*. (1888.)

Clark, G. N., *The Seventeenth Century*. (1929.)

Clyde, W., *The Struggle for the Freedom of the Press from Caxton to Cromwell*. (1934.)

Commons' Journals, 1640–1660.

Constitutional Documents of the Puritan Revolution, ed. S. R. Gardiner. (1906.)

Cunningham, W., *The Growth of English Industry and Commerce*. (1919.)

Curtler, *The Enclosure and Redistribution of our Land*. (1920.)

Davies, G., " The Parliamentary Army under the Earl of Essex, 1642–45 ", *English Historical Review*, January 1934.

D'Ewes, Simon, *Journal*, ed. Notestein. (1923.)

Dietz, F. C., *English Public Finance, 1558–1641*. (1932.)

Dowell, S., *A History of Taxation and Taxes in England*. (1888.)

Engels, F., *The Peasant War in Germany*. (1927.)

Firth, C. H., *Clarke Papers*. Camden Society Publications, New Series, Vols. XLIX, LIV. (1891, etc.)

—— *Cromwell's Army*, 3rd edition. (1921.)

—— *Oliver Cromwell, and the Rule of the Puritans in England*. (1900.)

—— *The House of Lords during the Civil War*. (1910.)

—— *The Last Years of the Protectorate, 1656–1658*. (1909.)

Fox, G., *Journal*. (Everyman Edition, 1924.)

Gardiner, S. R., *History of England, 1603–1642*. (1883.)

—— *History of the Great Civil War*. (1893.)

—— *History of the Commonwealth and Protectorate*. (1903.)

—— *Oliver Cromwell*. (1901.)

—— *Reports of Cases in the Courts of Star Chamber and High Commission*. Camden Society Publications. (1886.) New Series, Vol. XXXIX.

Gasquet, F., *Henry VIII and the English Monasteries*. (1888–89.)

Gonner, C. K., *Common Land and Enclosure*. (1912.)

Gooch, G. P., *Political Thought in England from Bacon to Halifax*. (1914.)

Gooch, G. P., and Laski, H. J., *English Democratic Ideas in the Seventeenth Century*. (1927.)

Gretton, R. H., *The English Middle Class*. (1917.)

Haller, Wm., *The Rise of Puritanism*. (1938.)

—— *Tracts on Liberty in the Puritan Revolution, 1638–47*. (1934.)

Harrington, J., *Oceana.*
Hobbes, T., *Leviathan.*
—— *Behemoth.*
Holdsworth, W., *History of English Law.* (1916, etc.)
Hutchinson, L., *Memoirs of Colonel Hutchinson.*

Inderwick, F., *The Interregnum.* (1891.)

James, M., *Social Problems and Policy During the Puritan Revolution.* (1930.)
James, Wm., *The Varieties of Religious Experience.* (1902.)
Johnson, A. H., *The Disappearance of the Small Landowner.* (1909.)
Jones, R. M., *Spiritual Reformers of the Sixteenth and Seventeenth Centuries.*
     (1914.)
—— *Mysticism and Democracy.* (1932.)
—— *Studies in Mystical Religion.* (1909.)
Jordan, W. K., *The Development of Religious Toleration in England.* (1932,
     etc.)

Kautsky, K., *Communism in Central Europe in the Time of the Reformation.* (1897.)
Keir, D., *The Constitutional History of Modern Britain, 1485–1937.* (1938.)

Laski, H. J., *The Rise of European Liberalism.* (1936.)
—— *Studies in Law and Politics.* Chaps. I, II, III. (1932.)
Laud, W., *Works.* (1842.)
Leonard, E. M., *Early History of English Poor Relief.* (1900.)
—— "The Enclosure of the Common Fields in the Seventeenth Century",
     Trans. Royal Hist. Society, N.S., Vol. XIX. (1905.)
Lichtenberger, A., *Le Socialisme Français au XVIIIème Siècle.* (1895.)
Liljegren, S., *The Fall of the Monasteries and the Social Changes Leading Up to*
     the Great Revolution. (1924.)
Lipson, E., *The Economic History of England.* (1934, etc.)
Lords Journals.
Ludlow, E., *Memoirs*, ed. C. H. Firth. (1894.)

MacIlwain, C. H., *The High Court of Parliament.* (1910.)
—— *The Political Works of James I.* (1918.)
Marriot, J. A. R., *The English Land System.* (1914.)
Masson, D., *The Life of Milton.* (1859–94.)
Merriman, R. B., *Six Contemporaneous Revolutions.* (1938.)
Miller, P., *Orthodoxy in Massachusetts.* (1933.)
Milton, J., *Works.*
Morley, J., *Oliver Cromwell.* (1904.)

Neal, D., *History of the Puritans.* (1843–4.)
Nef, J. U., *The British Coal Industry.* (1932.)

Oman, C., *The Great Revolt of 1381.* (1906.)
Owst, G., *Literature and Pulpit in Mediaeval England.* (1935.)

Parliamentary History of England. (1758.)

Pease, T. C., *The Leveller Movement.* (1914.)

Price, W. H., *The English Patents of Monopoly.* (1906.)

Prothero, *Statutes and Constitutional Documents, 1558–1625.* (1894.)

Reid, R., *The King's Council in the North.* (1920.)

Rogers, R., *Six Centuries of Work and Wages.* (1884.)

—— *A History of Agriculture and Prices in England.* (1887.)

Rushworth, J., *Historical Collections.*

Sabine, G. H., *A History of Political Theory.* (1937.)

Scott, W., *Joint Stock Companies.* (1910–12.)

Shaw, W. A., *A History of the English Church during the Civil Wars and under the Commonwealth.* (1900.)

Smith, R., *Harrington and his Oceana.* (1914.)

Tawney, R. H., *Religion and the Rise of Capitalism.* (1938.)

—— *The Agrarian Problem in the Sixteenth Century.* (1912.)

Tindall, W. Y., *John Bunyan, Mechanick Preacher.* (1934.)

Trevelyan, G., *England under the Stuarts.* (1930.)

Troeltsch, E., *The Social Teaching of the Christian Churches.* (1931.)

Unwin, G., *Industrial Organization in the Sixteenth and Seventeenth Centuries.* (1904.)

—— *The Gilds and Companies of London.* (1938.)

Usher, R. G., *The Rise and Fall of the High Commission.* (1913.)

—— *The Reconstruction of the English Church.* (1910.)

—— *A Critical Study of the Historical Method of S. R. Gardiner.* (1915.)

Victoria County Histories, The.

Wade, C. E., *John Pym.* (1912.)

Webb, S. and B., *History of the English Poor Law.* (1927.)

Weber, M., *The Protestant Ethic.* (1930.)

Whitelocke, B., *Memorials of English Affairs.* (1732.)

Woodhouse, A. S. P., *Puritanism and Liberty.* (1938.)

Wright, C. B., *Middle-Class Culture in Elizabethan England.* (1935.)

SUPPLEMENTARY
BIBLIOGRAPHY

a) Two further works by Winstanley have come to light since Petegorsky compiled his list:

i) *Englands Spirit Unfoulded* (1650 – probably early). Edited by G.E. Aylmer and printed in *Past and Present*, XL. (1968.)

ii) A letter to Lady Eleanor Davies [Douglas], the prophetess (4 December 1650). Edited by P.H. Hardacre and printed in *Huntington Library Quarterly*, XXII. (1959.)

b) Other tracts relevant to the Diggers include:

Light Shining in Buckinghamshire (December 1648.)
More Light Shining in Buckinghamshire (March 1649.)
A Declaration of the Wel-Affected in the County of Buckinghamshire (May 1649.)
The Speeches of the Lord General Fairfax and the Officers of the Armie to the Diggers at St Georges Hill in Surrey and the Diggers several Answers and Replies thereunto (31 May 1649.)
A Declaration from . . . Iver (May 1650.). Edited by K.V. Thomas and printed in *Past and Present*, XLII. (1969.)

c) Modern editions of Writings by Winstanley are listed in the Supplementary Bibliography *below*.

d) Works published since 1940

Alsop, J. D., "Gerrard Winstanley: Religion and Respectability", *Historical Journal*, XXVIII. (1985.)
—— "Gerrard Winstanley's Later Life", *Past and Present*, LXXXII. (1979.)
—— "A High Road to Radicalism? Gerrard Winstanley's Youth", *Seventeenth Century*, IX. (1994.)
Achinstein, S., *Milton and the Revolutionary Reader*. (Princeton, 1995.)
Armytage, W. A. G., *Heavens Below: Utopian Experiments in England, 1560–1960*. (Toronto, 1961.)
Ashley, M. P., *John Wildman: Plotter and Postmaster*. (1947.)
Aylmer, G. E., ed., *The Interregnum: The Search for Settlement*. (1972.)

—— ed., *The Levellers in the English Revolution*. (1975.)
—— ed., *'Englands Spirit Unfoulded'*, Past and Present, XL. (1968.)
—— "Gentlemen Levellers", *Past and Present*, IL. (1970.)

Badstock, A., "Sowing in Hope: the Relevance of Theology to Gerrard Winstanley's Political Programme", *Seventeenth Century*, VI. (1991.)
Barber, F. *et al.*, eds., *1642: Literature and Power in the Seventeenth Century*. (Colchester, 1981.)
Barg, M. A., *Lower Class Democracy in the English Bourgeois Revolution*. (Moscow, 1967 – in Russian.)
Baxter, N., "Gerrard Winstanley's Experimental Knowledge: the Perception of the Spirit and the Acting of Reason", *Journal of Ecclesiastical History*, XXXIX. (1988.)
Brailsford, H. N., *The Levellers and the English Revolution*. (1961.)
Brink, A., "Gerrard Winstanley", *Journal of the Friends Historical Society*, III. (1960.)
Brockway, F., *Britain's First Socialists*. (1980.)
Burns, J. H. and Goldie, M., eds., *The Cambridge History of Political Thought, 1450–1700*. (Cambridge, 1991.)

Capp, B., "Godly Rule and English Millenarianism", *Past and Present*, LII. (1971.)
—— *The Fifth Monarchy Men*. (1972.)
—— *The World of John Taylor the Water Poet*. (Oxford, 1994.)
Carlin, W., "Leveller Organisation in London", *Historical Journal*, XXVII. (1984.)
Caute, D., *Comrade Jacob*. (1961 – a novel.)
Cole, C. R., and Moody, M. E., eds., *The Dissenting Tradition*. (Athens, Ohio, 1975.)
Cornforth, M., ed., *Rebels and their Causes*. (1978.)
Corns, T. N., *Uncloistered Virtue: English Political Literature, 1640–1660*. (Oxford, 1992.)

Dalton, L., "Gerrard Winstanley and the Experience of Fraud", *Historical Journal*, XXXV. (1992.)
Davis, J. C., "The Levellers and Democracy", *Past and Present*, XL. (1968.)
—— "Gerrard Winstanley and the Restoration of True Magistracy", *Past and Present*, LXX. (1976.)
—— *Utopia and the Ideal Society: a Study of English Utopian Writing, 1516–1700*. (Cambridge, 1981.)
—— *Fear, Myth and History: The Ranters and the Historians*. (Cambridge, 1986.)
—— "Fear, Myth and Furore: Reappraising the Ranters", *Past and Present*, CXXIX. (1990.)

—— "Puritans and Revolution: Themes, Categories, Methods and Conclusions", *Historical Journal*, XXXIII. (1990.)

Dell, E., "Gerrard Winstanley", *Modern Quarterly*, IV. (1949.)

Dow, F., *Radicalism in the English Revolution*. (Oxford, 1985.)

Elmen, P., "The Theological Basis of Digger Communism", *Church History*, XXIII. (1954.)

Erskine-Hill, H. and Storey, G., eds., *Revolutionary Prose of the English Civil War*. (Cambridge, 1983.)

Frank, J., *The Levellers: A History of the Writings of Three Seventeenth-Century Social Democrats (Lilburne, Overton and Walwyn)*. (Cambridge, Mass., 1955.)

Fernstein, C. H., ed., *Socialism, Capitalism and Economic Growth*. (Cambridge, 1967.)

Firth, K. R., *The Apocalyptic Tradition in Reformation England, 1530–1645*. (Oxford, 1978.)

Friedman, J., *Blasphemy, Immorality and Anarchy: The Ranters and the English Revolution*. (Athens, Ohio, 1987.)

Fuz, J. K., *Welfare Economics in English Utopias from Bacon to Smith*. (The Hague, 1952.)

Gentles, I., *The New Model Army in England, Ireland and Scotland, 1645–1653*. (1992.)

—— "London Levellers in the English Revolution: The Chidleys and their Circle", *Journal of Ecclesiastical History*, XXIX. (1978.)

George, C. H., "Protestantism and Capitalism", *Church History*, XXVII. (1958.)

—— "Puritanism as History and Historiography", *Past and Present*, XLI. (1968.)

—— *Revolution: European Radicals from Hus to Lenin*. (Glenview, 1971.)

Gibb, M. A., *John Lilburne the Christian Democrat*. (1947.)

Gibbons, B. J. *et al.*, "Debate; Fear, Myth and Furore: Reappraising the Ranters", *Past and Present*, CLX. (1993.)

—— "Richard Overton and the Secularisation of the Interregnum Radicals", *Seventeenth Century*, X. (1995.)

Gimmelfarb-Brack, M., *Liberté, Egalité, Fraternité, Justice: La Vie et L'Œuvre de Richard Overton*. (Bern, 1981.)

Gleissner, R., "The Levellers and Natural Law: The Putney Debates of 1647", *Journal of British Studies*, XX. (1980.)

Greaves, R. L., "Gerrard Winstanley and Educational Reform in Puritan England", *British Journal of Education Studies*, XVII. (1969.)

—— *The Puritan Revolution in Educational Thought*. (New Brunswick, 1969.)

—— and Zaller, R., eds., *Biographical Dictionary of British Radicals in the Seventeenth Century*. (3 vols, Brighton, 1982–84.)

Gregg, P., *Freeborn John*. [John Lilburne]. (1961.)

Haller, W., and Davies, G., eds., *The Leveller Tracts*. (New York, 1944.)

Haller, W., *Liberty and Reformation in the Puritan Revolution*. (New York, 1955.)

Hamilton, L. D., ed., *Gerrard Winstanley: Selections from his Works*. (1944.)

Hampsher-Monk, I., "The Political Theory of the Levellers: Putney, Property and Professor Macpherson", *Political Studies*, XXIV. (1976.)

Hardacre, P., "Gerrard Winstanley in 1650", *Huntington Library Quarterly*, XXII. (1959.)

Harris, M., *Communists and Kings*. (New York, 1972.)

Hayes, T. W., "Gerrard Winstanley and Foxe's *Book of Martyrs*", *Notes and Queries*, CCXXII. (1977.)

—— *Gerrard Winstanley the Digger: a Literary Analysis of Radical Ideas in the Puritan Revolution*. (Cambridge, Mass., 1979.)

Hill, C., "Land in the English Revolution", *Science and Society*, XIII. (1948.)

—— ed., *The English Revolution of 1640*. (1940.)

—— *Puritanism and Revolution*. (1958.)

—— *The World Turned Upside Down*. (1972.)

—— ed., *Winstanley: The Law of Freedom and Other Writings*. (1973.)

—— *Anti-Christ in Seventeenth-Century England*. (Oxford, 1974.)

—— *Change and Continuity in Seventeenth-Century England*. (1975.)

—— *Milton and the English Revolution*. (1977.)

—— *The Religion of Gerrard Winstanley*, Past and Present, Supplement No. 5. (1978.)

—— "Debate: The Religion of Gerrard Winstanley – A Rejoinder", *Past and Present*, LXXXIX. (1980.)

—— *The Experience of Defeat*. (1984.)

—— *Collected Essays*. (3 vols, Brighton, 1986–87.)

—— *A Turbulent, Seditious and Factious People: John Bunyan and his Church*. (Oxford, 1988.)

—— *The Bible and the English Revolution*. (1992.)

Hill, C. and Dell, E., eds., *The Good Old Cause: The English Revolution of 1640*. (1949.)

Himbury, M., "The Religious Beliefs of the Levellers", *Baptist Quarterly*, XXIII. (1954.)

Hollorenshaw, J. [Needham, J.], *The Levellers and the English Revolution*. (1939.)

Holstun, J., ed., *Pamphlet Wars: Prose in the English Revolution*. (1992.)

—— "Ranting at the New Historicism", *English Literary Renaissance*, XIX. (1989.)

Howell Jnr, R. and Brewster, D. E., "Reconsidering the Levellers: the Evidence of *The Moderate*", *Past and Present*, XLVI. (1970).

Hudson, W. S., "Gerrard Winstanley and the Early Quakers", *Church History*, XII. (1943.)

—— "Economic and Social Thought of Gerrard Winstanley: Was he a Seventeenth-Century Marxist?" *Journal of Modern History*, XVII. (1946.)

Ives, E. W., ed., *The English Revolution*.   (1968.)

Jacob, M. and Jacob, J., eds., *The Origins of Anglo-American Radicalism*. (1984.)
James, M., "The Political Importance of Tithes", *History*, XXVI.   (1941.)
Jones, C., Newitt, M. and Roberts, S., eds., *Politics and People in Revolutionary England: Essays in Honour of Ivan Roots*.   (Oxford, 1986.)

Kenny, R. W., ed., *The Law of Freedom in a Platform*.   (New York, 1941.)
Kenyon, T., *Utopian Communism and Political Thought in Early Modern England*.   (Princeton, 1989.)
—— "Labour – Natural, Property – Artificial: The Radical Insights of Gerrard Winstanley", *History of European Ideas*, VI.   (1985.)
Kishlansky, M., *The Rise of the New Model Army*.   (Cambridge, 1979.)
—— "The Army and the Levellers: Roads to Putney", *Historical Journal*, XXII.   (1979.)
—— "Consensus Politics and the Structure of Debate at Putney", *Journal of British Studies*, XX.   (1981.)

Lindsay, J. D., "Gerrard Winstanley's Theology of Creation", *Toronto Journal of Theology*, IV.   (1988.)
Lutaud, O., "Le Parti Politique Niveleur et la Premiére Revolution Anglaise", *Revue Historique*, CCXXVII.   (1962.)
—— *Winstanley, Socialisme et Christianisme sous Cromwell*.   (Paris, 1976.)
—— *Les Niveleurs, Cromwell et la République*.   (Paris, 1978.)
—— ed., *Les Deux Revolutions d'Angleterre*.   (Paris, 1978.)

MacGregor, J. F. and Reay, B., eds., *Radical Religion in the English Revolution*. (Oxford, 1984.)
McMichael, J. and Taft, B., eds., *The Writings of William Walwyn*.   (Athens, Georgia, 1989.)
MacPherson, C. B., *The Political Theory of Possessive Individualism*. (Oxford, 1962.)
—— "Hampsher-Monk's Levellers", *Political Studies*, XXV.   (1977.)
Manning, B. W., ed., *Politics, Religion and the English Revolution*.   (1973.)
—— *The English People and the English Revolution*.   (1976.)
—— *1649: The Crisis of the English Revolution*.   (1992.)
Morrill, J., *The Nature of the English Revolution*.   (1993.)
Morton, A. L., "The Place of Lilburne, Overton and Walwyn in the Tradition of English Prose", *Zeitschrift für Anglistik u. Amerikanistik*, VI.   (1958.)
—— *The Matter of Britain*.   (1966.)
—— *The World of the Ranters*.   (1970.)
—— ed., *Freedom in Arms: A Selection of Leveller Writings*.   (1975.)
Mulder, D., *The Alchemy of Revolution: Gerrard Winstanley's Occultism and Seventeenth-century Communism*.   (New York, 1990.)

Mullett, M., *Radical Religious Movements in Early Modern Europe*. (1980.)

Mulligan, L., Graham, J. K., and Richard, J., "Winstanley: A Case for the Man as he said he was", *Journal of Ecclesiastical History*, XXVIII. (1977.)

—— "Debate: The Religion of Gerrard Winstanley", *Past and Present*, LXXXII. (1980.)

Murphy, W. E., "The Political Philosophy of Gerrard Winstanley", *Review of Politics*, XIX. (1957.)

Orwell, G. and Reynolds, R., eds., *British Pamphleteers*, I. (1948.)

Padgden, A., ed., *The Language of Political Theory in Early Modern Europe*. (Cambridge, 1987.)

Parkin-Speer, D., "John Lilburne: a Revolutionary interprets Statutes and Common Law Due Process", *Law and History Review*, I. (1983.)

Parry, R. H., ed., *The English Civil War and After*. (1970.)

Patrick, J. M., "The Literature of the Diggers", *University of Toronto Quarterly*, XII. (1942.)

—— "William Covell and the Troubles at Enfield in 1659: A Sequel of the Digger Movement", *University of Toronto Quarterly*, XIV. (1944.)

Pennington, D. H. and Thomas, K. V., eds., *Puritans and Revolutionaries: Essays in Honour of Christopher Hill*. (Oxford, 1978.)

Petegorsky, D., "Class Forces in the English Civil War", *Science and Society*, VI. (1942.)

Pocock, J. G. A., ed., *Three British Revolutions*. (Princeton, 1980.)

Polizolto, C., "Liberty and Conscience: The Whitehall Debates of 1648–49", *Journal of Ecclesiastical History*, XXVI. (1975.)

Poynter, F. N. L., "William Walwyn: 'Health's Student'", *British Medical Journal*, (1949.)

Pulsford, J. S. L., *The First Kingston Quakers*. (Walton-on-Thames, 1973.)

Ratcliffe, E., *Winstanley's Walton, 1649*. (Stevenage, 1994.)

Richardson, R. C. and Ridden, C. M., eds., *Freedom and the English Revolution*. (Manchester, 1986.)

Richardson, R. C., ed., *Town and Countryside in the English Revolution*. (Manchester, 1992.)

Robertson, P. B., *The Religious Foundations of Leveller Democracy*. (New York, 1951.)

Rowse, A. L., *Reflections on the Puritan Revolution*. (1986.)

Rush, P., *Freedom is the Man*. (1946 – a novel.)

Sabine, G. H., ed., *The Works of Gerrard Winstanley*. (New York, 1941.)

Sanderson, J., "The Digger Apprenticeship: Winstanley's Early Writings", *Political Studies*, XXII. (1972.)

Schenk, W., *The Concern for Social Justice in the Puritan Revolution.*
    (1948.)
—— "A Seventeenth-Century Radical", *Economic History Review*, XIV.
    (1941.)
Sharp, D., *Political Ideas of the English Civil Wars.* (1983.)
Sharpe, K., *Politics and Ideas in Early Stuart England.* (1989.)
Shaw, H., *The Levellers.* (1968.)
Shulman, G. M., *Radicalism and Reverence: The Political Thought of Gerrard
    Winstanley.* (Berkeley, 1989.)
Slater, M., *Englishmen with Swords.* (1949 – a novel.)
Smith, N., ed., *A Collection of Ranter Writings.* (1983.)
—— *Perfection Proclaimed: Language and Literature in English Radical Religion,
    1640–1660.* (Oxford, 1989.)
Solt, L. F., "Anti-Intellectualism in the English Revolution", *Church History*,
    XXV. (1956.)
—— "Winstanley, Lilburne and the Case of John Fielder", *Huntington
    Library Quarterly*, XXV. (1982.)
Stripp, F., "The Anti-Clericalism of Gerrard Winstanley", *Historical
    Magazine of the Protestant Episcopal Church*, XXIII. (1954.)

Taft, B., "The Council of Officers' Agreement of the People, 1648/9",
    Historical Journal, XXVIII. (1985.)
Taylor, D. C., *Gerrard Winstanley in Elmsbridge.* (Elmsbridge, 1982.)
Thomas, K. V., ed., "Another Digger Broadside: *A Declaration from . . .
    Iver*", *Past and Present*, XLII. (1969.)
—— "The Date of Gerrard Winstanley's *Fire in the Bush*", *Past and Present*,
    XLII. (1969.)
Thompson, C., "Maximilian Petty and the Putney Debates on the
    Franchise", *Past and Present*, LXXXVIII. (1980.)
Tolmie, M., *The Triumph of the Saints.* (1977.)

Vann, R. T., "From Radicalism to Quakerism: Gerrard Winstanley and
    Friends", *Journal of the Friends Historical Society*, XLIX. (1956.)
—— "Diggers and Quakers: a Further Note", *Journal of the Friends
    Historical Society*, L. (1962.)
—— "The Later Life of Gerrard Winstanley", *Journal of the History of Ideas*,
    XXVI. (1965.)
—— *The Social Development of English Quakerism, 1685–1755.* (1969.)

Waltzer, M., *The Revolution of Saints: A Study of the Origin of Radical Politics.*
    (1973.)
Webster, C., *The Great Instauration.* (1975.)
Williamson, H. R., *Four Stuart Portraits.* (1949.)
Wolfe, D. M., ed., *Leveller Manifestoes of the Puritan Revolution.* (New York,
    1944.)

—— *Milton in the Puritan Revolution.* (New York, 1941.)

—— "The Unsigned Pamplets of Richard Overton, 1641–49", *Huntington Library Quarterly*, XXI. (1958.)

Woolrych, A. H., *Soldiers and Statesmen: The General Council of the Army and its Debates, 1647–48.* (Oxford, 1987.)

Zagorin, P., *A History of Political Thought in the Puritan Revolution.* (1954.)

—— ed., *Culture and Politics from Puritanism to the Enlightenment.* (Berkeley, 1980.)